Th *'ron*

ISBN 978-1-291-98641-9

2

Index

Acknowledgements

This book would not have been possible without the help of a number of people to whom I owe a debt of thanks. These include the readers who gave up their time to review drafts and make constructive suggestion regarding plot and character development. Foremost of these were Jessica Allen, Rosemary Riches, Dave Simkins and a cousin of mine Graham Watkins who always claims I was named after him. His grammatical corrections and patience as I stumbled from one comma to the next were invaluable. Patricia, my Wife, also deserves my thanks for putting up with my withdrawal from family life as I battled with heroes and villains from another century.

Introduction

The period between 1780 and 1833 was a golden age for some. For others a time of misery and hardship. Fortunes are made in wartime and Britain was going to war. It was an opportunity the Iron Masters of Merthyr Tydfil would seize with both hands to make their fortunes. Men like Richard Crawshay, Francis Homfray and Josiah Guest built huge iron foundries employing thousands of men. The foundries of Cyfartha, Dowlais, Penydarren and Abercynon roared like thunder as they fed the war machine with cannon. The iron masters built canals and railways to get their wares to market. They fought, tricked and connived together. Anything was possible and nothing stood in the way of these powerful men.

Cannon production was important enough for Admiral Nelson to visit Merthyr to see for himself. 'Cheer you buggers, It's Nelson,' commanded Richard Crawshay, to his workmen, when the Admiral arrived.

Thomas Carlyle visited Merthyr writing that the town was filled with such 'unguided, hard-worked, fierce, and miserable-looking sons of Adam I never saw before. Ah me ! It is like a vision of Hell, and will never leave me, that of these poor creatures broiling, all in sweat and dirt, amid their furnaces, pits, and rolling mills.'

The story of the rise and ultimate decline of Merthyr which during the Napoleonic Wars was the biggest industrial city in the world, is very real. To avoid upsetting partisan opinions, I've used fictional characters but the events you will find them entangled in did happen and theirs is fascinating adventure.

Part 1 1780 - 1786

Chapter 1

Nye Vaughn glanced down at the crude coffin. It looked smaller in the grave, too small to contain his mother's body. 'Eternal rest grant unto her, O Lord,' intoned the minister.

His mother's death had been cruel. Consumption devouring her body and destroying her mind. Once, she had been a strong woman. Full of life. She had made a good home and kept it well. Nye had listened to her coughing and her cries as demons tormented her dreams. Nye's father had deserted the marriage bed to spend the evenings in the ale houses of Llangadog, to forget his sick wife. The town was alive with drovers, gathering to walk animals to the profitable English markets. Every room was occupied. Drovers, unable to find a bed, slept in barns and outhouses. On the nights when Nye's father came home, he slept in a chair by the kitchen fire. The farm, too, was neglected. Hedges needed repairing. The barn roof had collapsed. The autumn nights were getting longer and there was no winter feed for the animals. Nye did his best to work the farm, more than anyone could expect of a boy of eighteen.

Nye looked across the grave at his father, hoping for a smile, a nod, a gesture of compassion, of shared grief but his father stood motionless, staring straight ahead. Father and son were never close. Nye imagined his mother's death would bring them together. He was wrong; a void existed, as big as the grave between them, that would never be bridged.

'May she rest in peace,' said the minister and threw a sod of earth into the grave. It landed on the coffin with a thud. Nye shuddered. His father put on his cap and strode out of the graveyard. The minister put his hand on Nye's shoulder. 'Your mother was a good woman. She isn't down there, Nye.

She's with God now,' said the minister and glanced up to the heavens. He closed his prayer book and followed Nye's father from the graveyard. Nye watched the gravediggers shovel earth into the grave.

It was raining as Nye walked back to the farm, a soft cold rain that penetrated his coat and chilled his back. Nye changed out of his Sunday clothes and did his chores. The animals had to be seen to. Nye collected eggs, shut the hens in and filled the carthorse's manger with hay. The cow, her udders heavy with milk, was waiting by the barn. He milked her and cleaned the cowshed. The rain grew heavier as he worked. The heavy muck barrow slid in the mud as he pushed it across the yard. When the jobs were finished, Nye lit the kitchen fire, dried himself and sat in his mother's chair. Her shoes were by the grate, her knitting still in a bag on the floor. The hearth mat his mother had woven with strips, cut from old clothes, looked shabby. Nye remembered cutting the cloth for her and helping make the rag rug. It was threadbare and greasy; ready to be discarded.
   'I'll clear everything out tomorrow,' he said to himself. He focused on the burning logs. Shadows danced on the walls as flames illuminated the room.

Nye was dozing when the clock struck ten. He stirred. The fire had burned low and the kitchen was dark, except for a faint glow from the embers. Nye added sticks to the fire. There was a noise outside, voices and scuffling. Nye stood up, looked at the door and the loaded gun hung above it. The door opened and his father lurched into the kitchen, followed by a woman.
   'What a dirty night. Let's get these wet things off,' laughed his father and grabbed at the woman. She giggled as he pulled at her coat. The woman noticed Nye and stopped laughing. Nye's father turned and saw his son.

'This is Jean. Jean, this is my boy, Nye,' said his father, swaying as he spoke.

'Mum's not even cold in the ground and you bring a woman into her house,' said Nye angrily.

There was silence as Nye's father digested what he said. Rain beat on the window. Drops of water came down the chimney. The fire hissed and spat a burning ember onto rug. Nye's father stepped forward and slapped his son across the face.

'Your mother is gone. This is my house and you've insulted my friend,' said his father. A trickle of blood ran down Nye's face. 'You'll apologise to Jean.'

Nye pushed past his father, snatched his coat from behind the door and ran out, into the darkness.

'Go after him,' said Jean.

'What for? He's got nowhere to go. He'll be back,' replied Nye's father.

The rug had begun to smoulder. Nye's father carried it outside and threw it in the mud. Jean watched from the doorway. Nye's father peered into the gloom, hoping to see his son but the farmyard was empty.

Chapter 2

Nye stumbled along the track in the darkness. Rain lashed his face and wind sucked the breath from his mouth. He pulled his coat tighter around his neck, pushed his hands deep into the pockets and curled his fingers around his pocket knife. The handle felt warm and reassuring. Nye passed the graveyard where his mother lay. A gloomy mist hung, shroud like, across the gates. Nye hurried on. He followed the track south east, towards the mountain. Something moved behind the hedge and startled Nye. He relaxed. It was a bullock, sheltering from the wind. The rain stopped and the clouds passed, revealing a bright moon that lit up the fields. An owl hooted nearby. A second, distant bird, answered. Nye's mother had always said the owl's call foretold of a death. He knew it was an old wives tale. A patrolling fox crossed the track ahead of him.

Nye saw a stone barn beside the track. Yellow eyes, shining in the moonlight, stared from within. Nye saw the loft and smelt the sweet fresh hay. He climbed over the gate in the doorway, pushed through the nervous sheep, climbed into the loft and slept.

'What are you doing in my barn?' demanded a voice. It was light and a man was standing over him. A dog was barking outside. The tines of a pitchfork rested on Nye's chest.

'I meant no harm,' answered Nye. The shepherd prodded with the pitchfork.

'What's your name? Where do you come from?'

'Vaughn, Nye Vaughn, I'm from Llangadog,' replied Nye.

'What are you doing here?' asked the shepherd and jabbed Nye again with the pitchfork.

'I argued with my father and left home last night,' replied Nye. The shepherd studied Nye for a moment, raised the pitchfork as if to strike and thrust it into the hay.

'Are you hungry boy?'

'Yes sir,' replied Nye.

'Follow me,' ordered the shepherd.

The cottage was warm. Fresh bread was cooling on the table. Stew simmered in the hearth. A flitch of bacon hung from the ceiling. The shepherd's wife filled a bowl with stew, cut a wedge from the loaf and told him to eat.

'Where will you go?' inquired the shepherd, filling his pipe.

'I don't know,' answered Nye with a mouth full of bread.

'I hear there's work to be had in the iron foundries at Merthyr,' said the shepherd and lit a spill from the fire. He held the flame to his pipe and sucked.

'I don't know anything but farming. What would I do in a foundry?' asked Nye.

'A strong lad like you would soon find something, labouring perhaps,' replied the shepherd and blew smoke across the kitchen.

'You could join a cattle drive to England,' suggested the shepherd's wife.

'That means going back to Llangadog. That's where they hire,' said the shepherd.

'I'm never going back. Where is Merthyr? Is it far?' asked Nye.

'Follow the drovers track east along the mountain. A day's walk will bring you to the road between Brecon and Merthyr. Turn right and go south. The road will take you over the mountain to Merthyr.'

'Then I shall go to Merthyr,' said Nye and wiped the bowl with the crust.

As he was leaving the shepherd's wife produced a small parcel.

'It's bread and cheese, for the journey,' she said and pushed it into his pocket.

The drover's track was wide and well trodden. Nye stopped after mid day and sat on a boulder to rest. He unlaced his boots. A blister had burst on his left heel. He wrapped the heel carefully with his handkerchief, replaced the boot and laced it tight. Nye remembered the packet from the shepherd's wife. The bread and cheese tasted good. He had finished eating when he heard a cry.

'Heiptrw Ho,' yelled a distant voice. There were more shouts and whistling. Nye stood up and walked towards the

11

voices. The shouts grew louder. He reached a ridge and saw animals in the valley below. Sheep, and cattle were moving along the track. Drovers called, as they herded the animals. Dogs nipped at the heels of stragglers, followed by a rider on a pony. The rider turned his pony and cantered up the slope towards Nye. He stopped and Nye saw he was holding a pistol.

'Why you are following us?' demanded the rider.

'I'm not,' replied Nye. The rider cocked his gun.

'Where's the rest of the gang?' he shouted. Other drovers ran up the slope.

'Is he one of them?' called a drover with an ugly scar.

'He's got to be, following us like that. Tie him up. We'll bring him along. The magistrate at Brecon can decide what to do with him,' ordered the horseman. The drovers seized Nye, tied his hands behind his back and placed a noose around his neck.

'Let's slit his throat and leave him for the buzzards. No one will find him on the mountain,' suggested one of the drovers.

'No, we'll do it properly,' said the rider and yanked Nye's halter.

'I haven't done anything. Why are you doing this?' shrieked Nye and stumbled.

'Get up or I'll drag you to Brecon through the gorse,' snarled the rider. Nye got up and lurched after the horse.

The drovers stopped at a stream to water the animals. Nye got on his knees and bent his head down to drink like one of the beasts. The rope tightened, dragging him back.

'No water for you,' said the rider. The drovers laughed. The rider dismounted and pulled Nye towards him.

'Was it you? Did you stab David, last night?' demanded the rider. 'He was only fifteen. Did you kill him?'

'I haven't killed anyone. Why would I want to?' answered Nye. He could taste the riders stale breath.

'Because he was guarding my cattle,' said the rider and tightened the noose. Nye began to choke.

'Finish him,' called a drover. The rider increased the pressure, lifting Nye onto his toes.

'Someone's coming,' warned one of the men. The rider relaxed his grip. Nye gulped for air. A tinker, leading packhorses was coming along the track. He greeted the drovers and walked on, ignoring the noose around Nye's neck. It didn't pay to interfere in other men's business. As the tinker passed, the rider regained his composure. He remounted and ordered the drovers to move the herd on.

It was dusk when they reached a clump of Scots pines. Beneath the trees stood an inn, a blacksmiths shop and a walled field. The buildings were at the junction of the drovers track and a dirt road. The landlord greeted the drovers and counted the animals into the walled field. The rider produced a purse.

'Half a penny per beast,' he said and counted seven shillings and six pence into the landlord's outstretched hand. 'Some of the beasts have lost shoes. Can you see to them?' he asked.

'I'll light the forge in the morning but your men will need to sort the cattle that need shoeing,' replied the landlord.

'You boys will sleep with the animals tonight and keep watch. Tomorrow, while the cows are shod, I'll take the rustler to the magistrate at Brecon,' said the rider.

The drovers sat Nye by a gatepost, lashed him to it and went into the tavern to eat, leaving a guard watching from the doorway. Nye eased himself upright with his back to the post.

The wet mud had soaked through his breeches. His legs were numb and his wrists throbbed where the rope had cut his skin. He wriggled around, twisting his coat to move the pocket containing his knife within reach. Eventually, he was able to push a hand into the pocket and pull out the knife. He tried to open the blade but the spring was strong. The knife slipped from his wet fingers and fell into the mud. Nye strained to retrieve it but the rope was tight. His hands didn't reach the ground.

Nye heard footsteps and looked up. The lookout was walking towards him with a tankard. It was the drover who wanted to cut his throat.

'Are you thirsty?' called the drover. Nye didn't answer. The drover took a mouthful of ale and spat it at Nye. He pulled a dagger from his belt and pressed it against Nye's neck. Nye felt the point pierce his skin.

'David was a good friend of mine. I'll be back, later,' whispered the drover. He made a slashing motion across his own throat, kicked Nye and ambled back to the tavern.
Nye reached for his knife. He turned sideways, to get one hand lower than before. The rope cut deep into his wrists. He felt the knife in the mud. He picked up the handle with the tips of his fingers and carefully raised it until it was cupped in both hands. He tried to prise open the blade, knowing that if he dropped the knife again it might vanish in the mud. The blade moved and sprang open. Nye turned the blade upwards and cut himself free. He couldn't see the lookout and wondered if he was still watching from the shadows. Nye waited until a cloud obscured the moon and crawled through the mud, away from the tavern. As he reached the track the sky cleared and there was a shout.

'He's getting away.' Drovers ran from the tavern. Nye stood and ran.

'There he is,' yelled one of the drovers. He heard a shot. The bullet hit a stone wall, showering him with fragments. Nye tripped, fell, got up and ran blindly into the night.

When he could run no further, Nye stopped and listened, straining to hear his pursuers through the darkness. At first, he heard nothing but his own panting but as he caught his breath there were voices, the drovers were calling to each other on the mountain. They seemed all around him. Nye lay down in the heather and tried to conceal himself. It was still dark when he woke from a restless sleep. He was cold and cramp knotted his legs. He rubbed them to restore the circulation. Nye listened for the drovers but the mountain was silent. He waited until the rising sun revealed the dirt track leading across the mountain. He remembered the shepherd's words.

'Follow the road south. It will take you to Merthyr.' Nye scrambled across the heather to the track, checked the sun was to his left and walked south.

Chapter 3

The track led him over a mountain pass and through a valley dotted with small farmsteads. Curious dogs approached, barking defiantly. Others were friendlier and came forward nervously, with their wagging tails between their legs and their heads down. Nye drank greedily at a waterfall, bathed his foot and continued on. He reached a milestone, 'Merthyr Tydfil 3 miles - Brecon 24 miles.' The track continued down the mountain and became a muddy lane, rutted and choked with overgrown hedges. He reached a row of cottages. A woman, beating a rug by her front door, smiled awkwardly. Barefoot children, playing noisily in a stream, ignored him. A tethered pony, grazing beside the lane, looked up briefly.

Nye came to a tavern. It was a shabby building with a faded star, hanging drunkenly, above the door. A man emerged from the tavern and hurried away. Nye ran his hands through his hair and entered. The bar was gloomy. Stale smoke hung in the air. A customer was laughing with a woman behind the counter. Drinkers, huddled by the fire, watched silently as Nye crossed the room. The landlady, a plump woman in her 40s, greeted her new customer with a smile.

'What can I get you?' she asked.

'Do you have any jobs that need doing?' replied Nye. The smile vanished.

'Jobs, what jobs?' She turned to the man at the bar, 'Do you hear that Will. He's looking for work.'

'I'll do anything, wash dishes, cut firewood, fetch coal,' offered Nye.

'Where are you from?' asked the landlady.

'Llangadog.'

'That's a long way off. How did you get here?'

'I walked,' answered Nye. The landlady's expression softened. There was something about him she liked and there were jobs a stout lad could do. She fetched some ham and a jug of beer.

'I don't have any money' said Nye.

'You can sleep in the outhouse behind the inn. Tomorrow, you will work,' answered the Landlady. 'My name is Meir,' she added, 'What's yours?'

'Nye Vaughn,' he replied.

The following morning Nye woke early and Meir gave him his orders.

'You can start by feeding the pig and when you've done that, muck her out,' said Meir and handed Nye a bucket of slops. 'Mouldy bread and stale beer, she loves it. Watch her, she's ready to farrow and can be nasty,' she added. The sow reared up with her trotters on the gate when Nye approached the pig pen. She was a large animal and her head was level with Nye's face. Nye advanced slowly, talking quietly,

'You're a big girl. Are we going to be friends?' The pig grunted. It smelt the food and was hungry. Nye filled the trough. Nye talked softly to the pig while she ate and, after eating, the sow allowed him to stroke her back. She had accepted Nye and a contented familiarity was established. Nye mucked out the pigsty, chopped wood, filled the coal scuttles, cleaned the grates, laid a fire in the bar, moved barrels in the cellar and was as useful as possible. That evening, Meir introduced Nye to Will Jones, the customer Meir had been talking with the previous evening.

'If you're looking for work there might be a chance of some labouring at Thomas' foundry,' suggested Will. 'I'm a pattern maker there, ask for Mr. Thomas.'

'What's a pattern maker?' asked Nye.

'I make the wooden patterns used for casting iron,' replied Will Jones.

The following morning, Nye walked to Thomas' foundry. In the yard, men were loading a wagon with iron cooking pots.

'Who do I see about a job?' asked Nye. One of the workmen pointed to the office,

'You need Mr. Thomas. He's in there.' Nye knocked on the door and entered. Two men were bent over a table, studying a drawing. One was elderly with white hair. The other had similar features but was younger. A young woman was at a desk writing in a ledger. All were well dressed.

'Do you really believe we can cast something this large?' asked the older man.

'I'm sure of it, father. It's a new method I've read about, invented by Henry Cort, an iron producer in Hampshire. His system of puddling the iron removes more impurities. The castings are stronger with less flaws and weaknesses,' replied the younger man. 'Imagine, Thomas ovens and cooking ranges. This would open up new markets for us,' he added enthusiastically.

'Yes?' asked the young woman looking at Nye.

'I'm looking for work,' answered Nye, removing his cap.

'We aren't hiring,' snapped the younger man, without looking up from the drawing.

'Isaac, if we're expanding we'll need more labour,' said the older man. 'I'm Mr. Thomas, this is my son, Isaac and my daughter Eira. What's your name?' asked Mr. Thomas.

'Nye Vaughn, sir,' replied Nye.

'Have you ever worked in a foundry, Vaughn?' asked Mr. Thomas.

'We don't need any more men,' said Isaac, testily.

'No sir but I'm strong and a quick learner,' answered Nye.

'Very well, you can start as a labourer 6 o'clock tomorrow morning. The wage is seven shillings a week. Eira, Vaughn will make his mark in the pay ledger.' Eira watched Nye slowly write his name.

'Your signature is neat Mr. Vaughn,' she said.

'My mother taught me letters and numbers. She made me practice every night,' replied Nye.

Nye returned to the Star Tavern to tell Meir his news. She was pleased and offered Nye the spare room above the bar.

'It will be good to have a paying lodger and you can lend a hand,' she explained.

'You're very kind, Meir,' said Nye.

'Am I?' she said and handed him the slop bucket.

Chapter 4

Labouring in Thomas' foundry was dirty, physical and dangerous but Nye was strong and hard work suited him. His job involved moving barrows of iron ore, coal and limestone, charging the furnaces and transferring molten metal to the

18

moulds. Accidents were common. One labourer slipped as he emptied a barrow of ore into the furnace. He let go of the barrow rather than being dragged into the fire and watched it disappear into the throat of the kiln. As the barrow hit the fire it erupted, belching flames and molten slag. He was badly burned and never worked again. Nye found puddling the metal one of the most difficult and unpleasant jobs. When the furnace was up to temperature and the molten contents boiling, it was stirred using long iron ladles that slowly dissolved into the mixture. The ladles weighed 25 pounds and it took a strong man to turn the thick porridge-like mix while facing a searing heat. Spikes of iron, like jagged icebergs, would float to the surface and had to be quickly stirred under before they oxidized. As each ladle melted and shrank it was replaced and the puddling continued, without stopping, for 30 minutes, the time needed to break up the impurities. The molten metal was then lifted from the furnace in 100 pound balls ready to be drawn; the next stage of the process. It was exhausting work.

Nye learned his job quickly and was soon accepted by the other men. He continued to lodge at the Star, helping Meir when asked, and became a drinking companion with Will Jones. Will encouraged Nye and the young labourer began to absorb the technical details of casting iron.

The new puddling process, suggested by Isaac Thomas, was a success and the improved quality of the iron which resulted, enabled Thomas and Son to progress from making cooking pots. Now, they were able to manufacture more complex products; cast iron stoves with intricate panels, special architectural orders, seats for distant towns and the most promising development of all; cannons. As the business expanded, Nye grew to appreciate the importance of Will

Jones' patterns. Without skilled pattern makers none of the intricate shapes could be cast.

Nye Vaughn's thirst for knowledge and willingness to work hard did not go unnoticed by Mr. Thomas. One morning, Nye was summoned to the office.

'How long have you been here Vaughn?' asked Mr. Thomas.

'Just over a year Mr. Thomas,' replied Nye.

'We're expanding and I need a new foreman for the furnaces. The men respect you. Do you want the job? It's a big responsibility but I'm confident you can do it,' added the foundry owner. Nye was surprised by the offer.

'If you're willing to give me the chance I won't let you down,' replied Nye and grinned.

'It's settled then,' said Mr. Thomas and the two men shook hands.

Mr. Thomas put on his hat and coat, turned to Eira who had been sitting quietly with her books and said,

'Tell cook, I'm eating out and won't be home for supper this evening.' Then he left. Eira and Nye were alone in the office.

'You're going up in the world Mr. Vaughn,' said Eira and smiled coyly.

'So it seems. Will you walk out with me on Sunday?' asked Nye. Just then, Isaac entered the office and demanded to know why Nye was there.

'I was here to see your father,' replied Nye.

'Well, he's not here and you're not paid to loaf about. Get back to work,' retorted Isaac. Nye shrugged and started for the door.

'I'll see you on Sunday after church, by the bridge,' called Eira, as he left.

'Stay away from him Eira. He's a labourer and he's living with the old woman who runs the Star Tavern,' said Isaac, venomously.

Eira's cheeks turned red, 'He's not a labourer. He's the foreman of the furnace gang,' she replied.

'Since when?' demanded Isaac.

'Since father promoted him just before you arrived,' she answered.

'Labourer, foreman, it makes no difference, he's a workman,' replied Isaac. and slammed the door as he left. His father might be a gullible fool but Isaac wasn't going to allow a farm boy like Vaughn get above his station.

Isaac was still angry when he saw his father in the street.

'You made Vaughn a foreman without telling me,' he shouted.

'This isn't the place to discuss our business. People can hear,' said Mr. Thomas.

'He's an upstart. Do you know Vaughn's got his eye on Eira?'

'Not here, Isaac. We'll talk about Vaughn later, at home' replied Mr. Thomas and refused to discuss the matter further. That evening, when Mr. Thomas returned home, Isaac challenged his judgement again. It started as a discussion but when Eira supported her father, Isaac lost his temper, called his father a fool and stormed out. Isaac's wife Delyth, who had sat quietly during the argument, picked up her things and followed her husband. Seeing her husband so annoyed intrigued Delyth. A man who Isaac found threatening, interested Delyth. Nye Vaughn, she decided, deserved further investigation.

The minister's sermon was longer than normal on Sunday and the town hall clock had struck twelve before Eira was able to slip away from the church. She hurried to the bridge.

'You're late. I didn't think you were coming,' said Nye.

'I nearly didn't,' replied Eira, 'You don't go to church?'

'My mother was a Methodist but she never managed to persuade me there is a God. Anyway, church is for masters and gentry,' replied Nye. The pair were unaware they were being observed. Isaac and Delyth had seen Eira leave the church and were watching from a distance.

'Your father is easily taken in, promoting him so quickly like that. It's indecent. Take care Isaac or Vaughn will be a partner one day,' said Delyth, 'You're the one who has made the foundry a success. Your father's no businessman. Left to him you would still be casting second rate cooking pots,' she added. They watched Nye and Eira stroll along the river bank towards the mountain. 'Or he might marry your sister and worm his way into the family,' said Delyth as they disappeared from sight. Isaac's eyes darkened as he stared into the distance. He didn't see the calculating, sideways glance his wife gave him.

Nye and Eira climbed to a cairn on the mountain and sat enjoying the view. The sun warmed their backs. Clouds floated over the valley, their shadows dancing across the landscape. An invisible skylark, was singing high above.

'Why did you say you nearly didn't come?' asked Nye.

'Isaac says you are living with a woman at a tavern. Is it true?' asked Eira. Nye laughed.

'You're brother really doesn't like me, does he? I am living with a woman but not in the way you think.' Nye explained how he lodged at the Star Inn and the landlady was old enough to be his mother. Eira was relieved and they sat in comfortable silence. When Nye took her hand she did not pull away. When he kissed her she responded with a warmth that surprised Nye.

'We should be getting back,' said Nye awkwardly and stood up.

As they walked down the mountain Nye held Eira's hand in his. The kiss had changed their relationship, offering a tantalizing promise of mutual trust and respect, an emotional adventure to come and private feelings to be shared with no one else. They didn't speak until they were back in Merthyr.

'I'll walk you home,' suggested Nye.

'No, it's better not to,' replied Eira.

'I'm not afraid of your brother,' said Nye.

As they parted she turned to him with a warning, 'Take care. Isaac can be spiteful.'

It was Tuesday evening and Nye was in the Star finishing his supper when a boy came with a message.

'The Thomas lady said can you come to the house at once,'

'What's happened?' asked Nye, grabbing his coat. The boy looked vacant and shrugged.

'Something must be wrong. You had better hurry,' said Meir. Nye ran most of the way and was out of breath when he reached the Thomas house. He rang the bell and was surprised when Delyth answered the door instead of the maid.

'I got a message from Eira. Is she all right?'

'She's perfectly well,' replied Delyth and invited him into the parlour. 'Sit down Nye,' she said and pointed to the sofa. Delyth took Nye's coat, placed it on a chair and sat beside him. 'The message was from me,' whispered Delyth. Nye felt uncomfortable. He could feel Delyth's hot breath on his cheek.

'Where is Eira?' he asked quietly.

'Don't worry. Everyone, including the servants, are at a magic lantern show in the town hall. They won't be back for hours,' she whispered and took his hand, placing it on her leg. Then she brushed his cheek with her lips and kissed him. It was a long penetrating kiss designed to arouse. For a moment Nye was lost in the excitement. He felt confused. Then he thought of Eira and felt ashamed. Exhilaration turned to disgust. He pushed Delyth away.

'Mrs. Thomas, you're married. What are you doing?'

'Isn't it obvious,' she said, laughing. She tried kissing him again. Nye stood up but Delyth was holding his shirt and would not let go. It ripped as he pulled away. Nye picked up his coat and left.

Delyth was crying when the family returned from the magic lantern show.

'Is your headache worse Delyth?' asked Eira.

'I've been attacked,' sobbed Delyth and threw off her shawl revealing her dress. There was a large tear down the side.

'Who did it,' demanded Isaac. Delyth told how a man had forced his way into the house and tried to rape her. She produced the torn rag she had ripped from her attacker's shirt. A brown button was hanging by a thread from the corner.

'Who was it?' asked Eira.

'One of the workmen, I think his name is Vaughn,' answered Delyth.

'This is a matter for the magistrate,' said Mr.Thomas angrily.

'I warned you father but you wouldn't listen. Vaughn's chanced his luck with Eira and now he's attacked my wife. I'm not having her honour debated by a magistrate or the people of Merthyr sniggering behind our backs. This is a private affair to be discussed with no one. Do you understand? I'll deal with Vaughn,' said Isaac.

Chapter 5

Nye returned to the Star and said nothing of what had taken place with Delyth Thomas. Seeing he was upset, Meir decided to wait until Nye was ready to talk and went to bed leaving him to lock up. He was alone in the bar when three large men burst in and dragged him outside to where Isaac Thomas was waiting. Thomas produced the torn cloth and brown button. It matched the tear on Nye's shirt. Nye protested his innocence but the brown button was all the evidence Isaac needed. Hearing shouting, Meir got up and peered through her bedroom window.

The first blow was a punch from behind. It landed on Nye's kidneys. Pain seared up his spine. His legs buckled. More blows followed. Nye stumbled and fell. Then, the thugs kicked him. He covered his face with his arms but they gave little protection from the heavy boots. Isaac Thomas watched as his ruffians did their work.

'That's enough. We don't want to kill him,' said one of the men. The three villains stood over their victim breathing heavily. Clouds of vapour hung in the damp air.

Isaac Thomas stepped forward, bent down and whispered to Nye, 'Vaughn if you ever again come near my family, I will kill you.' Then he stepped back and lunged forward to deliver a powerful kick. Nye heard his ribs crack before pain overwhelmed him and he passed out.

Delyth recovered her composure surprisingly quickly when Isaac announced he would deal with Vaughn. Eira was sitting with Delyth when they heard a crash from upstairs followed by moaning. They found Mr. Thomas sitting on the landing.

'What's wrong father?' asked Eira. Mr. Thomas tried to answer but his words were incomprehensible.

'What's wrong with his face?' said Delyth. The right hand side of Mr. Thomas's face was contorted and he was dribbling.

'Help me get him to his room,' said Eira and the two women manhandled the old man, who was a dead weight, to bed.

In the morning the doctor examined Mr. Thomas and told them he had suffered a massive stroke.

'Did something upset him last night?' asked the doctor.

'Will he recover?' asked Isaac, ignoring the doctor's question.

'I can't cure him. There is a possibility he will recover some movement, God willing, but for now he's bed ridden and will need constant nursing. There is something else. He has lost the ability to talk and it's unlikely he will ever speak again,' added the doctor.

Delyth waited until she was alone with Isaac. 'You know what this means? Now the old fool won't be there to interfere with the way you run the foundry,' she said and smiled at her husband. Isaac was surprised by Delyth's remark.

'You never liked my father. Why is that?' he asked.

'Rubbish, I'm just thinking how much better it will be now you have a free hand,' she lied.

When Nye regained consciousness and tried to move, there was a sharp pain in his chest. Slowly, he moved his hand down the front of his body. It was tightly bandaged. Nye lay still and tried to focus but his left eye would not open. He was in a double bed in a strange room. A water jug painted with flowers stood on a washstand by the window. A framed embroidery sampler, with a quote from the bible, hung on the wall behind the door. Rays of sunlight illuminated the room, revealing particles of dust floating in the air. He could hear distant laughter and shouts. Children were playing outside. Then, black oblivion returned.

The next time Nye woke the room was dim. Meir was sat on a chair beside the bed.

'I'm dry. Can I have some water?' Nye drank awkwardly from the cup Meir held to his lips. His face was swollen and he could feel a large cut across his mouth. He touched his face and winced. His nose was broken. Meir went downstairs and returned with a bowl of broth which she fed to him with a spoon. 'Where am I?' asked Nye.

'At the Star, in my bedroom,' replied Meir. Then he slept again.

Nye was in bed for six days. The kicking had broken three ribs, knocked out a tooth and left him cut and bruised. Both eyes were black and his nose was twice its normal size.

'You were lucky they didn't kill you,' said Meir as she washed him. 'Why did they beat you?' Nye didn't answer. The next day Meir asked again and Nye began to talk. As he described what happened, Nye tried to understand but nothing made any sense. He held nothing back from Meir, describing how Delyth had kissed him, how she ripped his shirt and how Isaac Thomas threatened to kill him.

'I had a son once,' said Meir, after a brief silence, 'He would be about your age.'

'I didn't know you were married,' said Nye.

'I wasn't. I was nineteen, working as a housemaid for a mine manager in Dowlais. He took advantage of me and I got pregnant. When I began to show, his wife found out and threw me on the street. All I had were the clothes on my back.'

'What happened?' asked Nye.

'The owner of this place, John Price, took me in and raised the boy as his own. He never married me but was good to me. John even left me the pub when he died.'

'Where is he now?' asked Nye.

'I told you he died.'

'No I meant the boy, your son. Where is he now?'

'He went down the mine when he was eight and was killed in an explosion. His real father, the old bastard, never acknowledged him, not once. Not even when I buried my boy. That's the masters for you. We can all rot in hell for all they care.'

Nye pushed back the blankets and asked for his clothes. 'Where are you going?' asked Meir.

'To see Mr. Thomas and talk to him. He's a decent man, he'll understand,' replied Nye.

'They won't let you see him. He's had a stroke. Some say he's gone mad,' said Meir and pushed Nye back into bed. The door opened and Will Jones came in. 'Will's been helping look after you. It was Will who carried you up here the night they gave you the beating,' explained Meir.

'How's the invalid today?' asked Will.

'My chest hurts like hell when I move or cough. What's happening at the foundry?' asked Nye.

'Isaac Thomas is strutting around like he owns the place. He's made quite a few changes,' replied Will.

'And Eira, have you seen her?'

'She came into the foundry one morning and there was a row. I heard Isaac tell her to go home where she belonged. He said she was no longer going to embarrass him by working in the office,' said Will, 'There is some other news which will interest you both,' he added.

'What's that?' asked Meir.

'We've made peace with the American colonists. The war's over. The Americans have won their independence,' replied Will.

Chapter 6

The news that peace had broken out in America did not please Isaac Thomas particularly when an order for cannons was cancelled by the Board of Ordnance. The ending of hostilities meant the army no longer needed the cannons.

Mr. Thomas' stroke left him paralysed and unable to communicate except by grunts and nods. Having been told she was not welcome at the foundry, Eira stayed at home and nursed her father but the humiliation she experienced in front of the workers made her angry. She resented her brother's arrogance but, realising how important it was to make sure her father was looked after properly, accepted her new role. Delyth had enthusiastically volunteered to help to look after Mr. Thomas but seldom visited the old man's room unless Isaac was at home. When he was, she made a point of bustling about and appearing indispensable.

It was a month before Nye was fit enough to look for work. He walked to the foundry at Dowlais and asked for a job. The manager went to speak to the owner and returned to say there were no positions. He was told the same thing at Pen-y-darren and Plymouth works. Isaac Thomas had spread the word. Vaughn was a troublemaker. Returning home, Nye saw Eira come out of the apothecary on Church Street. He ran towards her and called her name. She stopped and glared at him.

'Stay away from me,' she shouted and hurried off.

Blacklisted by the foundries, Nye took any work he could find. He pushed coal tubs to the washing tables at Abercynon mine, where women sorted stones from coal. He laboured as a blaster's mate in Gurnos limestone quarry, using a sledge hammer to drive six foot metal drills into the rock face, ready for the explosive charges to be set. When there was no work, he scavenged for coal on the slag heap above the town. His life had become brutal and uncertain. He considered giving up and returning to his father's farm. Meir didn't complain when Nye had no money for rent. Instead, she encouraged him like his mother would have done.

One evening, Meir and Nye were alone in the bar when Will Jones burst through the door. He was angry.

'What's wrong with you?' asked Meir.

'That bastard, Thomas, he's finished me,' replied Will.

'So now there are two of you without jobs,' she said and handed a beer to Will.

'Why don't we start our own foundry?' suggested Nye suddenly.

'Don't be stupid,' replied Will.

'Listen to me, Will. I don't mean anything grand, like Thomas', just a modest workshop where we make small, quality items. What would we need? A small furnace, sand pits, some patterns - you can make them - and raw materials,' explained Nye.

'We aren't businessmen and you're forgetting something else that's rather important; we haven't got any money,' said Will.

'I have,' said Meir, quietly, 'John Price left me £885 in a bank account.'

'That's a lot of money. You didn't say he was rich,' said Nye.

'I didn't know what to do with the money, so I left it where it was. It's still there,' added Meir. They discussed Nye's idea until the early hours of the morning and shook hands agreeing a partnership between Nye and Will. Meir would provide her inheritance as a loan. Will would manage production while Nye promoted the business and found customers. The three drank a toast to their success.

'I still think it's a mad idea,' said Will.

'What about premises?' said Nye.

'There is an old water mill by the river,' suggested Will.

'You mean Castle Mill. It's been empty for years. Maybe we could rent it,' said Nye.

The owner of Castle Mill, Mr. Griffiths, a genial self made man, owned a number of properties in Merthyr. He watched as the two young men explored the building.

'We can build the furnace by the far wall. The water wheel still works. I can adapt it to drive the bellows,' said Will, enthusiastically.

'Do you boys seriously think the mill can work as a foundry?' asked Mr. Griffiths.

'We certainly do. If we can agree a fair rent this place will soon be producing ironware,' replied Nye. Will nodded.

'I wasn't thinking of renting. I prefer to sell,' answered Mr. Griffiths.

'I understand that but we don't have the money. What if we leased the mill for £300 per annum?' suggested Nye.

'That's a good offer Mr. Vaughn. More than it's worth,' said Mr. Griffiths. Nye realised he had blundered.

Mr. Griffiths smiled. He was dealing with novices.

'What are you going to manufacture?' he asked. Nye explained they were going to make small iron products like flat irons, cooking pots and firebacks.

'What about competitors like Thomas and Son, they won't like what you are doing?' said Mr. Griffiths. The partners didn't answer. 'I'll tell you what I'll do. In return for the rent you offered, and a ten year lease, which my lawyer will prepare, I'll give you a six month rent free period. That gives you time to repair and convert the mill,' offered the owner.

'We agree but can we keep our arrangement secret?' said Nye.

'I'll have my solicitor draw up the papers and don't worry; Isaac Thomas is no friend of mine. Gentlemen, you can rely on my discretion. Good luck with your new business. I offer my hand to settle our agreement,' said Mr. Griffiths. They shock hands, the deal was done.

As they were leaving, Mr. Griffiths asked the name of their new company. It was something that Will or Nye hadn't thought about. Mr. Griffiths suggested 'Castle Iron Works' as suitable because the mill was already known as castle mill and a castle signifies strength, an ideal metaphor for iron goods.

The partners started converting the premises the day the lease was signed.   The roof was repaired. Labourers constructed a furnace and ramp along the side of the mill to give wheelbarrow access to the throat of the furnace. Will modified the waterwheel to drive bellows, forcing air through the furnace and dug a new culvert from the River Taff to increase the flow of water. Workmen tore up wooden floors and covered the earth with sand to create a casting area. While Nye managed the conversion of the mill, Will carved wooden patterns for their new range of products. Stout wooden doors were fitted to make the foundry secure and a sign was positioned high above the entrance. Meir, Will and Nye watched as it was lifted into place;

'Castle Iron Works – Proprietors Vaughn and Jones'

The activity at Castle Mill did not go unnoticed by Isaac Thomas. At first, he was idly curious to learn who was rebuilding the mill. None of his acquaintances seemed to know and that made him more inquisitive. He asked around but was no wiser until his coal supplier mentioned that the new owners had negotiated a price for regular deliveries and placed an order. He quizzed the merchant and discovered what Vaughn and Jones were doing. The idea of a farm boy and a pattern maker, with no money or experience in commerce, trying to start a business amused him but when he shared the news with Delyth she told him they were a threat. Isaac protested that one more foundry in the town was of no consequence but Delyth was adamant.

'Someone with money must be backing them. They know who your customers are and can copy your products,' she warned. Isaac told Delyth she was obsessed but when she suggested a plan to put Castle Iron Works out of business he agreed it was a good idea. If it worked there would be one foundry less in Merthyr Tydfil.

Production started at the new foundry on the 1st March 1784. Nye and Will carefully poured the molten metal into the moulds. When the metal had set, Will broke open a mould and shook out the sand, revealing their first product, a boot scraper. Nye used tongs to lift up the scraper and examined it. The hot iron shone like silver. They looked at the flower patterns on the sides

'It's flawless,' said Nye triumphantly.

'It's only a boot scraper,' said Will modestly.

'No Will, this is our future,' replied Nye.

Chapter 7

The Thomas house settled into a new routine. Isaac went to the foundry early and returned for dinner each evening. In the morning Eira fed her father. Then, washed and shaved him before a housemaid helped turn the old man on his side to relieve the bedsores on his elbows and heels. Delyth rarely appeared from her room before lunchtime and no longer made any pretence of helping to care for Mr. Thomas, even when her husband was in the house. On some afternoons Delyth went out, without saying where she was going and returned shortly before her husband. Delyth and

Eira rarely spoke except when they passed on the landing or in the hallway.

The mood of the house was sombre, as if Mr. Thomas' ill health had infected the fabric of the building. Eira would sit with her father. His eyes looked tired and vacant, like windows of an empty house, seeing nothing and revealing nothing of within. Occasionally a tear would run down Mr. Thomas' cheek and Eira wept with him. Once she saw a twinkle in his eye and laughed as if to share a private joke. Her father would never walk or talk again but his mind was active, imprisoned in a crippled body. Eira was also trapped, in a silent house with no human contact except her father. She talked to him and, when a reply was needed, she answered for him. Some of the conversations were idle chatter about the weather or gossip from the town. She told her father how Isaac was expanding the foundry, about the new competitor at Castle Mill and of more personal matters, sharing her innermost secrets.

Nye Vaughn's visit to Blacks Iron Merchants of Whitechapel, London went well and Nye was disappointed when Mr. Black didn't place an order. During his business trip, other retailers had been more forthcoming. Mr. Black complimented Nye on his samples and agreed to study the catalogue and pricelist in more detail but declined to buy anything. Nye had hoped Mr. Black would buy some stock but the ironmonger would not be drawn.

Apart from the disappointment at Blacks, the sales tour had been a success and Nye was happy to be returning to Merthyr. He settled back in his seat as the coach slowly made its way across the Heads of the Valley. The blustery weather on the mountain rocked the stage and cold air whistled through the ill fitting windows. Nye thought of the unfortunate souls sat on the roof in the perishing wind. No one would be falling asleep and dropping off the coach today. The stage picked up speed and headed downhill, towards Merthyr, slowing to a trot over the cobbles on Dowlais High Street. Nye viewed the familiar scene. He'd been away for four weeks but it seemed as if he had been gone for months.

Nye flourished his order book triumphantly, when he got to the foundry. Will Jones flicked through the contracts and grinned. Then, he handed Nye an envelope. 'What's this?' asked Nye.

'It came yesterday from London. Have a look,' said Will. Nye opened the letter. It was from Mr. Black of Whitechapel. Nye read the contents aloud;

> *'Sirs,*
> *Blacks Iron Merchants require delivery at your earliest convenience but for   certain before the thirty first day of July the following items namely;*
> *Quantity*
> *200 barley twist newel posts - catalogue number CIW 602,*
> *300 barley twist spindle balustrades - catalogue number CIW 614,*
> *360 flower motif bowed balustrades - catalogue number CIW 217,*
> *100 firebacks - catalogue number CIW 165.*
> *Our terms of payment are 30 days following satisfactory delivery and completion of our order.'*

'It's the biggest order we've ever had. Can we cast that many pieces in time?' asked Nye.

'I've already started but we are going to need an extra shift and more raw materials,' replied Will.

'There's a footnote,' said Nye, *'Subject to our customers approval we anticipate placing similar orders on a regular basis.'* That evening Nye, Will and Meir celebrated.

When the coal merchant refused to deliver to Castle Iron Works unless he was paid in advance Nye wondered why. The merchant's account had always been paid on time. Then, other suppliers demanded payment and stopped supplying. Without regular deliveries of materials the foundry was in trouble. Completing the order for Blacks was impossible.

'We can't pay suppliers in advance. We don't have the money,' said Will dejectedly.

'Then we must borrow,' replied Nye. The partners knew none of the banks in Merthyr would lend without collateral and were still discussing the problem when the landlord, Mr. Griffiths, came striding across the yard.

Mr. Griffiths came straight to the point. 'I've been warned you can't pay your rent. Is it true?'

'Yes, it probably is,' replied Nye and told Mr. Griffiths about the sudden reluctance of suppliers to give credit.

'Apart from your current cash flow problem, is the business sound?' asked the landlord. Nye confirmed it was and produced the order book to prove his point. 'Without money we are in trouble,' he admitted.

'I'll put money into Castle Iron Works, enough to pay your creditors but I want a share in the business,' said Mr. Griffiths, 'The way I see things, without my money you are finished. On the other hand, with my money and experience, which you do also need, we can all become wealthy men,' said Griffiths. Mr. Griffiths was taking advantage but the partners knew he was right. Without his money they faced bankruptcy and making him a partner was a good idea. His knowledge of deal making and commerce would be invaluable to the business. Nye and Will had no choice and agreed to Benjamin Griffiths becoming a partner.

As Griffiths was leaving Nye asked, 'Who told you we're in trouble?'

'The same man who's been telling all your suppliers you're insolvent, Isaac Thomas,' replied Mr. Griffiths.

All the suppliers except one resumed their deliveries after being paid. Gurnos quarry, where Nye had once swung a sledgehammer, sent Castle Iron Work's next purchase order for limestone back with the words , 'We regret we are unable to meet your requirement on this occasion,' written across the bottom. Thomas had threatened to withdraw his substantial custom from Gurnos quarry if it continued to supply Castle Iron Works. Without limestone, there was no way of removing impurities from the iron ore and the furnace was useless. Nothing could be made. Benjamin Griffiths and Nye went to see the quarry owner.

'Why won't you deliver? We've paid your account,' demanded Nye.

'I'm sorry but I've sold our entire output for the next six months. Try another supplier,' replied the quarry owner.

'I don't believe you and we don't have the time to find another supplier,' said Nye.

'Sir, I'm not accustomed to being called a liar,' snapped the owner.

'Gentlemen, I have an idea which might help us all. Castle Iron Works would like to buy your quarry. Let's discuss a price shall we?' said Benjamin Griffiths.

'We can't afford to buy a quarry. You should never have done the deal,' said Nye.

'Don't worry my boy, I have collateral, we'll borrow the money,' replied Benjamin, adding, 'Look at it this way. We've secured our limestone supply for the future and added the quarry's profit margin to ours. It makes perfect business sense. You have to be prepared to think big if you want to make money.' Nye was seeing Benjamin Griffiths in a different light. He wasn't a genial old man with money, Griffiths was an astute businessman with a nose for profit.

'So when do we buy our first coal mine?' asked Nye.

'You're learning fast,' replied the older man and grinned. Limestone deliveries to Castle Iron Works resumed the next day.

Mr. Thomas was woken by an argument in the early hours of the morning. It was a warm, dark night and the windows were open. He could hear Isaac and Delyth's raised voices coming from their bedroom.

'You lost another order to Vaughn. When will you learn? You were stupid to let them buy Gurnos quarry,' shouted Delyth.

'It's only one customer. What would you have done different?' snapped Isaac.

'I would arrange an accident to destroy their foundry and put them out of business,' said Delyth.

'You're mad,' replied Isaac.

'And you're spineless. Remember it was me who sorted Vaughn out last time. If I hadn't done something he would be your brother in law by now,' yelled Delyth.

'I don't understand what you're saying. What did you do?' replied Isaac.

'Nothing,' shouted Delyth.

'Keep your voice down or father will hear,' said Isaac.

'Let him hear. He can't talk. Your father's a vegetable. He can't do anything,' screamed Delyth. The argument continued with lowered voices and Mr. Thomas struggled to hear what they were saying. When he woke in the morning he thought he had been dreaming.

That afternoon, as Eira talked to her father, his right hand moved slowly across the bed and touched her arm, as if to console her. The following day, Mr. Thomas could hold a pencil and scrawl short messages on a notepad. The writing was childlike and the effort quickly tired the old man but he could communicate. He wrote a note asking for his solicitor to be summoned. The solicitor, Mr. Jacobs, stayed alone with Mr. Thomas for more than an hour. Mr. Jacobs returned the next morning accompanied by his clerk. They arrived with them a last will and testament Mr. Thomas had asked to be drafted. Eira was asked to leave so the confidential document could be read to Mr. Thomas. After the solicitor had read the will to Mr. Thomas, he scrawled his name and the visitors signed as witnesses. Then, the solicitor left, taking the will with him for safe keeping. Eira showed the visitors out and returned to her father's room. Mr. Thomas was holding a note. Eira read it, got up and closed the door. Her father wanted a private moment with her.

Three men stood in front of Isaac Thomas' desk.

'What sort of accident?' asked one.

'Furnaces can be dangerous things. They have been known to burst, especially if gunpowder is added to the mix,' said Isaac.

'How do we pour gunpowder into a hot furnace without blowing ourselves up?' asked another.

'You don't. The furnace at Castle Iron Works is being relined on Saturday. It's been allowed to cool and the work will be completed by Saturday night. On Sunday afternoon, the furnace will be recharged with coal, iron ore and limestone ready for firing by the first shift on Monday morning. Your job is to place the gunpowder in the furnace on Sunday night,' explained Isaac.

'Someone might get hurt,' said the third man.

'An accident like that would put them out of business. Twenty guineas is a lot of money for an hour's work,' replied Isaac and spread the gold coins tantalisingly across the desk.

Eira Thomas looked up at the shabby sign. She had never been in a tavern. She took a deep breath and opened the door. The shift had just ended at Castle Iron Works and the smoke filled bar of the Star Tavern was crowded with foundry-men, washing the day's grime from their throats. The tap room fell silent as she entered. Meir hurried from behind the bar, shuffled Eira into a side room and shut the door. She listened while Eira explained the reason for her visit. Then she sent a boy to the foundry to fetch Nye and Will.

'You need to hear what Miss Thomas has to say,' said Meir. Her story astonished them.

Nye Vaughn walked back across the town with Eira. 'You're brave, coming to warn us,' said Nye.

'What are you going to do?' asked Eira.

'I don't know,' replied Nye. They stopped by the town hall.

'Don't come any further in case Isaac is about,' said Eira. Nye took her arm and kissed her on the cheek. She drew away.

'This doesn't change anything between us,' said Eira.

'It doesn't alter how I feel about you,' replied Nye. Eira looked at him. She wanted to ask if Delyth's accusations were true, but she couldn't find the right words.

'Goodbye Mr. Vaughn,' said Eira and walked away.

Chapter 8

'What time is it?' whispered Will.

40

'I don't know,' replied Nye. The partners were sitting in darkness in the foundry.

'Do you still think the bombers will come?' asked Will. It had been a long night. The first glimmer of dawn was beginning to push the black of night west. Dark clouds hung low across the sky. A cockerel crowed in the distance. The first shift would be arriving soon to begin the day. Will stood up, stretched and said, 'They won't come now. Let's get some breakfast.'

'Sh,' said Nye and pulled his companion down.

There was a squeaking noise outside. The squeak grew louder and stopped. There was a murmur of voices. Wood splintered. Someone was forcing the doors. They watched as the doors opened and three men entered the gloomy foundry, two were pushing a barrow loaded with a keg.

'You should have oiled that wheel,' said one.

'Shut up and bring the powder,' said another.

'Stand still or we'll shoot,' shouted Nye and cocked a pistol. A bomber raised a gun and aimed at Nye. The others turned and ran for the door. Nye fired at the man with the gun. The bomber dropped the gun. It hit the ground and discharged. He stumbled out through the doors. Will lit a lantern and walked over to the discarded weapon. 'There's blood on the floor. You hit him Nye,' he said retrieving the gun.

They found the bomber outside the door. Nye's bullet had passed though his chest. He was dead.

'I know him. He's one of the ruffians who gave me a beating,' said Nye.

'What are we going to do with him?' asked Will.

'Give me a hand,' said Nye. They lifted the body onto the barrow and wheeled it to the river. Nye broke open the gunpowder keg and emptied the contents into the river then they tipped the body into the water. 'Promise me Will, to tell no one or we will both hang,' said Nye. They watched the body float downstream.

'What about the other two?' asked Will.

'They can't say anything. If they do they would have to explain what they were doing here and there's no evidence,' replied Nye. They returned to the foundry and covered the bloodstains with sand as the morning shift arrived to light the furnace.

Isaac Thomas listened while his thugs told how they were ambushed.

'What happened to Sam?' he asked.

'We don't know. Haven't seen him since,' replied one. Isaac told the men Sam was probably drunk somewhere spending his gold. He gave them an extra five guineas and told them to keep their mouths shut.

Delyth was angry when she learned the plot had failed. Had Vaughn discovered their plan? She accused Isaac of telling someone but he was adamant, he hadn't. Then, she remembered the night of the argument and Isaac's father asleep in the room next door, or was he?

The following afternoon, Delyth announced she was going for a walk and made her way to the George Hotel. She entered the hotel, walked through the bar, up the stairs and into room eleven. The solicitor, Marcus Jacobs was sitting on the bed waiting for her. She kissed him and undid his shirt. Later, while Delyth was dressing the solicitor began to tease her. 'I wrote a will last week.'

'How interesting,' replied Delyth in a disinterested way

'It concerned a certain foundry.' Delyth's ears pricked up.

'What foundry might that be?' she asked.

'It seems your husband has lost part of his inheritance. He's only going to get a legacy. Old man Thomas has left the foundry in a trust for Eira and the workers,' said the solicitor and grinned. He was enjoying himself. Delyth thought for a moment.

'Marcus, where's the will now?' she asked.

'Don't worry. It's quite secure. It's locked in my desk,' replied the solicitor.

Delyth didn't tell her husband about her afternoon with Marcus Jacobs. There were pleasures a woman was entitled to keep private and as a result she could hardly tell Isaac about the will. The fact that the old man had disinherited Isaac, infuriated her. In her mind the foundry was Isaac's by right. Wasn't he the one who was building it up? Her husband deserved the foundry, more importantly she wanted it. Who else knew about the will, Delyth wondered? Had the old man told Eira? Delyth decided to find out. She found Eira sewing in the parlour.

'What did the solicitor, Mr. Jacobs, want with father the other afternoon?' she asked innocently.

'Presumably, they had some business to conduct,' replied Eira, guardedly.

'I thought he might have been making a will. Has he said anything to you about a will?' asked Delyth.

'A will, I believe he made one several years ago. Why do you ask?' replied Eira.

'No particular reason. So he hasn't spoken to you about his will,' asked Delyth.

'No Delyth. My father hasn't spoken a word to me about any will,' replied Eira testily. Satisfied with the answer, Delyth left Eira alone, to continue sewing.

That night as the maid was clearing the dinner table Delyth declared she had a headache and was retiring early. Delyth went upstairs to Mr. Thomas' room and quietly closed the door. The old man was dozing but woke with a start as his unexpected visitor approached the bed.

'Isaac worked hard to make the foundry a success and you want to steal it from him. That isn't right, is it?' whispered Delyth in the old man's ear. Mr. Thomas' eyes were wide open. He tried to speak but no sound would come.

'You never liked me,' she added and pulled the pillow over the old man's face.

Delyth pressed down hard on the pillow until the old man stopped moving. Then, she replaced the pillow under Mr. Thomas' head, straightened the sheets and retired to her own room. When Isaac came to bed, Delyth pretended to be asleep. On her way to her room, Eira cracked open the door to look in on her father and seeing him sleeping comfortably she closed it again. The maid discovered Mr. Thomas' body the following morning when she opened the bedroom door and recognised the smell of death.

'It was to be expected. His suffering is over now,' said the doctor after examining the corpse. He wrote 'heart failure' on the death certificate.

Thomas and Son Foundry shut on the day of the funeral and the workforce walked behind the dead man to his final resting place. Some of the men wanted to show their respect. Others, aware they would lose a day's pay, were less charitable towards the Thomas family. After the funeral service in St. Tydfil's Church, Mr Thomas' coffin was carried, shoulder high, through the streets of Pen-y-darren where it was transferred to a horse drawn hearse for the journey through Dowlais to the family vault at Caeharris. A priest led the procession, ringing a small corpse bell to frighten away evil spirits. Isaac walked behind the hearse. Eira and Delyth followed in a carriage. The men of Castle Iron Works stood erect and removed their caps as the cortege passed. Nye

Vaughn saw Eira slumped in the carriage but her head was down and she did not see him. Pen-y-darren Iron Works, Dowlais Iron Works and other smaller foundries closed as a mark of respect. Workers lined the streets in silence as the procession of mourners trudged by.

After Mr. Thomas' interment, there was a funeral feast at the town hall for friends and dignitaries. The Thomas' were seated in the main room, accepting condolences. Eira was tearful. Her brother looked uncomfortable. Delyth was beside her husband and appeared to be enjoying the attention. Nye Vaughn approached cautiously to express his sympathy.

'I'm sorry that your father has passed away Mr. Thomas. He was a good man,' said Nye. Isaac Thomas ignored Nye and turned to speak with another mourner. 'I'm sorry Eira, I shouldn't have come,' said Nye and left.

'The impudence, coming here and gloating like that,' said Delyth and put a protective arm around her sister in law's shoulder.

The following day Isaac, Eira and Delyth went to the solicitor's for the reading of Mr. Thomas' will. Marcus Jacobs sat on the large leather chair, behind his desk and surveyed the family. All three were dressed in black. Black veils hid the women's faces. Jacobs produced an envelope from the desk drawer, with a theatrical gesture, opened it, placed the contents on his desk and began to read;

> *"This is the last will and testament of me Richard John Thomas of Bryncoch in the parish of Dowlais in the county of Brecon iron manufacturer. Subject to the payment of my just debts funeral and testamentary expenses I give the sum of four hundred pounds unto my son Isaac Thomas of Bryncoch in the parish of Vaynor upon trust to invest the same upon mortgage of freehold*

or leasehold property in England or Wales or in any investment authorised by law for trust funds with power to vary the investments thereof from time to time and to supply the income thereof towards the support of my daughter Eira Thomas of Bryncoch in the parish of Dowlais. I give the sum of three hundred pounds to Marcus Jacobs of Dafadfa Uchaf in the parish of Dowlais in the county of Brecon. The remainder of my property of whatever nature or kind soever I give to my son Isaac Thomas and I appoint him sole executor of this my will. I revoke all former wills made by me and declare this to be my last will and testament in witness whereof I have hereunto set my hand on this sixth day of August one thousand seven hundred and eighty four. Signed Richard John Thomas."

'It's quite straight forward. Mr. Thomas has provided an income for Eira and left the bulk of his estate including of course the foundry to Isaac,' offered the solicitor by way of explanation.

'That isn't what he told me before he died. My father said the works would be placed in a trust, I can prove it,' said Eira.

'I assure you the will is perfectly in order. I was with him when he signed it,' said the solicitor.

'Yes and suddenly you are a beneficiary,' snapped Eira. Her invective electrified the room.

'Eira you're upset. You don't know what you are saying,' said Isaac, trying to calm her.

'You told me your father never told you about a will. If you have proof, produce it,' said Delyth.

'I said my father never spoke about a will. He couldn't. He wasn't able to speak but I still have the notes my father wrote. They clearly show what he wanted. They're in my room. I'll fetch them,' said Eira and stood up.

'I'll take you in the carriage,' said Isaac and escorted her from the room.

Delyth lifted her veil and smiled at Marcus Jacobs. 'The trust fund for Eira was a nice idea, especially with Isaac controlling the money,' she said.

'You can't leave her with nothing. It would look odd. Even you aren't that heartless Delyth,' replied the solicitor, 'If she has kept notes her father scribbled they won't be a problem. The will is a legal document renouncing all other wills. That includes hand scribbled notes that someone might have forged. You realise she is slandering me. If she defames my character in front of others I shall sue.'

'I'm sure that won't be necessary Marcus,' said Delyth with a grin.

Isaac followed Eira upstairs to her bedroom. She opened the drawer of her chest and felt under her clothes for her father's notes. They had gone. Someone had been through her things and removed them. Isaac had never heard his sister tell a lie before and wondered why she was behaving so strangely.

Chapter 9

Richard Thomas' will was proved by Isaac's oath and, being the sole executor, administration of the estate was immediately granted to him. The assets were transferred to his name making him the new owner of Thomas Iron Works. Eira could do nothing to prevent the transfer and, since he also controlled the small trust fund provided for her, Eira's financial future was in his hands. At home, Delyth started to make changes. She threw out the old man's personal effects, ordered new furniture, moved into the large front bedroom and made it obvious that Eira lived in Delyth's house under sufferance. With the death of her father, Eira's circumstances had changed. She was now Delyth's poor relation, subject to pity and scorn in equal measure.

Castle Iron Works prospered. Retailers sold the products quickly and were sending repeat orders. Blacks Iron Merchants were a particularly good customer, ordering cast iron stair posts and balustrades to be delivered to houses being constructed for wealthy clients across Britain. Benjamin Griffiths' book keeping gave the partners more control. He showed them how to cost overheads and accurately calculate profit margins. Benjamin offered customers discount for paying promptly and liquidity improved. Despite giving discount, the business was profitable and, because customers settled their accounts early, Castle Iron Works accumulated cash to repay the loan on Gurnos quarry.

On the other side of the valley, Thomas' ironworks had stopped making iron goods for the domestic market and was concentrating on manufacturing cannons for the Board of Ordnance. Procurement for the army and navy was a gentlemanly affair Isaac Thomas was able to charge what he liked. He inflated prices beyond what was reasonable. There was no competition between the foundries and little friction between Isaac and Nye. When they met, at civic functions, the two men ignored each other. Both foundries were making money and a tacit truce existed between them.

'Have you seen this? Two men have flown across the English Channel in a balloon,' said Will Jones and handed the newspaper to Nye Vaughn. Nye read about the daring two and a half hour flight, made on the 7th January 1785, smiled and returned the paper to his partner. 'Trust a

Frenchman to come up with a mad idea like that. I read that he once jumped out of a balloon and floated down to earth on a device he's called a parachute,' added Will.

'Perhaps we should market a cast iron balloon,' suggested Nye. The partners laughed and agreed that neither balloon nor parachute would ever have a practical use.

'We've been asked to take part in the St. David's Day parade. The other foundries always do something. What do you think?' asked Nye. Neither man could think of anything suitable. Meir suggested a float depicting Saint Tydfil's life and a picnic for the foundry men's families after the parade and the partners agreed to her idea.

Tuesday, 1st March was a bright sunny day and Merthyr was on holiday to celebrate the life of Saint David, the patron saint of Wales. The foundries stood idle. Men loitered on street corners, smoking and exchanging greetings. Women scrubbed their children clean and dressed them in their Sunday clothes. During the morning, people drifted towards the town centre to watch the parade. The wagon from Castle Iron Works was drawn by two shire horses dressed with polished leather harnesses and brasses that shone in the sunlight. The bed of the wagon was covered with green matting to represent the farmland where Tydfil was slain. A boy dressed as the Welsh Chieftain, Brychan, stood grieving, unconvincingly while his dying daughter Tydfil, a young girl dressed in white, tried to look saintly as a bleating lamb tied next to her struggled to escape. Tydfil's handmaidens waved to onlookers and boys armed with wooden spears completed the wagon's tableau.

The parade set off. Will and Nye walked alongside the horses. Behind the wagon, boys representing the heathen Picts, who murdered Tydfil, shouted and ran about. As the pageant progressed around the town, the Picts became more unruly. Mock sword fighting degenerated into a general rumpus leaving unrepentant boys bloodied and bruised. A mother grabbed her son, clipped him round the ear and shouted,

'Elwyn, if you don't behave there'll be no picnic.' Elwyn returned to the fray and walloped a boy on the head with his sword.

The procession was moving along Quarry Row when Nye saw Eira at the back of the crowd. She was alone. He left the parade, pushed his way through the people and stood beside her. She looked tired.

'How are you Eira?' asked Nye.

'I'm well thank you, Mr. Vaughn,' she answered frostily.

'Nye, please?'

'I'm well thank you, Nye,' she replied. They stood watching the passing floats. Many were decorated with St. David's flag; a golden cross on a black field. A marching band, playing popular tunes, set the tempo. Women in the crowd linked arms and danced. Others cheered and whistled their appreciation. A company of soldiers with leeks pinned on their tunics marched past, led by an officer with drawn sword.

'Come on,' yelled Nye, above the din and guided Eira along the road.

'Where are we going?' she shouted.

'You'll see,' answered Nye. The parade finished on the meadow by the River Taff where there was a fair. Riders on the flying chairs were screaming and laughing. Others paid a farthing and waited for their turn. Music echoed across the valley. Young daredevils, eager to impress the girls, pushed the swing boats as high as possible. A boisterous crowd listened to a man, at the boxing booth, daring any stout fellow to come up and stay inside the ring with the champion

50

for one round to win a shilling. When a challenger, goaded on by his friends stepped forward, they cheered. Nearby, a horseshoe tossing competition was taking place. Families were picnicking on the grass.

The float from Castle Iron Works stopped on the far side of the meadow, by the river. Nye steered Eira towards it. The tethered horses grazed, contentedly on the lush grass. A table was laden with hams, pies, cheeses and pickles. Another overflowed with fancy breads, bara brith, welsh cakes and savoury puddings. Shortbread and cakes were piled around bowls of jelly and custard. Meir was serving beer from a barrel.

'We're having a picnic,' announced Nye and handed Eira a plate.
After the meal, there were races and games. The men of Dowlais Works challenged Castle Iron Works to a tug of war. It was a noisy affair with shouting and good natured cheating on all sides. No one could agree who won but it didn't matter and the men agreed to a rematch the following year. Eira laughed with the others and, for the first time since her father's death, felt happy.

Eira and Nye sat by the river. A heron was standing, motionless, by the far bank waiting for its supper to swim by.

'What happened in the house with Delyth?' asked Eira. Nye explained, how a boy brought a message, how Delyth forced herself on him, about the beating he received and how Isaac broke his ribs with a kick.

'You must hate them both,' she said. Nye didn't reply.

'I hate them,' said Eira.

'Why should you hate them? They've done nothing to you,' answered Nye. At first, Eira struggled to explain but, as she unburdened, she grew more confident, impatient to share her secrets for the first time. She told Nye how she nursed her father, about the will, the missing notes written by her father and what they contained, why she couldn't prove her father's will had been forged, the solicitor's threats to sue her and how, without her own money, she was trapped in a house ruled by Delyth. Eira wept as she spoke. Nye put his arms around her.

'You don't have to live a wretched existence.'

'I have nowhere else to go,' she replied.

'Yes you have. I'll take you if you'll have me?' asked Nye.

'What do you mean have me?'

'I'm asking you to marry me,' replied Nye.

Nye waited for her answer. The heron pounced, shooting its beak into the water and emerging with a fish. The bird tossed the struggling fish in the air and swallowed it head first. They watched as the outline of the fish slid down the bird's gullet. Eira didn't answer. She didn't know what to say. The proposal of marriage had stunned her. She wanted to say yes but was it the right thing to do? She liked Nye a great deal but he was a lodger in a tavern. He might have started a business but he was living by his wits and had no money or social status. How would they live? Where would they live? What would her brother do? Eira thought of her father and wished he was alive, to advise her.

'I want you to be my wife. Not so you can escape, but for us, for our future and the future of our children. Forget your brother and his wife. This is about us,' said Nye.

'I can't marry you, Nye,' replied Eira.

'Why not?' asked Nye.

'My father has only been dead for half a year. I'm still in mourning. It wouldn't be right. What would people say?'

'But will you marry me after your mourning is over?' asked Nye.

'Yes I'll marry you Nye but we must wait,' she replied.

They sat by the river making plans until the sun disappeared behind the mountain and the dew settled on the grass. The field behind them was empty. The last of the revellers had gone home. Eira shuddered.

'We must go,' she said. Walking back, they agreed to tell no one. The engagement would be their secret for another six months. There was no need for Isaac or Delyth to know their plans, not yet. When Eira's mourning was over the whole world would know. They stopped by the bridge to say goodbye.

'We'll meet here on Saturday?' said Nye and kissed her.

When Nye got back to the Star tavern he was grinning. Meir asked why he was in such high spirits. She had seen him with Eira by the river and, having her suspicions, wanted to know more. Nye refused to say and she teased him, probing to discover the reason for his good humour. Still, he refused to answer. Nye was bursting to share the good news with friends but kept his promise.

Nye's mind was racing as he went to bed. There were things to do. He needed a house for his new bride, one suitable for a respectable woman. Eira's treatment by Isaac and Delyth, infuriated Nye.

'Did he hate them?' Eira had asked. He hadn't answered her but he did and now, knowing the evil done to the woman he loved, he hated them more than ever. Thinking about Eira, defenceless, in a house with her brother and his scheming wife, angered Nye. Rage and euphoria competed, tempest like, in his head.

'Yes,' he said to himself, 'There are things to do.'

The house was dark when Eira arrived home. She closed the front door and walked slowly towards the stairs, feeling her way. The parlour door opened, casting a beam of yellow light across the passage and illuminating the stairs. Isaac's silhouette appeared in the doorway.

'It's late. We have been waiting for you. Come into the parlour for a moment we have something to tell you,' said Isaac. Eira followed her brother into the room.

'Come and sit down we have some news for you,' said Delyth and patted the sofa.

'You tell her Delyth,' said Isaac and stood with his back to the fire. Delyth smiled at her sister in law.

'These last few months haven't been easy for you. We know you took father's death badly, after nursing him for so long. His passing has made you ill Eira. Nobody in their right mind would have said the terrible things you said about poor father's will. We were lucky not to have had a scandal. If Mr. Jacobs hadn't been reasonable who knows what might have happened. We'd have been the laughing stock of Merthyr. Eira, we're worried about you. You mope about the house, you don't eat. Look at you. You must have lost a stone in weight. Face it Eira, you aren't well. Do you understand what we're saying?'

'I'm listening but I don't understand,' said Eira.

Delyth paused, 'Perhaps you can explain better, Isaac.'

'Delyth is trying to say, you need a break. Some time away from Merthyr will do you good. I have business in England. You and Delyth will come and stay with Delyth's Aunt Lily while I'm in Birmingham,' said Isaac.

'When?' asked Eira.

'We leave in the morning. I've already packed you some things,' said Delyth.

'I won't go,' said Eira.

'Rubbish we'll only be away for a few days. You can't stay here on your own. We'll take the landau. If it's nice we'll put the roof down. You'll enjoy it,' said Isaac.

The bags were strapped on the back of the landau by the time Eira had finished breakfast,

'Come on. We need to get going,' called Isaac from the hall. Isaac and Delyth were climbing into the carriage as Eira emerged from the dining room. The maid held the front door open. Eira handed her a letter.

'Will you make sure this gets delivered,' she said and joined the others in the landau.

'I've forgotten my amethyst brooch,' announced Delyth and hurried back into the house. Moments later, she returned and they set off.

The carriage stopped at Abergavenny and they lunched at the Angel Inn. The sun shone in the afternoon and the driver lowered the roof so they could enjoy the views. The road was clear and the carriage progressed at a steady trot. Approaching Hereford the horses slowed to a walk as they passed livestock being driven along the road. The carriage reached the England's Gate Inn, their overnight stop, as the church clock struck six. It was Wednesday, market day in Hereford and the town was busy. Farmers, who seldom left their farms, were making the most of the visit. Drovers were drinking in the taverns. A boy shepherded a flock of geese along the street. A groom ran from the stables and held the horses. Isaac helped the women from the carriage and led them into the coaching inn.

Eira was tired and retired immediately after dinner. She lay in the unfamiliar bedroom and listened to the rowdy drinke's in the bar below. It had been a pleasant day. Even Delyth had been civil to her.

'Perhaps,' she thought, 'they were right. A few days away from Merthyr will do her good. Nye would still be there when she got back and he would have got her letter by now.'

Delyth also retired early, leaving Isaac talking with a doctor from Wrexham. They had ordered a third bottle of wine and it would be some time before he joined her. Delyth removed an envelope from her pocket, placed it on the wash stand and undressed. She finished her toilet, opened the letter and read the contents. Delyth smiled as she read the last line.

'I'm sorry about Saturday but we will soon be together my love. For ever, yours, Eira.' Delyth tossed the letter in the grate and watched it burn.

Chapter 10

The weather deteriorated during the night. A storm blew up bringing heavy rain and gusty winds. Isaac, who had stayed up late, had a hangover and sat in the carriage with his eyes shut. The roof was up and there was little to see as they continued the journey. Delyth was in good spirits and talked about her aunt.

'You'll like Aunt Lily. She's old but active for her age. She has a beautiful rose garden. She lives in Herefordshire. It's a large house for a woman living alone but she has servants and wants for nothing except some company.' Eira listened but her mind was elsewhere.

They arrived at Aunt Lily's house late in the afternoon. Aunt Lily received her visitors in the drawing room. A servant brought tea and cakes. Isaac stayed for an hour, announced he would be back in four or five days and departed. Delyth chatted with her aunt and Eira sat quietly, feeling like an outsider. Aunt Lily didn't move from her chair. Eira was daydreaming when Aunt Lily raised her voice,

'Young lady are you listening. I asked you to ring the bell. I wish to withdraw.' Aunt Lily pointed to a bell rope beside the fireplace. Eira got up and pulled the sash. A manservant entered the room with a bath-chair. He lifted the old lady into it and pushed her towards the door.

'We dine at seven,' announced Aunt Lily and disappeared.

'You didn't tell me your aunt was an invalid,' said Eira.

'Didn't I,' answered Delyth.

Dinner was a gloomy affair. A small oil lamp lit the table but darkness crowded in from the corners of the dining room. Eira shivered. The room was cold.

'How's cousin, Charles?' asked Delyth.

'I haven't seen my son for months. He only visits when he wants his gambling debts paid,' replied Aunt Lily. On the second evening, they ate in silence. Eira was beginning to dislike Aunt Lily and her sad house. She wanted to leave, to see Nye again and was counting the days to their departure.

Eira woke early the next morning. There was a gentle breeze blowing from the south, the sky was clear and it was a beautiful spring day. Eira dressed and left the house before breakfast. She wandered around the flowerbeds and reached a gate leading to a walled vegetable garden. She went through the gate and found a man planting potatoes. He lifted his cap.

'Morning Miss. Can I help you?' he asked.

'Good morning. What a lovely day after all that rain. Can I walk to the village from here? How far is it?' asked Eira.

'Two miles, Miss, but the lane is muddy and there is nothing to see except a few houses,' replied the gardener and returned to his digging. Eira abandoned her plan of walking to the village and returned the house.

That afternoon, Delyth spoke to Eira about her future plans.

'You are looking so much better Eira. The country air has put colour in your cheeks. I've been thinking about your future. You only have a small allowance and you can't live with us forever. Aunt Lily is lonely and needs a companion. The position would suit you admirably and solve all your problems,' said Delyth.

'I don't want to live here with your Aunt,' replied Eira.

'I admit she's formidable but that's just her manner. Let's talk about it again, when you've had time to consider the idea,' said Delyth.

Eira was relieved when Isaac returned. She packed, ready, for the journey home the following day and went to bed. In the morning, she woke early and went down for breakfast. Aunt Lily was in her usual seat at the head of the table. No other places were laid for breakfast.

'Where are Isaac and Delyth?' she asked.

'They left an hour ago,' replied Aunt Lily, 'I've arranged for you to take your meals with the other servants. I'll expect you in the morning room, at ten, to read to me.'

'I'm not your servant,' replied Eira angrily.

'Eira, you're impertinent. Consider your position. You have no husband and money. I'm doing you a kindness. My servant will move your things to your new room and I'll see you in the morning room at ten o'clock.' said Aunt Lily and continued with her breakfast.

Nye was excited. He had been making plans for the future and wanted to tell Eira. More importantly, he wanted to see Eira again, to hold her, to tell her how much he loved her and surprise her with the news of the house they were going to build together. Nye waited on the bridge, as they had arranged. He was early. Nye could see the church clock. Five minutes and they would be together. The clock chimed the hour and Nye looked along the road. There was no sign of Eira. By quarter past, Nye was concerned. He hadn't expected her to be late. When the church bell struck half past

Nye was worried. Was Eira alright? He walked to the Thomas house and knocked on the front door. The maid opened it.

'Tell Miss Thomas that Mr. Vaughn is calling on her,' instructed Nye.

'There is no one home Sir. Mr. Thomas is in Birmingham on business. Mrs. Thomas and Miss Eira have gone with him to visit an aunt,' replied the maid.

'When do they return?' asked Nye.

'Towards the end of the week,' answered the maid. Nye hesitated for a moment, thanked the girl and was leaving when she called him.

'Didn't you get Miss Eira's letter. Mrs. Thomas promised it would be delivered?' The maid told how Eira had been surprised by the sudden trip to Birmingham and how Delyth had snatched Eiras' letter, addressed to him, as she left.

Nye returned to the house the following Thursday. The Thomas' were at home. Delyth told the maid to show him to the parlour.

'What does he want?' said Isaac.

'Let's go and ask him,' replied Delyth.

'I've come to see Eira,' said Nye.

'What business do you have with my sister?' asked Isaac.

'It's a private matter between us.'

'She isn't here,' said Delyth, 'she's taken a position as a lady's companion in England.'

'Where in England?' snapped Nye.

'That doesn't concern you. She doesn't want to see you. Now, we want you to leave,' said Delyth.

'Tell me where she is,' shouted Nye.

'My sister's whereabouts is nothing to do with you. My wife has asked you to leave. Now go,' snarled Isaac.

'I'm going to find her and if you've harmed her, God help the pair of you,' warned Nye. Isaac held the parlour door open.

'That was easier than I expected,' said Delyth after Nye had gone.

'Why, were you expecting him?' asked Isaac and poured a whisky.

'Let's say, I had my suspicions,'

'You never said anything to me,' said Isaac.

'Didn't I,' replied Delyth and shrugged.

Nye went to Birmingham to search for Eira. Enquiries led him to Thomas' business contact but the man couldn't help. Nye rode back to Merthyr hoping Eira had returned, for a message or a letter asking him to come but there was no news of Eira. Weeks passed. Nye lost interest in the foundry and spent his time in the Star Tavern. His friends tried to raise his spirits but the energy that fired Nye's enthusiasm and motivated him had gone. His plans for a new house were forgotten. Why build a house when there is no one to share it? When he slept, Nye dreamt of Eira. In the dreams, they were in a strange place. She would tease him, laughing and waving from a distance. Nye would run towards her but his legs grew heavy until he couldn't lift them from the ground. In his worst nightmares, Eira called him from beyond the grave but, try as he may, he could not reach out to her.

'I'm worried about him, Will,' said Meir one evening, 'He's acting strangely. He's going to do something stupid,'

'Then we must watch him,' replied Will.

Nye began to drink heavily. He became loud and easily angered, revealing a temper his friends hadn't seen before. Hung-over, he was sullen and morose. One evening, when he was drunk, Nye left the Star Tavern and wandered out into the night. Will followed his friend through the streets to

Isaac Thomas' house. He saw Nye stagger forward and take something from inside his coat. It was a pistol. Will ran towards his friend,

'Don't be a fool. What are you doing?' he asked.

'I'm going to kill them,' replied Nye and tried to cock the weapon.

'Then you'll hang. Isn't one killing enough? This isn't the answer,' hissed Will and took the gun from Nye. Nye wept as his friend led him home.

Aunt Lily's routine was rigid. Eira read to her in the morning and after lunch they would embroider. In the afternoon, Eira served Aunt Lily tea, in the garden if it was sunny, or the drawing room. Aunt Lily treated Eira like a servant. Her only free time was before breakfast, when she would walk in the garden. Eira wanted to get away but she had no money and no means of travelling from England back to Wales. Escape was impossible. She wrote Nye a letter asking him to come but how could she send it? The servants couldn't be trusted. They were watching her. Eira resolved to stay calm and pray to be rescued. She tried hard with Aunt Lily but, as the weeks passed, the old woman's vinegar disposition slowly crushed her spirit.

Marcus Jacobs didn't know how long he dozed but he woke to find Delyth still in his arms. The lovers untangled themselves. He waited until Delyth was comfortable,

'You did alright for yourself,' said Jacobs.

'What do you mean?' said Delyth pulling the sheet up to her chin.

'Isaac got the old man's money, the foundry and now Eira has vanished. What nasty surprise are you planning next?' asked the solicitor.

'Since old Thomas died my poor husband has been working too hard. He needs some help, someone trustworthy. A family member who can watch his back. I've asked my Cousin Charles to come to Merthyr and give him a hand.'

'Does Isaac know?' asked the solicitor.

'Not yet, but he won't object,' replied Delyth. Marcus Jacobs got up and began to dress.

'It hardly seems fair. You have a fortune and all I got was three hundred pounds,' he said.

'It's what we agreed,' replied Delyth.

'I know but my part was worth more.'

'What do you mean, more?' asked Delyth.

'Another three hundred.'

'Marcus, I don't have three hundred pounds. All the money's in Isaac's name. Anyway, why should I give you more money?' replied Delyth.

'To keep me from producing the real will,' said the solicitor.

'You still have it! You're a fool. It would destroy both of us,' said Delyth and sat up.

'No Delyth. It's my insurance and I want a fair share.'
Delyth considered what Marcus Jacobs was doing and decided to humour him.

'It'll take time to get the money.'

'I knew you would be reasonable,' said Marcus Jacobs and smiled.

'What's the matter, Miss, have you hurt yourself?' Eira looked up. The gardener was standing a few feet away. She dabbed her eyes with a handkerchief.

'No, I'm alright,' replied Eira recovering her composure. The gardener shook his head and went back to work.

'Oh Nye, where are you?' she whispered.

Chapter 11

Benjamin Griffiths signed the lease for Garngoch Colliery on the 5th August 1785. Six months had passed since Eira's disappearance and although Nye was not completely himself, he was beginning to show a renewed interest in the company. Castle Iron Works continued to grow. With a coal mine and a quarry now part of the company Castle Iron was a major employer in Merthyr Tydfil, one of the foundries that dominated the town. Benjamin Griffith's next objective was to acquire the mineral rights for the mountains above Vaynor and Trefechan. To achieve this, negotiations were well advanced with Lord Dynevor's agent. The foundry now included four furnaces which smelted iron continuously. To provide the extra air, bigger bellows were installed and a second waterwheel added to power them. A new culvert diverted water from the River Taff to a large pond, above the foundry providing a constant water supply.

Delyth Thomas was surprised when Isaac came home early. It was only 2 o'clock. He looked angry.

'Where's my wife?' he shouted at the maid.

'In the garden room, Sir,' replied the maid. Isaac marched through the house to the garden room.

'I've had enough. He has to go.'

'Who has to go?' asked Delyth.

'Your Cousin, Charles. He's been thieving from us,' snapped Isaac, 'The accounts clerk has discovered he's been falsifying ledgers and taking money.'

'How much money has he taken?' enquired Delyth.

'Four hundred pounds,' shouted Isaac, 'and he claims you told him to take the money. Is it true or is he a liar as well as an embezzler?' demanded Isaac.

'It's partly true,' replied Delyth, 'let me try and explain.'

Delyth told Isaac how Marcus Jacobs suggested altering Mr. Thomas' will and how the solicitor was blackmailing her, threatening to produce the real will. She explained how in

63

desperation she asked Charles to help find the money to pay Jacobs.

'I've given Jacobs three hundred pounds and he still had the will. Now, he wants more money. I only did it for you Isaac. You must believe me,' she said.

'We must expose Jacobs for the blackmailer he is,' said Isaac.

'I always wanted to expose him but I had to protect you. Jacobs threatens to say you told him to change the will. Don't you see you're the one who gained? Exposing him will ruin you,' said Delyth.

'Why would Jacobs want to alter my father's will?' demanded Isaac.

'Isn't that plain enough. He bequeathed himself three hundred pounds and now he's blackmailing us for more money.'

'Where has the other hundred pounds gone?' asked Isaac.

'I don't know. Perhaps Charles took it to settle gambling debts,' replied Delyth.

Isaac Thomas thought about his wife's story. He suspected she was lying but in one respect he knew she was right; if they exposed Jacobs as a blackmailer, his own reputation would be damaged and he might lose control of the foundry. Isaac was trapped in a web of deceit.

'So Eira was telling the truth,' he said, 'what do we do about her?'
Delyth paused before replying, 'Do nothing Isaac. She's settled and happy with her new life. Leave her with Aunt Lily. More importantly, what are you going to do about Jacobs?'

'Why didn't you tell me what was going on?' said Isaac.

'I was frightened of Jacobs and frightened you wouldn't still love me,' replied Delyth, 'You do love me?'

'Yes Delyth. I love you but I want no more of your games,' said Isaac.

Eira's early morning walks in the garden pleased Tom. He liked to see her but wondered why she always looked sad. One morning, while he was weeding, he heard footsteps on the gravel and knew it would be Eira. Tom stood up, removed his cap and offered her a rose.

'Thank you,' said Eira and smelt the flower's scent.

'What ails you, lass?' asked Tom. His familiarity surprised Eira.

'Can I trust you with a secret, Tom?' she asked.

'I'm a simple gardener Miss. No one asks me if I know any secrets,' replied Tom.

He followed Eira to a bench, by the potting shed, where she invited him to sit with her. Tom listened carefully to Eira as she explained how she belonged elsewhere and asked for his help. Tom didn't understand all she said, it sounded complicated for a gardener like him but he agreed to do what she asked.

The next day was a Sunday and Tom's day off. He met Eira in the vegetable garden and she handed him a letter to Nye.

'I've never had a letter Miss. I can't read,' said the gardener sheepishly. Eira told him to take the letter to Leominster and give it to the postmaster.

'How do I find the postmaster?' asked Tom.

'There will be a wooden post, probably outside one of the inns with a sign that says Royal Mail on it. The post master waits by the post for mail riders to deliver and collect letters. He will take the letter from you and send it on its way,' explained Eira. Then she remembered, Tom was illiterate, 'Just ask someone where it is.'

'Do I need to pay him, Miss?' asked Tom.

'No Tom he won't want any money. The recipient pays when the letter is delivered,' replied Eira. Tom didn't know what a recipient was but didn't ask.

'It's important that you give it to the post master and no one else,' said Eira as he was leaving.

Tom walked to Leominster, made his way to the town centre and asked a stranger where he might find the post master. The man told him the post master didn't work on a Sunday and offered to take the letter on his behalf. Tom was about to part with the letter when he remembered his sister lived in Leominster. He stuffed the letter back into his tunic and went to ask her advice. His sister was married to a baker and was, in Tom's opinion, a clever woman. She would know what to do. Tom's sister made a fuss, when her brother arrived unexpectedly and insisted he stayed for a meal. Tom forgot the purpose of his visit to Leominster and it was not until he was leaving that he remembered the letter. He repeated Eira's story as best he could, omitting the bits he didn't understand and the whole family sat looking at the letter in the centre of the kitchen table.

'It's a very important message,' said Tom.

'Then we will deliver it to the post master tomorrow,' promised the baker. Satisfied that his job was done, Tom bade his sister and her husband farewell and walked home.

Marcus Jacobs and his clerk arrived at Thomas and Son's office at three o'clock, as the summons had instructed. They were shown into the boardroom and asked to wait. Jacobs, normally a confident man, felt uncomfortable. He selected a chair on one side of the long polished table, sat down and wondered why they had been sent for. Perhaps Isaac had discovered the affair with Delyth but if so why ask him to come to the office and why tell him to bring his clerk? Then, there was the will. Surely, Delyth had not been foolish enough to tell her husband about it. It was half past the hour when the boardroom door opened and Isaac Thomas entered.

'Thank you for coming. Don't get up,' said Isaac and sat down opposite his visitors. Marcus Jacobs relaxed. The meeting had started cordially and Thomas didn't appear to be angry.

'I need some professional advice. It's a complicated matter so your clerk might want to make some notes,' said Isaac and gestured to writing materials at the end of the table. Isaac Thomas continued by telling the solicitor and his assistant a convoluted story about a financial dispute he was involved with. The clerk wrote quickly but struggled to keep up and interrupted to ask for clarification several times. When Isaac had finished he sat back and invited Marcus Jacobs to give his legal opinion on the matter.

'If the facts you have told me are correct, and I am sure they are, there is no need to issue a writ. A statutory demand for the money including a threat to bankrupt should bring the affair to a speedy and satisfactory conclusion,' said the lawyer.

'Can you tell me how a statutory demand works?' asked Isaac. Jacobs began to explain. While he was talking, the door opened and a man entered the boardroom carrying a large carpet bag. He put the bag on the floor, nodded to Isaac Thomas and left without speaking. Jacobs considered the interruption rude, ignored the man and continued talking. Suddenly, Isaac produced his pocket watch and stood up.

'I'm sorry gentlemen but it's almost five o'clock and I have another appointment,' he said and ushered the confused visitors out.

Walking back to his office, Marcus Jacobs saw smoke coming from the direction of the high street. Getting closer, he found a crowd gathered in front of his office. It was on fire.

Jacobs watched helplessly as the tinder dry building became an inferno. Windows shattered and flames roared through the building. The roof collapsed inwards sending burning debris into the street. Nothing could be done to save the building or its contents.

The man carrying the carpet bag returned to the boardroom after the solicitor's departure.

'Did you do exactly as I told you?' asked Isaac.

'Every scrap of paper in his desk,' replied the man and pointed to the bag.

'Was there a secret compartment in the desk?'

'Not very secret, It opened with a crowbar,' replied the man.

'And the fire?' asked Isaac.

'An oil lamp got knocked over. I made it look like an accident. No one will ever know I've been there,' replied the man and left.

Isaac emptied the contents of the carpet bag on the table, sorted through the papers and found his father's original will. It was in a bundle of documents tied with ribbon. He read the will, screwed it up and threw it into the burning fire. Then, out of curiosity, he examined the other documents. It appeared that Marcus Jacob's law practice had a number of wealthy clients. The contents of the solicitor's desk included title deeds, mortgages, contracts and other valuable documents whose loss would be a major embarrassment to the solicitor. Isaac was about to burn the papers when a promissory note, from the Bank of Haverford West, for fifty pounds gave him an idea. Attached to the promissory note was a letter authorising it's bearer to purchase livestock, for transportation to London. Isaac picked up a pen dipped it into the ink pot and started to write.

The following day, Marcus Jacobs was picking through his burnt out office when he was told the magistrate, a friend of his, wished to see him. He made his way to the magistrate's house, expecting sympathy and was surprised to be greeted formally.

'Is this yours?' demanded the magistrate, pointing to a carpet bag being held by a constable. Jacobs said the bag did not belong to him and was asked if the contents of the bag were from his office. He looked at the papers, confirmed they were and asked how the constable had come by them.

'It seems your office was burgled and set alight to conceal the crime. The bag was found this morning by the river. The thieves must have dumped it thinking the papers were worthless to them,' said the magistrate.

Marcus Jacobs gathered up the documents and thanked his friend for his help.

'You don't know how important recovering my papers is to me,' he said.

'It's not quite that simple,' said the magistrate and held out the promissory note. Jacobs took the note, examined it and saw the payees name had been changed. His own name had been crudely substituted in place of the real payee. Other documents in the bag had also been altered indicating that Marcus Jacobs was embezzling from his clients.

Marcus Jacobs' trial took place at the Michaelmas Quarter Sessions in Brecon. Witnesses confirmed they were the rightful owners of the papers in Jacob's possession and had not authorised him to make any changes. The jury concluded that Jacobs was a forger who had altered the documents to enrich himself. Things looked bad for the solicitor; a man could be executed for stealing five shillings. Jacobs was horrified when the judge placed a black cloth on his head and sentenced him to be hanged for the crime.

Tom's brother in law kept his promise and gave Eira's letter to the post master at Leominster. It was delivered to Castle Iron Works three days later. Nye recognised the handwriting immediately. He ripped the letter open and read it. At last, he knew where Eira was.

It took Nye two days to ride to Aunt Lily's house. He hammered on the front door and pushed past the servant who answered, calling Eira's name. She was in the garden room reading to Aunt Lily. Eira closed the book and stood up.

'I shall be leaving now so you will have to read for yourself. Goodbye,' said Eira and dropped the book into Aunt Lily's lap. Then she ran into the hall and Nye's open arms.

The couple returned to Merthyr discussing the future and agreed there was no reason to delay their wedding. A year had passed since Eira's father's death and her mourning period was over. Until the wedding, Eira would stay with a cousin. There was a lot to do. Nye arranged for the banns of marriage to be read at Vaynor Church. He instructed the architect to begin the new house and rented a cottage to serve as their married home while the house was being built. The wedding took place at Vaynor on the 8th October 1785. It was a small ceremony. Will Jones was best man and Benjamin Griffiths escorted Eira down the aisle. Meir cried as she watched. They celebrated at the Star Tavern before Nye and Eira left by carriage for a short honeymoon.

Although he was a convicted fraudster, Marcus Jacobs still had friends in the legal profession. Strings were pulled and the sentence was commuted to transportation to the penal colony of New South Wales. The disgraced solicitor left Wales, in irons with 774 other felons, in the first fleet of prison ships bound for Australia on the 18th August 1786.

Once they were at sea, Jacob's chains were removed and he was allowed free reign of the ship. Solicitors were scarce in New South Wales and, as he would soon discover, a law practice in Australia could be very profitable, particularly for a man with his particular talents.

Chapter 12

The Vaugn's honeymoon started with a ride over the mountain to Brecon where they turned west along the road to Nye's old village, Llangadog. Nye helped Eira down from the carriage and she followed him into the graveyard. They searched for his mother's grave but there was no marker.

'The skinflint wouldn't even pay for a headstone,' muttered Nye and took Eira to the minister's house. The minister greeted Nye and agreed to arrange for a monument to be erected and inscribed with Nye's mother's name. Nye gave the minister some money.

' Are you going up to the farm to see your father?' asked the minister.

'There's no point. We have nothing to say to each other,' replied Nye.

'Did you know, he remarried after your mother died? They have a baby son. You should go and see your brother,' said the minister. Eira agreed with the clergyman's suggestion but Nye was adamant. There were too many painful memories and he refused to go. That night, they took the best rooms in the King's Head, Llandeilo. They were eating supper when the landlord approached the table, apologised and told them the room was required by two gentlemen who had just arrived from London.

'Who are these impertinent fellows?' demanded Nye.

'A Mr. Paxton, late of India and his associate Captain Williams. They are in the bar waiting for their bags to be brought in,' replied the innkeeper.

'I shall have a word with Mr. Paxton, late of India,' said Nye. He told Eira he would be back shortly and went to confront the strangers who were upsetting their evening.

William Paxton, recently retired master of the Calcutta Mint, was a pugnacious Scot, dark skinned from years in India and reputedly the wealthiest man in Britain. Paxton was a soldier, a protégé of Clive of India and a capable businessman. The gentry with their old money referred disparagingly to such rich men returned from India as Nabobs but never, if they were sensible, to their faces. His companion, Captain David Williams, was a sailor with an distinguished record of service with the East India Company. Paxton and his friend were in Wales, searching for a country estate to buy. Paxton had insisted on the best rooms on their arrival and would accept none other.

Nye Vaughn went over to the men, stood facing Paxton and said,

'Gentlemen, you are going to have to find other rooms this night. My wife and I have no desire to move.'

'Sir, there are other rooms suitable for you and your good woman to sleep,' replied Paxton and moved closer to Nye. The two men were inches apart. Neither intended to give way.

'Perhaps if we compensated you for your inconvenience it would resolve our impasse,' suggested Captain Williams.

'Let's step outside and resolve our impasse,' replied Nye angrily, unaware that Eira had followed him from the dining room.

'Nye we're on our honeymoon. It's not worth it. Let them have the room,' she implored. Nye didn't move. Paxton studied the young man confronting him. Few men had the spirit to challenge William Paxton and the young fellow, who he was starting to admire, clearly was not going to back down. Paxton thought of his own wedding, planned for the

72

following year, smiled and decided he no longer needed the best rooms.

'Your honeymoon! Sir, it would be a shame to spoil your features with a bloody nose on such an occasion. Captain William's and I both apologize for our rudeness. What is more, we would like to pay for your accommodation as a wedding gift. Will you accept my apology?' he asked and proffered his hand.

The next day, Nye and Eira visited St Teilo's Church and the saint's holy spring before leaving Llandeilo. They rode to Aberystwyth and took a room in an inn overlooking the harbour. The honeymooners visited Devil's Bridge to see the waterfalls. They explored the brigand's cave and heard how two brothers hid there after murdering a man who refused to part with his purse. Both were surprised how small the cave was and agreed it was an unlikely tale. From there, they travelled to Hafod Uchtryd, the great mansion completed two years earlier by Thomas Johnes. Eira marvelled at the 160ft long conservatory filled with exotic plants and the huge library filled with books. The housekeeper told them that the owner's grandfather made his fortune as an ironmaster in Herefordshire.

'One day we will own a house like this,' whispered Nye and kissed his bride.

Riding back to Merthyr, Nye's thoughts turned to business. His mind was full of new ideas; new ways to grow Castle Foundry. His old enthusiasm had returned and life was good.

Chapter 13

Tom, the gardener, was surprised to receive a letter and happy to part with a halfpenny to take possession of it. The following Sunday, he hurried to Leominster and presented the letter to his sister so that she might tell him what it said. Tom sat by the kitchen table and watched with anticipation as she carefully broke the seal, unfolded the letter, spread it flat on the table and read the contents;

My Dearest Tom,

It is with great happiness that I write to thank you for your kindness. The letter you took the trouble to take to Leominster and give to the post master resulted in my rescue from a terrible plight. There is no need for me to explain more except to tell you that I am now happily married and beginning a new life with my husband. Without your help I would have remained trapped in a life with no joy, no future and no hope.

I will always be your friend and enclose a token of my gratitude.

Thank you again.

Eira Vaughn

Tom's sister examined the piece of paper that was enclosed. She counted the sheep in the corner. There were ten.

'Well I never did, it's a ten pound note,' she exclaimed, 'How much do you earn a week, Tom?'

'Eight shillings,' replied Tom.

'Well, my lad, your friend has just sent you half a year's wages,' said his sister. Tom took the letter and the ten pound note from his sister refolded them, put them in his pocket and grinned.

Delyth Thomas was indifferent to Marcus Jacobs' fate. There were other men to be used. She was equally disinterested in her Cousin Charles' dismissal. Later, when Charles begged her for money to pay his creditors, she refused. She had considered Charles the ideal person to insinuate, as her ally, into Isaac's business but Charles had shown himself to be unreliable and untrustworthy. Aunt Lily's failure to keep Eira securely tucked away at Leominster annoyed Delyth. She had no more use for Aunt Lily or her son Charles and quickly forgot them. Eira's marriage to Nye was less easy to disregard. The fact that Delyth's sister-in-law was happy infuriated her and she hadn't been invited to the wedding. Delyth would not forget the insult and she began to scheme again.

'We are going into a new line of business,' announced Nye Vaughn arriving back at the foundry.

'And what might that be?' asked Benjamin Griffiths.

'Bigger, more profitable castings,' replied Nye. The partners listened as Nye explained his plan. Castle Iron was going into the armaments business. Manufacturing cannons, particularly the naval guns Nye was proposing would require bigger furnaces, large casting pits and new cranes.

'For the scheme to succeed we must invent more efficient ways of handling raw materials,' said Nye.

'Castle Iron Works is a small foundry. We're not set up to produce heavy castings,' said Will.

'It would take a huge investment. We are already mortgaged to the limit. Where's the money going to come from?' asked Benjamin.

'Ben, do you remember what you said to me the day we bought Gurnos quarry? You said, you have to be prepared to think big if you want to make real money. We'll find the money,' replied Nye.

'We'll be fighting against Thomas. Can we seriously compete with him? Isaac won't like us taking his business, assuming that we can find a way to beat him. He's well established with the Board of Ordnance. Why should they buy from us?' asked Will.

'That, Will, is my problem. Think of it. Between us we are going to build Castle Iron Works into the biggest iron works in the world,' said Nye.

'We already have a good profitable business. Why risk it by chasing after markets we know nothing about?' cautioned Benjamin.

'Our future success depends on growing and this is the right way forward. Don't get cold feet now Ben. This isn't the time. I need your support if we are going to succeed,' said Nye.

'Are you sure this isn't some sort of personal vendetta?' asked Will. Nye didn't answer.

The next year was a busy time at Castle Iron works. Benjamin Griffiths negotiated a lease on adjacent land and construction began to expand the foundry. Three new 50 foot tall blast furnaces were built. Two puddling furnaces and a rolling mill, using Henry Cort's new puddling system were added alongside the blast furnaces. The water powered bellows were replaced with more powerful pumps. Benjamin Griffiths persuaded Banc y Llong, Aberystwyth to advance a loan to finance the work. Boring machines, needed to machine the gun barrels, were purchased from Birmingham. Castle Iron Works was now capable of producing more than 100 tons of iron a week. The first prototype cannons produced at Castle Iron were a failure. Proving the guns required them to be test fired with an explosive charge 25% larger than normal. Guns burst during the tests. Cutting the gun barrels along the damaged sections revealed the cause of the failures, small cracks in the metal. The quality of the iron had to be improved but how? Will Jones and his men were already working at the limit of their knowledge. If Castle

Iron didn't find a solution, the business faced ruin. Benjamin Griffith's warning was becoming a possibility.

Will Jones was convinced the answer lay in the puddling process, used to separate impurities from the molten iron. Isaac Thomas was manufacturing cannons successfully using the puddling method invented by Henry Cort. To compete they had to learn the secret and, knowing Thomas would never share it with them, the partners decided there was only one possible course of action.

Henry Cort was a Royal Navy pay agent, collecting and distributing retired officer's pensions. He married and joined his wife's family business in Gosport which had a lucrative contract to supply the navy with iron mooring chains. Cort built an iron works at Fontley, Hampshire to fulfil the orders. Cort improved the quality of his iron by stirring the molten metal, removing carbon and making it less brittle. Nye wrote to Cort asking to visit Fontley. The letter from Nye Vaughn of Castle Iron Works interested Cort and he agreed to a meeting.

Nye and Will travelled to Hampshire and were greeted by Cort.
'What can I do for you gentlemen?' asked Cort. Will explained their problem and asked how it might be solved.
'It sounds to me as if you have almost solved the problem of removing impurities yourselves except for one thing,' said Cort.
'What is it we've missed?' asked Nye.
'The secret is how you roll the pig iron. I'll tell you my secret for nothing but if you ever use it to manufacture you will have to pay me,' said Cort and explained his puddling and rolling process was covered by a patent taken out in 1783. Cort agreed a licensing agreement allowing Castle Iron

Works to use his process, in return for a royalty of ten shillings per ton of iron produced. As they shook hands, Nye asked a question.

'Thomas and Son in Merthyr manufacture cannon using your method. Do they pay you a royalty?'

'Do they indeed?' replied Henry Cort and summoned his works manager to discuss the technical details with Will. The partners returned to Merthyr with the expertise they needed to cast high quality iron and were eager to get started.

The Vaughns continued to live in a rented cottage but Eira was expecting their first child and it was about to become crowded. Building their new home had stopped. Nye needed every penny for the foundry. Eira gave birth to a son on the 15th July 1786. They christened him Rhys, at Vaynor Church. As the christening party emerged from the church, Will pointed towards the mountain where some of Castle Iron's men were waiting. Will waved his hat in the air. There was a puff of smoke followed by the boom of a cannon that echoed across the valley, saluting the new arrival.

Chapter 14

'What does it mean?' demanded Isaac Thomas. The lawyers on the far side of the table were prepared for their client's questions.

'It means, Mr. Thomas, you are going to lose,' replied the leading advocate, calmly.

'What goes on in my foundry is my business. Why should I lose?'

'Because Mr. Cort has evidence that you have been infringing his patent for the last three years,' explained the lawyer.

'But Thomas and Son have been puddling the same way since 1781, long before any patent,' said Thomas.

'It makes no difference. Of course, if you instruct us, we will dispute Cort's right to the patent and thereby ask for his claim to be struck down but I warn you again, you will lose,' said the lawyer.

'You've spoken to his legal team? How much does he want?' asked Isaac.

'One pound for every ton produced since the patent was granted which calculates as £15,312 plus punitive damages of £11,000 and, in addition, his costs, still to be calculated, depending on how much you continue to fight the claim,' answered the lawyer.

'Will he negotiate a lower settlement?'

'I'm afraid the matter has dragged on too long for that. You either pay up or see him in court,' replied the lawyer.

Isaac Thomas sat back and surveyed his well dressed visitors. They had already charged him a fortune in fees. What had he got in return; nothing. The only advice they could give was to settle and pay Cort. Isaac faced a painful decision. Thomas and Son was profitable but the damages being claimed by Henry Cort would swallow up more than two years profit and, more seriously, the company didn't have enough liquidity to pay the claim. If Cort was bloody minded enough, he could bankrupt the business. Nine months of lawyers negotiating had achieved nothing. Isaac regretted trying to brush off the claim in the first instance. He stood up and peered through the window overlooking the foundry. Acrid smoke billowed from the furnaces. A bell rang, signalling the change of shift. Workmen scurried through the gates, encouraged by the foreman's shouts. He watched the gates being closed and a latecomer pleading to be let in.

'These are my instructions. Offer Cort's representatives £12,000 payable in six equal instalments as full settlement of his claim, including his legal costs. You'll also tell him that if he refuses my offer I will liquidate the foundry and he'll get nothing,' said Isaac. 'There's something else Cort must agree.'

'What's that?' asked the lawyer.

'To make it possible for me to pay him, I must have a licensing agreement for future production. Without it, my company will be unable to meet its obligations,' replied Isaac.

Henry Cort's answer was immediate and uncompromising. He issued a writ. The case came to trial at the Court of Chancery, London in the autumn of 1787. After protracted and costly legal arguments, Henry Cort won his claim in full. To avoid bankruptcy, Isaac Thomas was forced to borrow against the foundry and mortgage his personal assets. It was a bitter pill to swallow, sweetened only by Cort's willingness to give him a licensing agreement for future manufacturing. Isaac Thomas had gambled and lost. He had taken a financial thrashing but was still in business and he still had the valuable Board of Ordnance contract.

Castle Iron Works continued to expand its domestic ironware sales but was less successful with cannons. Nye Vaughn was naïve thinking it would be a straight forward matter to sell weapons. His approaches to the Board of Ordnance, exclusive purchasers of armaments for the army and navy, were rejected out of hand. The board, originally established as the Office of Ordnance by Henry VIII in 1544, had its headquarters in the Tower of London. Letters addressed to Field Marshal, His Grace, Duke of Richmond, Master General of Ordnance, were returned by his secretary with a standard reply;

Dear Sirs
His Grace and the directors of the Board of Ordnance thank Mr. Vaughn and Castle Iron Works for their interest but regret to inform that existing procurement contracts preclude the need for further suppliers. Consequently, I am instructed by His Grace to advise Mr. Vaughn that the board will not be considering his enquiry.
Your faithful servant
William Sturgeon
Secretary

'What do we do now?' asked Will.

'Somehow, we have to get His Grace's attention,' replied Nye.

'But he won't see you. You can't just walk up to the portcullis of the Tower of London, knock and demand to be let in.'

'I know that. We need a demonstration of some kind,' said Nye.

'We have cannons we can show him,' suggested Benjamin.

'What, blow a hole in the curtain wall of the Tower of London and stroll in? It would be one way to enter the castle but His Grace might take offence. He'd probably keep us in the tower on a permanent basis,' said Will. The absurdity of Will's suggestion was apparent, or was it. Nye needed to think, to find a way past the intimate relationships other suppliers had established with the Board of Ordnance.

The expansion of Castle Iron put financial pressure on the business. Without orders for cannons, the new furnaces were under employed and, although domestic product sales were up, the company, with its increased overheads, was haemorrhaging cash. Benjamin Griffiths' warning was becoming a reality. Castle Iron was overstretched and vulnerable. Another injection of funds was needed, but from where and how were they going to solve the impasse with the Board of Ordnance?

Nye didn't share his business troubles with Eira. She was fully occupied with Rhys, who was a year old and had just learned she was expecting again. Meir helped, fussing around Rhys like a doting grandmother, but Eira was having a difficult start to this pregnancy. It showed in her drawn features and sunken eyes.

An invitation to a dinner to celebrate the election to Parliament of Lieutenant Colonel Sir Charles Morgan 2nd Baronet, representing Breconshire, was unexpected. Sir Charles whose most notorious ancestor was Captain Henry Morgan, the pirate, was a Tredegar Morgan, the oldest and richest family in Glamorgan. The county had once been a kingdom, ruled by the Morgans. Nye was not an acquaintance; he moved in different circles.

'What do you think? It says evening dress. Shall we go?' he asked.

'You go. I'm tired and need to look after Rhys,' replied Eira.

82

'An evening in adult company will do you good. Meir can look after the boy,' said Nye.

Nye and Eira arrived by carriage at the Castle Hotel. They walked through the vestibule to the cloakrooms, removed their coats and joined the queue of guests waiting to be announced. The master of ceremony took their invitation.

'Mr and Mrs Vaughn,' he shouted and they moved forward in the greeting line. Sir Charles and his wife thanked them for coming, shook hands and passed them on to the next dignitary in the line, the mayor. Nye and Eira looked at the seating plan and circulated, exchanging small talk with other guests. Nye felt his wife stiffen. Delyth was walking towards them.

'Eira, Nye, it's been a long time. How well you both look. It's good to see you. How's your son?' she asked.

'Rhys is in good health, thank you Delyth,' replied Eira, abruptly. Delyth ignored the frosty reply.

'Good. Eira, you must bring him to visit one afternoon and tell me all your news.' Isaac Thomas joined the group. 'Good evening Vaughn, Eira,' he said.

'My Lords, Members of Parliament, Your worship Mr. Mayor, ladies, gentlemen, honoured guests. Will you please take your seats,' called the master of ceremony.

'Excuse us,' said Nye, taking hold of Eira's arm and guiding her to their table. As Nye was helping his wife sit down he heard a familiar voice.

'We meet again Mr. and Mrs Vaughn. I trust your honeymoon was a success. May I introduce my wife Anne? We have just returned from our own honeymoon in Scotland,' said William Paxton. It was a convivial meal. Paxton's new wife, a magistrate's daughter from Aylesbury, who was considerably younger than her husband, entertained the table with charm and good humour. The banquet finished with a loyal toast, allowing the men to light their cigars and enjoy a brandy during Sir Charles' speech.

Sir Charles, who enjoyed the sound of his own voice, embarked on a long winded account of international affairs. He began with North America and the War of Independence, blaming the French for the loss of the colonies. From there, he turned to Europe and the crisis developing in the Dutch Republic of Austrian Netherlands. 'I warn you, 40% of British government debt is held by Dutch bankers. It's a dangerous situation. The French are already fermenting unrest in the Netherlands which we will have to deal with by force of arms. Gentlemen, war in Europe is coming and we must prepare. We must arm ourselves with new regiments of foot, new squadrons of cavalry, new mortars, new batteries of cannon and new ships to defend our shores. All that is required to ignite the fuse of war is a strong French leader, unfettered by the past and ambitious for his country.' Sir Charles paused for effect and sipped his drink. Then he continued, 'My warning will worry the faint hearted but the truth is, it presents both a challenge and an opportunity for the iron foundries of Merthyr Tydfil to arm the nation, ready for the coming battle.' Sir Charles sat down to loud applause.

'What are your intentions for the future, Mr. Paxton?' asked Eira.

'We plan to buy a country estate where Anne will bear and raise ten children while I will tend to my business interests,' replied Paxton. Anne sniggered.

'Only ten, William, whatever will I do to keep myself busy?' she said and gave her husband a playful nudge.

'May I ask, what line of business you're in?' said Nye.

'I have a company in London that looks after money invested from India but I am always looking for other opportunities to invest,' answered Paxton.

As the guests were departing, Nye found an opportunity to speak with William Paxton alone.

'I have a business opportunity which might interest you.'

'Then perhaps we can discuss the matter at a more appropriate time,' replied Paxton. They agree to meet the next day at Castle Iron Works.

Isaac Thomas approached Sir Charles, congratulated him on the clarity of his speech and asked the baronet's opinion of the army's readiness for war.

'We are still repatriating our troops from North America. They are battle hardened but it will take time to prepare for action on the European mainland,' replied Sir Charles.

'Do you really think there will be war in Europe?' asked Delyth.

'Madam, you can be assured there will,' answered Sir Charles.

'And you sir, will you return to active duty if called to serve again?' asked Isaac.

'My fighting days are over, Mr. Thomas. My duty, now, is to manage Tredegar and serve my country as a parliamentarian,' answered Sir Charles.

'Speaking of Tredegar, the minerals on your estates will be valuable if there is war,' commented Isaac.

'You make an astute observation. Of course, if the right offer is made I might be prepared to lease the mineral rights to an ironmaster with enough foresight to understand the potential,' said Sir Charles.

'On an exclusive basis?' asked Isaac.

'For the right price, it might be arranged.'

'I'm sure we could agree suitable terms.'

'Then, I will instruct my land agent to contact you and negotiate the details. Good evening Mr. Thomas, Mrs. Thomas. If you'll excuse me, my wife is ready to leave,' said Sir Charles.

'What would the exclusive rights mean?' asked Delyth.

'Control of iron production in South Wales,' replied Isaac.

'Did he agree?'

'Yes, Delyth, he agreed!' said Isaac, acidly. She was stung, but not surprised, by the sharpness of his reply. In Delyth's opinion the fact that the land agent would be negotiating meant nothing was agreed. But there was more to Isaac's answer than that. Since Isaac had caught Delyth's nephew embezzling, he had been cold towards her. Isaac no longer discussed his business with Delyth and showed no interest in what she was doing. At home, meals were eaten in silence. Delyth believed Isaac was unaware of her infidelity and didn't understand his change in behaviour. In public, Isaac was well-mannered but in private he was rude and ignored the normal rules of courtesy. They rarely made love, except when he had been drinking and when they did, he was brutal and selfish. Delyth didn't love her husband, love was not a word in her lexicon, but she had done her best to help him in ways she would never be able to disclose. His change in behaviour changed her feelings and the two of them were becoming strangers.

Chapter 15

William Paxton arrived at Castle Iron works with Captain Williams, his companion from India. Nye Vaughn had already briefed his partners about the previous evening's conversation and both Will and Benjamin agreed an injection of funds from Paxton was a good idea, subject to certain conditions; principally that the three partners retained control of the business. Before the meeting began, Nye took the visitors around the foundry. Nye explained each part of the works and answered questions from William Paxton, which showed his understanding of manufacturing.

'For a sailor you seem to know a great deal about industrial methods, Mr. Paxton,' said Nye.

'After he left the navy, Paxton was the Master of Calcutta Mint,' explained Captain Williams.

'What did that involve?' asked Nye.

'Minting silver rupees for trade and to pay East India Company employees. Manufacturing the money was the easy part. The real profit came from shipping silver bullion to Great Britain on behalf of our wealthier clients,' replied Paxton.

'Did you know Lord Clive?' asked Nye.

'I knew him well. Robert Clive was my mentor when I arrived in India. He was a great man. Without Clive there would be no British interests in India. Those who claim Lord Clive committed suicide, cutting his own throat with a penknife, are scoundrels,' said Paxton as the party returned to the office.

William Paxton listened quietly while the partners explained the company's position. Nye began with an appraisal of sales then Will Jones' gave an overview of production. Captain Williams took notes. When Benjamin Griffiths started to explain the financial state of the business, Paxton interrupted him,

'In a nutshell you've run out of money and need to sell cannons to the Board of Ordnance, who won't talk to you. I can help with both.'

Paxton invested £30,000 in Castle Iron Work in return for non-voting preference shares, explaining that he had full confidence in Nye and his partners and had no wish to interfere in the running of the company. The money and terms suited all sides.

'How can you help with the Board of Ordnance?' asked Nye.

'I'll give you a letter of introduction to a friend, Sir Henry Strachey. Strachey was Lord Clive's Private Secretary in India. Since returning to Britain, he has served as Storekeeper to the Board of Ordnance and is now Under Secretary of State for the Home Department,' said Paxton.

'You have powerful friends, Mr. Paxton,' said Nye.

'Sometime you need friends to open doors,' said Paxton.

'We're grateful for any doors you can open,' said Nye.

'There is another customer you should approach, the East India Company. The company has a Royal Warrant allowing it to operate a fleet of armed merchantmen. What's even more important is they are building a new ship, at Northfleet, due to be launched next year. It's called the Earl of Abergavenny and will carry 26 cannon,' said Paxton.

'Why so many guns on a merchant ship?' asked Will.

'East India ships carry opium from India to China before returning to Britain and the South China Seas are swarming with pirates,' replied Paxton.

'Who should we approach?' asked Nye.

'I'm a Director of the East India Company. You can talk to me to begin with,' said Paxton and smiled, 'but I warn you, my colleagues on the board are businessmen and will drive a hard bargain.'

Sir Charles' land agent, Evan Jenkins, was a short, stocky man with a red face, a sharp tongue and a liking for port; a habit learned at university. When his father gambled and lost the family's fortune, he was forced to abandon his studies and find a job working for others, of his previous social class, who had been more prudent with their wealth. Jenkins' fall from a position of privilege to one of servant made him resentful. He never revealed the bitter side of his character to his master; he was too clever for that, but people who were still, in his opinion, inferior were less fortunate. In short, Evan Jenkins was a bully. When Sir Charles told him to meet Isaac

Thomas and arrange a lease for mineral rights on advantageous terms for the Tredegar Estate, he understood what was expected of him. Sir Charles was a gentleman and not interested in the details. It was Evan Jenkins job to squeeze the maximum benefit out of the deal and he relished the challenge.

The first meeting between Jenkins and Isaac Thomas began badly. Sir Charles' offhand manner had led Isaac to expect few complications but he soon realized his mistake. Evan Jenkins' pugnacious approach made it clear that the deal was far from in the bag. The prospect of exclusivity, dangled tantalizingly by Sir Charles, was no longer a foregone conclusion. Jenkins scoffed at Isaac's offer of eleven shillings per ton of ore, despite it being above the market price and the tone of the meeting deteriorated. When Jenkins suggested it would be more appropriate to put the mineral rights out to tender to all the iron masters, Isaac started to panic. The meeting was going dreadfully wrong. He needed time to think, to find a way to bring the negotiation back from the brink.

'It's clear that you have the better of me, Mr. Jenkins and I've insulted you by not preparing myself properly for our meeting, so I have a suggestion,' said Isaac.

'What's your suggestion?' asked Jenkins.

'It's getting late in the day. Let's adjourn our discussions until 9 o'clock tomorrow morning. That gives me time to check my costs and I'm confident I'll be able to make a substantially better offer, which Sir Charles will find agreeable,' said Isaac.

Evan Jenkins was in good humour the following morning and expecting a compliant Isaac Thomas, prepared to pay top price.

'Did you have time to examine your costs and revise your offer?' he asked.

'I did and you will be pleased to hear that my offer is substantially improved,' said Isaac.

'How much?'

'Nine shillings a ton,' said Isaac.

'You offered eleven, yesterday. Are you increasing your offer by nine shillings to twenty?' asked Jenkins. There was a note of doubt in his voice.

'No. My new offer, which Sir Charles will be pleased with, is exactly what I said, nine shillings per ton,' explained Isaac.

Evan Jenkins sat wondering if it was a joke. Isaac watched, waiting for his response. 'Why would Sir Charles be happy with a lower offer?' he asked.

'Because you'll be pleased with the price and, in turn, you'll tell Sir Charles that he's pleased with the price,' replied Isaac.

'What game is this? You insult my intelligence, Sir,' said Jenkins and stood up.

'Sit down Mr. Jenkins and let me explain. You'll be pleased because I'll also remit to you personally a royalty of one shilling for every ton of ore extracted from the ground. That amounts to several hundred pounds a year, making you a man of considerable substance,' said Isaac.

Jenkins sat down. He was breathing heavily and his face was scarlet. 'How do I know I can trust you?' he whispered.

'Have no fear on that account. We're both honourable men and no one will ever learn of our arrangement from me. To show my good faith here is an advance on your royalty,' said Isaac and spread one hundred pounds, temptingly, across the table. Evan Jenkins stared at the money. It offered a chance to amount to something again. He hesitated, scooped up the money, stuffed it into his pocket and nodded. The deal was done. Isaac Thomas smiled.

Delyth had also been busy. She had written a letter to Eira explaining how her actions had all been with the best intent, apologizing for any distress caused, asking Eira's forgiveness and a chance to begin again. Eira read the letter and burnt it. Delyth wrote a second letter to Anne Paxton, who she had briefly spoken to at the dinner, inviting her to afternoon tea. Grateful of some company while her husband was occupied with his business, Mrs. Paxton accepted. Delyth made enquiries about the Paxtons and learning that William Paxton was extremely wealthy, she determined to cultivate a friendship. Anne Paxton arrived in an excited state. She had just learned she was pregnant and the two women spent an animated afternoon discussing babies, a subject that Delyth had no knowledge of or interest in. Anne invited Delyth and her husband to join the Paxtons for dinner, at the Castle Hotel, the following Friday. It was to be a small gathering including William Paxton's London business partner, Charles Cockerell, his wife and Captain Williams.

'Have you heard? Captain Williams has sold a quantity of diamonds he bought back from India. He's purchased an estate in Carmarthenshire with the money,' said Anne Paxton as she was leaving.

When Isaac and Delyth arrived for the dinner she engaged the captain in conversation and contrived to sit beside him. During the evening, she put her hand on his thigh and smiled at him. He put his hand on hers and for a moment their eyes met. The implication of the intimate gesture under the table was not lost on the captain. Isaac didn't see Delyth's hand on the captain's leg but he knew his wife was flirting. William Paxton also noticed Delyth's ungracious behaviour and spoke to his wife after their guests had departed,

'It would be prudent to keep a distance from Delyth Thomas. She's a strumpet and her husband, a sour fellow. They are both best avoided.'

'Why do you embarrass us like that? Everyone noticed,' said Isaac, as they rode home in the carriage.

'I don't know what you mean,' answered Delyth.

'You were performing for Captain Williams like a lovesick puppy,' snapped Isaac. Delyth didn't reply.

Chapter 16

Second Lieutenant Bonaparte stood on the rampart, looking across the River Rhone. Bonaparte, the son of a prominent Corsican family, was not popular with his comrades and preferred to keep his own company. His Corsican accent was a source of amusement with other officers but he ignored their jibes and concentrated on his studies. Bonaparte read a great deal but he never fully mastered the written French language. Although he couldn't spell, his numeracy was remarkable and he solved complex mathematical problems with ease. Because of this skill, the artillery school at Valence, Bonaparte's present posting, suited the young officer ideally. He had once considered joining the British Royal Navy but chose, instead, to enrol at the elite Ecole Militaire in Paris where he astounded his tutors by completing the two year training in twelve months. Bonaparte was the first Corsican to attend the prestigious military college. To be accepted as an artillery officer it was first necessary to overcome the 'three degrees,' serving as a gunner, corporal and sergeant. Only when a cadet had learned every task, required to operate a cannon, would he be considered for promotion. Being an artillery officer was technically demanding, a fact not fully understood by officers in other branches of the military. They regarded the dash of a cavalry charge or the advance of infantry with fixed bayonets as the true glory of battle. Artillery men knew different. Well directed cannon fire cleared the battlefield of enemies and won wars. It required a logical mind to calculate the range of an enemy, size and type of shot required, angle of elevation and strength of gunpowder charge. Commanding a battery of guns was a scientific business.

Lieutenant Badeau, one of Bonaparte's few friends joined him. 'Have you heard, King Louis has called an assembly of 'Notables'. It's the first assembly for more than 100 years,' announced Badeau.

'What else can he do? He's bankrupted France with his American war against the British and lost our American colonies. Now, he needs someone else to sort out the mess,' replied Bonaparte.

'What do you mean, sort out the mess?' asked Badeau.

'Look around you, Badeau. We have humbled the British but at what cost? The price of bread has doubled and doubled again. While the people complain, the king dithers in his palace at Versailles, an absolute ruler with no ideas, no vision and no grasp of what's needed. Have you seen the pamphlets criticizing the government? People are demanding everything from release from servitude to freedom of religion?' said Bonaparte.

'Be careful my friend. You are talking like a republican,' said Badeau.

'A republican? No Badeau. I'm a loyal Corsican,' replied Bonaparte.

Bonaparte's view of the political situation did not surprise his friend. The unrest was everywhere. Some blamed King Louis, others the bishops and the nobility. There were even rumours that Queen Marie Antoinette, hated for her promiscuity and lavish spending, was an Austrian provocateur who sympathized with France's enemies.

'I have a copy of Benjamin Robin's gunnery treatise which you should examine. His argument for rifled barrels is compelling and the use of calculus to work out the ballistic pendulum ingenious. It's a German translation by Leonhard Euler but quite understandable,' said Bonaparte. His friend agreed he would look at it and changed the subject.

Back in Merthyr, Eira had been feeling mild contractions for several hours when there was a sharp pain. The strength of the contraction doubled her up. Meir, playing 'peek-a-boo' with Rhys in the kitchen, heard Eira's cry. She snatched up the toddler and went to see what was wrong. Eira was squatting by a chair, panting like a dog. 'Is it time?' asked Meir.

'My waters have broken. I'm soaking wet,' said Eira, through clenched teeth. The contractions continued through the afternoon and evening. By the early hours of the morning the midwife was getting concerned; Eira was exhausted. The baby had crowned but Eira had lost the strength to push. Even with the help of forceps the baby was stuck. Both mother and baby were in danger. Something needed to be done quickly to ease the child's entry into the world. Eira screamed as the midwife cut but the baby, a healthy boy, was safely delivered. A second baby, a girl, arrived stillborn a short while later. Eira was exhausted. The midwife gave her a draught of laudanum, stitched and washed her and told her to sleep. The boy, born on the 21st October 1787, was christened Brynmor. For the rest of his life, he would be known as Bryn. They named the girl Cerys. Her tiny pine coffin was buried on the same day her birth was recorded in the parish register.

William Paxton's investment made a significant difference to Castle Iron Works. Creditors could be paid promptly and the improvements to the foundry completed. Paxton's letter of introduction to Sir Henry Strachey worked and Nye was invited to meet the Under Secretary of State in March 1888.

Nye took the stage coach to Cardiff and the ferry to Bristol. It was a bright clear morning and the water in the estuary was brilliant blue as the cutter ran before a stiff breeze. Nye arrived in Bristol in time to catch the evening Royal Mail service to London. The coach sped through the night arriving at Charing Cross the next day. Nye looked at his watch. It was nearly noon. They had made good time. The journey from Bristol had only taken sixteen hours.

Nye felt tired and needed a shave as he stepped down from the coach. He stood, absorbing the strange sounds and sights of London. Costermongers shouting for trade, carriages clattering across the cobbles, gentlemen with tall hats strode past, servants hurried by on urgent business, drunks, ragamuffins, gaudily dressed women: all manner of humanity filled the square. The smell of soot, rotting vegetables, sewage, wet horses and stale sweat assaulted his nostrils. A nearby wagon had shed a wheel, spilling coal across the road. The driver was shouting at boys stealing lumps of the precious cargo. Northumberland House, the magnificent London mansion of the Duke of Northumberland, stood on the far side of the square. An equestrian statue of Charles I stood in the centre.

'Carry your bag, mister?' A scruffy boy looked up at him. The boy, who wasn't much bigger than the bag, struggled to carry it to the Golden Cross Inn. Nye gave him a penny and booked a room. He unpacked and lay on the bed. The room overlooked the square and the mail coaches arriving and departing made sleep impossible. After a short rest, Nye got up, shaved, dressed and left the inn. Paxton's London office was on Exeter Street, a ten minute walk away. A large crowd was pushing slowly east along The Strand. People were laughing and joking as they went.

'Where is everyone going,' Nye asked a man.

'To Newgate for the execution,' replied the man.

'Who's being executed?' asked Nye.

'A coiner. She's being strangled and burnt,' answered the stranger and disappeared into the crowd. Counterfeiting coins was a capital offence but the idea of choking a woman until she was semiconscious and burning her alive, to entertain a crowd, appalled Nye. He found Paxton's office and read the brass plate on the door, 'Paxton, Cockerell, Trail & Co – Merchant Bankers'. The building was unassuming, concealing the wealth managed from within. Inside was different. The décor, fittings and furniture were opulent. No expense had been spared. They had only met once but Charles Cockerell greeted Nye cordially and insisted on taking him to dinner that evening. They dined at Cockerells' club, Brook's on St. James' Street where a steward led them through the gaming rooms to the dining salon.

'Do you gamble?' asked Nye as they were served.

'Not often at the tables but my name's in the book,' replied Cockerell.

'What's the book?'

'It's where private wagers between members are recorded.'

'What sorts of things are bet on?' asked Nye.

'See the gentleman seated by the window?' asked Cockerell. Nye nodded.

'He's Lord Chomondeley. He paid Lord Derby two guineas and in return will receive five hundred guineas when Derby has his way with a woman in a balloon, one thousand yards above the earth. The wager is written in the book,' said Cockerell and watched for his guest's reaction. Nye coughed and grinned.

'Did he win the five hundred guineas?'

'He's still waiting,' replied Cockerell.

After dinner, Cockerell suggested joining one of the gaming tables, where a game of whist was about to begin. Nye declined the offer.

'Perhaps you prefer a different form of amusement,' said Cockerell and told a waiter to, 'Fetch Harris'.' The steward returned with a book and handed it to Nye.

'Harris's List,' was written on the cover. Nye opened it and read first page;

Harris's list
of
Covent Garden Ladies
or
Man of Pleasures
Kalander
1788
First edition published in 1773

The volume contained a list of London prostitutes, to suit gentlemen of every taste and income. After reading an entry for, 'Miss Fisher who is lusty, has dark hair and good teeth but will not yield to an embrace for less than three guineas which, in the author's opinion, is value for money,' Nye thanked Cockerell for the meal, returned Harris's list, explaining he was tired and would walk back to his hotel.

'No one walks through London alone at night. There are cutthroats and footpads in every alleyway. My carriage will take you,' said Cockerell and summoned the coach.

The next morning, Nye rose early, ate breakfast and walked along The Strand to the Navy Board's offices in Somerset House. His letter of appointment was examined at the gate and he was directed across the courtyard to the Under Secretary of State's chambers in the south wing. The Admiralty had recently taken over Somerset House's west wing and the courtyard was busy with workmen. Nye passed the victualling offices where suppliers were queuing to see the buyers. Nearby, a man was chained to a pillory with a sign hung around his neck. Nye stopped to read it, 'I swindled His Majesty's Navy.' Nye entered the south wing, leaving behind the bustle of the courtyard.

Sir Henry Strachey's office was on the upper floor, on the corner of the building overlooking the Thames. The river was crowded with vessels. Ships listed at awkward angles on the mud, waiting for the tide to return and lift them clear. Others, swung on their moorings with the flow of the river. Black rigging filled the skyline like an enormous spider's web.

Nye introduced himself and was directed to a settee near the window.

'How is Paxton?' asked Sir Henry, 'I haven't seen him since Calcutta. I hear he's married.'

'He's well and sends his regards to you,' replied Nye. A clerk entered with a tray of refreshments.

'Can I offer you tea, Mr. Vaughn, it's a private stock. I have the leaves imported from Assam. Drink it with a slice of lemon. It's very refreshing,' said Sir Henry as the clerk poured the tea.

'Let us get down to business. You're aware I left my position as Storekeeper of Ordnance some time ago and have no authority at the Board of Ordnance. Consequently I am unable to influence any buying decisions?' said Sir Henry.

'Mr. Paxton told me so but he also said you might be able to recommend me to someone at the Board of Ordnance with whom I might establish an honourable business relationship, possibly at a lower level than His Grace the Master General of Ordnance,' answered Nye.

'An honourable business relationship, you say. Am I to understand you are not looking for someone to bribe or offering me an incentive to help?' said Sir Henry.

98

Nye studied Sir Henry, trying to read him, for a sign; was he asking for an inducement? The stakes were high, if he gave the wrong answer the meeting would be over.

'No Sir Henry, I'm not interested in paying bribes to you or anyone else,' answered Nye. Sir Henry stood up and looked out of the window.

'Do you see the brig over by the wharf?' said Sir Henry, pointing towards the river.

'I'm not a sea going man, Sir Henry. Which ship is it?' asked Nye.

'The vessel with two square rigged masts. Her owner tried to cheat the navy of five hundred pounds by falsifying his ship's manifest. He offered me money to conceal the theft. I confiscated his ship and had him flogged. Today, the owner is in Fleet Prison,' said Sir Henry. Nye looked at the brig. It was a trim looking vessel, one the owner would have been proud of.

'There is someone I can recommend. His name is Thomas Baillie and he's a man of proven integrity. Let me tell you about him. Thomas Baillie was a naval captain before being appointed in 1774 as Governor of Greenwich Royal Hospital for Seamen. Two years later, he published a report exposing fraud, malfeasance and other abuses being perpetrated by the directors of the hospital. His report contained over 160 pages of evidence.'

'What happened?' asked Nye.

'Lord Sandwich, who Baillie's report exposed as a scoundrel, sacked Baillie and brought a libel action against him. It nearly broke the man. Baillie refused to withdraw the allegations. Baillie's defence was sound and he won his case but was ruined. Sandwich refused to reinstate him or give him a sea going appointment. Sandwich used his influence to block every attempt Baillie made to return to active service even when the case was brought before the House of Lords. Thomas Baillie is your man,' said Sir Henry.

'He may be honest but if he's unemployed what assistance can he offer me?' asked Nye.

'The Duke of Richmond, Master General of Ordnance, has appointed Captain Baillie to be his Clerk of the Deliveries. You see, Richmond and Sandwich don't get on. The Clerk of Deliveries is a full time office with considerable influence. I'll tell him to expect your approach,' answered Sir Henry.

Nye thanked Sir Henry for his courtesy and was leaving when Sir Henry added a final comment, 'There is a point that vexes me. You will have gathered I detest dishonesty and self serving officials. My last post in India was assisting Lord Clive root out cronyism and establish good governance. If there is corruption at the Board of Ordnance give me proof and I'll expose the culprits.'

Nye reflected on his visit to London and the meeting with Sir Henry during the journey home. He was disappointed Sir Henry was unwilling to intercede himself and unsure how Thomas Baillie, a discredited Clerk of Deliveries with powerful enemies, might help. It was a question he wished he had asked Sir Henry during their exchange. Back in Merthyr, Nye drafted a letter of introduction to Thomas Baillie asking for the opportunity for Castle Iron Works to tender for future business and explaining that Sir Henry had suggested the enquiry. He posted it, enclosing a prospectus for Castle Iron works and waited.

Chapter 17

While he was at Valence, Lieutenant Bonaparte courted Louise Adelaide de Saint Germain, a beautiful brunette and the daughter of a retired general. Bonaparte asked her father for permission to marry.

'This coarsely spoken junior officer has no future,' announced her father and refused to give his consent. On the 1st June, Bonaparte's regiment was transferred 90km to Auxonne, ending the brief courtship. Six days later, residents of Grenoble took to the streets, challenging the right of the Archbishop of Toulouse, the king's Controller General, to levy new taxes. Soldiers, sent to disperse the rioters, found the mob had climbed buildings and were waiting in ambush. As the troops approached, roof tiles rained down on them and the soldiers withdrew from the town. 'The Day of Tiles', as the confrontation became known, was the first physical manifestation of revolution. To address the unrest, King Louis allowed a meeting of the three estates; the nobility, the clergy and the bourgeoisie (middle classes) to convene. The meeting made several demands, including a relaxation of taxation in the province and an ending of arbitrary imprisonment, all of which the king accepted. Despite the king's concessions, the fuse of revolution was burning and the political situation continued to deteriorate.

'We are ordered south to Grenoble,' said Lieutenant Badeau. Bonaparte had already heard the news. The regiment was drawn up ready to move when conflicting orders arrived and there was confusion. Bonaparte ordered his men to unlimber their guns, feed the horses and wait. Badeau wandered across to discuss the situation.

'What do you think?' he said.

'I think moving a regiment of artillery 300 kilometres to sort out a few peasants shows we are led by amateurs,' replied Bonaparte. The company waited, in marching order for six hours until a messenger arrived with a third set of orders; return to barracks.

Isaac Thomas trembled with cold or nervous excitement, he wasn't sure which. The doorway he was sheltering in offered no protection from the wind. Isaac wiped a drop of water from his nose and waited. He saw Delyth cross the street and stepped back into the shadow. She preened herself in front of a window and entered the hotel. Minutes later, Captain Williams arrived. Isaac's suspicion was confirmed; Delyth was an adulterer. Why else would they be meeting? Isaac's hand gripped the pistol, concealed in his coat. He followed the captain into the hotel and found the pair in the bar, drinking and laughing together. Delyth saw her husband and froze. The captain, who was looking away from the door, turned around to face Isaac.

'Mr. Thomas, we were just talking about you. Come and join us, I'll order another glass,' said the captain, smiling. He seemed unperturbed by Isaac's arrival.

'Delyth, you are behaving like a whore and you Sir are a rascal who deserves to be whipped,' snapped Isaac. The smile vanished from Captain Williams face. He stood up and took a step towards Isaac but stopped when Isaac produced the pistol and levelled it at him.

'Thomas, you're a fool and a coward. You've questioned your wife's reputation and insulted me,' said Williams, 'If you intend to shoot an unarmed man, do so and be damned.' Captain Williams turned his back on Isaac.

'Excuse me Delyth, I need to get some air,' said the captain, pushed past Isaac and left.

William Paxton's efforts to dissuade Captain Williams were futile and he, reluctantly, agreed to act in the matter. Isaac Thomas was in his office when Paxton arrived.

'What can I do for you?' asked Isaac.

'I have come on behalf of Captain Williams to make the arrangements.'

'Arrangements! What arrangements?' asked Isaac.

'You've impugned the captain's honour and he intends to defend it. I act as his second,' replied Paxton.

'His second! A duel, I'm not a military man. This isn't India,' said Isaac, 'I'll apologize to him if that's what he wants.'

'I need the name of your second, Mr. Thomas,' said Paxton.

'And if I refuse?'

'Then Sir, you are, in the captain's words, a coward. Are you refusing?'

'I didn't say that,' answered Isaac.

Delyth was surprised her husband had been called out to fight a duel and tried to persuade him to ignore the challenge.

'He can't do anything if you don't go,' she said.

'Do you see what you've done, Delyth? If I fight you will be a widow. If I don't I'm a coward,' said Isaac. Delyth didn't want a cowardly husband and the prospect of widowhood was not unappealing. Delyth reflected on the possibilities and agreed that Isaac, being a gentleman, had to accept the challenge.

The duellists met on a cold overcast morning. There had been heavy rain during the night and the field was muddy. Isaac Thomas removed his coat and handed it to his second. William Paxton produced a brace of pistols and the seconds carefully loaded the weapons, while the umpire watched. Satisfied the guns were both correctly loaded, the umpire carried them to where Captain Williams and Isaac were waiting.

'Mr. Thomas since you have been challenged you have the choice,' said the umpire and offered the pistols to Isaac. Isaac took one. His hand was shaking. Captain Williams took the second gun and held it upright.

'Captain Williams, before we proceed. If Mr. Thomas apologises to you, for the offence he has caused, will your honour be satisfied?' asked the umpire.

'It will not,' replied the captain staring straight at Isaac. Isaac could not meet his opponents gaze and lowered his eyes.

'Very well, you are the offended party Captain Williams. What's your choice, one shot, first blood or death?' asked the umpire.

'First blood,' replied the captain.

'First blood it is. If you both miss, the pistols will be reloaded by your seconds and you will fire again. If, after three volleys, there are no wounds the duel will be over and satisfaction given,' said the umpire.

The two men stood back to back, pistols raised and waited. Isaac could feel William's shoulders pressed against him, hard and unmoving. The umpire dropped his handkerchief and began to count, marking the duellist's strides. At the count of ten Isaac spun around and fired. The bullet went wide. Captain Williams lowered his pistol and took aim. Isaac began to shake uncontrollably. He could clearly see William's eye looking along the pistol's barrel. Williams fired. The bullet's impact knocked Isaac to the ground. Captain Williams walked over to Isaac and stood over the prostrate figure lying in the mud. Isaac whimpered and clutched his shattered arm.

'Gentlemen, blood has been drawn. Captain Williams, is your honour satisfied?' asked the umpire.

'I am satisfied,' replied the captain and handed his pistol to Paxton.

Benjamin Griffiths looked at the parcel. It had been delivered by messenger and bore an admiralty seal. He wanted to open it but because of the official seal he controlled his curiosity and waited for Will and Nye. When the partners arrived, they found the box contained a smaller box packed in wood shavings and two large envelopes.

The first envelope contained a letter from Thomas Baillie, inviting Castle Iron Works to submit a tender to manufacture twenty cannons, five hundred cannon balls and five hundred rounds of canister shot. The envelope contained a sheaf of papers, detailing the Board of Ordnance's terms of purchase and delivery instructions. The second envelope was filled with technical information relating to the design. There was a specification of the metal quality required, drawings showing the details of the gun barrel and windage tolerances to allow for irregularities and wear. Another set of drawings showed the gun's mount and carriage.

'What's in the box?' asked Benjamin. They opened it and discovered a scale model of the finished gun.

'What a beautiful model. What calibre, does it say?' asked Nye.

'Six pounder, it's a mobile field gun' replied Will, referring to the drawing.

The partners spent a week preparing the quotation. Every word and figure on the document was checked and rechecked. There could be no mistakes. Satisfied everything was right, Nye returned to London, took a room at the Golden Cross Inn and went straight from there to the Board of Ordnance offices in the Tower. He wanted to make sure the quotation arrived safely and would deliver it personally.

When he arrived at the Tower of London, Nye was directed to Thomas Baillie's office in the White Tower. He climbed the steps, leading to the inner keep, and made his way to the Clerk of Deliveries room. Baillie's office was large with a vaulted ceiling. A small window high enough to reveal nothing but a patch of sky provided the only light. The sparsely furnished room was well ordered but it smelt musty. Thomas Baillie, a thin faced man in his late forties, wore a powdered wig to conceal his receding hair. He greeted Nye politely, took the quotation and offered his visitor a glass of sherry. He spoke slowly, picking his words with care.

'How long have you known Sir Henry?' he asked.

'I've met him once,' replied Nye.

'He speaks highly of you, says you have integrity.'

'I believe I act with good faith in my affairs,' said Nye. There was silence as Baillie studied Nye. The Clerk of Deliveries was a cautious man.

'This is only a small order Mr. Vaughn, one I can issue without board approval. If your offer is accepted, the quality of the ordnance you supply proves satisfactory and you deliver in a timely fashion I will be able to draw you to the attention of The Board as a possible supplier for more substantial contracts,' said Baillie.

'When will you be placing the order?' asked Nye.

'When I have considered all the offers,' replied Baillie as he stood up and took Nye's half full glass.

'If you will excuse me, I have work to do,' said Baillie and ended the audience. Baillie's abruptness surprised Nye. Nye had built his hopes up, before the meeting and the Clerk of Deliveries manner left him feeling disappointed.

Nye returned to Merthyr and waited. Two months passed with no news. Nye had given up hope when a purchase order arrived, from the Board of Ordnance. The tender they had so carefully prepared had won the business. Confusingly, a second, identical, order arrived days later. Nye suspected the second order was a duplication of the first and wrote to Thomas Baillie for clarification. Baillie's reply confirmed the second order was in addition to the first. Castle Iron Works had entered a new market.

'Tell me if you like the design?' asked Will as he unveiled the wooden carving. Nye stepped back to get a better look. The carving showed a castle, a cannon in the foreground and a pyramid of shot. The barrel of the cannon pointed outwards and the words 'Castle Iron Works' were in relief across the bottom.

'It's good. I like it. Are you going to hang it by the gates?' asked Nye.

'Better than that, it's a pattern. I'll cast an iron one and the design shall be our trade mark,' replied Will.

'Castle Iron Works, cannon manufacturers of Wales,' said Nye with a flourish.

'Of Great Britain!' added Will.

'Of the World!' yelled Nye.

During the summer of 1788, very little rain fell in France. The crop failed. Peasants were unable to pay rent to their landlords. There were rumours of a conspiracy to starve the poor. When it did rain, there were floods to compound the misery. The autumn brought snow. Hard frosts destroyed the vines and the olive orchards of the south. Chestnut and fruit trees died. Marauding bands of men scoured the countryside searching for food. Villagers armed themselves for protection. As the country slid towards anarchy, King Louis XVI vacillated, hoping something would happen and the next year would be better. On the 12th September, Lieutenant Bonaparte was ordered back to Valence with his regiment. The La Fere Artillery Regiment was the finest artillery regiment in France. The 100 officers and 900 men had a reputation for skill and good spirit. It was commanded by professional soldiers, unlike other branches of the army where officers were appointed purely because of their social rank. Bonaparte's ability' had been recognised by his superiors. He was promoted and made responsible for teaching battlefield tactics.

Chapter 18

Delyth was confused, after Isaac's duel. She didn't love Isaac but her husband had proved he wasn't a coward and she was glad he was alive. The confrontation in the hotel, when Isaac produced the gun, had frightened her. If Isaac had arrived a few minutes later, when they had finished their drinks and gone upstairs, the outcome would have been far more unpleasant. Delyth would still deny any wrong doing, if asked, but Isaac never mentioned the matter again. She decided to repair her marriage and become the dutiful wife she had always pretended to be. To begin with, her attempts at conversation were ignored by Isaac. She assumed Isaac's reserve was because of his injury and hoped his depression would pass given time.

Weeks passed. Isaac regained some use of his arm but his melancholy remained. Isaac Thomas had become bitter and seldom spoke. Delyth was surprised when he arrived home one evening and announced they were going to Birmingham on a business trip. She grew excited when he explained the importance of the trip. It was the first time, in months, he had discussed his business affairs. His eagerness for the trip was contagious and Delyth began to plan what they would do in Birmingham.

'Where will we stay?' asked Delyth.

'I normally stay at Dadley's Hotel on Temple Row. The rooms are clean and there's a good cellar,' replied Isaac.

'Is there a theatre in Birmingham we can attend?' asked Delyth.

'There is. New Street Theatre is next to an excellent coffee house. We must visit. The other place I want to show you is the Panorama. It opened last year. You stand on a platform in the middle of an enormous room, completely surrounded by a tall painting. When I last went, I saw the grand fleet under sail. It's as if you are actually there,' said Isaac and smiled. He was enjoying his wife's interest. 'If you like, we can visit Aunt Lily.'

The preparation for the visit to Birmingham changed the atmosphere in the house. Isaac suggested different things to do and Delyth, unsure what clothes to take, repacked several times. When they got to Leominster, Aunt Lily's was as terse as ever. Delyth joked with Isaac that her aunt's bad manners resulted from looking in the mirror and seeing how ugly she was. Isaac agreed and they laughed.

During the night, Isaac complained of a stomach pain, blaming the fish they had eaten and went downstairs in search of a glass of milk. Delyth went back to sleep. She didn't hear him return. When she woke, she was alone in the bed. Aunt Lily was waiting downstairs, for her niece to appear for breakfast. She knew Delyth would be upset to learn that Isaac had gone back to Merthyr without her but would console her niece with the news that Delyth had a new home; as Aunt Lily's companion.

'What do you think of it?' asked Paxton. Paxton and Captain Williams had ridden to the top of a hill overlooking the Towy valley. They dismounted, tied their horses to a tree and stood enjoying the view. Below them, the river meandered through lush farmland. To the east they could see the ruin of Dryslwyn Castle, on a bluff and beyond it the Black Mountains filled the skyline.
'How much land is there?' asked the captain.
'Middleton Hall comes with 2600 acres including the ruined castle and the villages of Llanarthney and Golden

Grove. I'm going to demolish the hall and build a new mansion. The plans have already been drawn and I've asked the landscape designer, Samuel Lapidge to create a country park with lakes and carriage drives. Where we're standing, I'm going to build a gothic banqueting tower to entertain my friends,' said Paxton.

'It sounds like you've already bought the estate,' said Captain Williams.

'Francis Middleton has no choice. He's in debt and has to sell quickly,' replied Paxton.

'Speaking of castles how's your investment at Castle Iron Works?' asked Williams.

'I'm pleased with it. Vaughn's doing a good job. The order for the Earl of Abergavenny has been fulfilled. The first cannons have been delivered to the army. I'm told the quality is satisfactory and more contracts are expected,' explained Paxton.

Chapter 19

In the spring of 1789 civil unrest spread to Paris. On April 28th a food riot was dispersed by troops who killed 25 people. Hearing that the peasants had no bread and were starving, the queen was said to have joked, 'Let them eat cake.' The news of her scornful comment spread like wildfire leading to more riots. Suspected ringleaders were arrested and incarcerated in the Bastille. Attempting to assert his authority and bring about new draconian laws, the king excluded the third estate, the bourgeoisie, from a congress. Confronted by soldiers with fixed bayonets, barring the way, the outraged delegates convened their own meeting on a tennis court, declared themselves to be 'The National Assembly' and swore an oath of allegiance to establish a new constitution. The king's strategy backfired. Excluding members from the congress created the first organized opposition to his rule.

On the 14th July a mob stormed the Bastille, releasing prisoners and killing the governor.

'What news from Paris?' asked Lieutenant Bonaparte.

'Mobs are rampaging through the streets killing and looting. I don't understand why the king doesn't order the army to clear the streets,' replied Badeau.

'Because he's weak,' said Bonaparte.

'How would you deal with the situation?' asked Badeau.

'If I were giving the orders, the streets would be swept with canister shot to establish order. Then, I would remove corrupt officials and replace them with men of principle, charged with governing fairly, but all of this is academic because I'm not in command and soon I won't be in France.'

'Where are you going?' asked his friend.

'I have been granted permission to return to Corsica,' replied Bonaparte.

'But if civil war is coming, you will miss the action.'

'Civil war is coming, Badeau you can be sure of it. When it does, Corsica will demand her freedom and, if needed, we will fight for it,' said Bonaparte. The friends parted knowing one day they might be fighting on opposite sides.

Isaac Thomas returned to Merthyr in good spirit. His deceitful wife, with her petty jealousies, acid tongue, lies and intrigues was gone from his life. He hated her for what she had done and blamed her for things that could not be undone; for not giving him children, for disgracing his name, for his crippled arm, his estranged sister and the unhappiness that had consumed him making him a twisted, bitter man. With Delyth gone, his mind cleared. He could see the future and Isaac's future was iron. Nothing and no one was going to stand in his way. Isaac Thomas' ambition was fired with new energy and focused on one thing; making money.

When Henry Dundas, summoned Captain Baillie and demanded to know why contracts had been placed with an unauthorized foundry, the captain was ready with his answers. As Admiralty Treasurer, Dundas was responsible for overseeing payments by the Board of Ordnance and, as far as he was concerned, the Clerk of Deliveries, whose parsimony he despised, had exceeded his authority. In his defence, Baillie produced board minutes, delegating power to award small contracts together with quotations to prove he acted properly. Castle Iron Works was significantly cheaper, delivered the cannons promptly and to the right quality, a fact he had reported back to the board with a recommendation to use Castle Iron Works to manufacture bigger weapons in the future. Baillie's paperwork was faultless and it annoyed Dundas intensely. He had reasons for preferring existing suppliers.

'Your authority was to process orders with existing foundries not to appoint new ones,' said Dundas.

'I don't agree. The minutes do not say I cannot use other iron works,' replied Captain Baillie icily.

'Damn you Baillie. You're impertinent. Get out,' blustered Dundas. Baillie gathered up his papers without replying, aware he had made a dangerous enemy. Henry Dundas was determined and ruthless. His duties as treasurer, a position he had held for seven years, offered many profitable opportunities for an enterprising man but Dundas had grander ambitions. In addition to being Admiralty Treasurer, Dundas was also a Member of Parliament and had cultivated the Prime Minister, William Pitt, hoping for a place in his cabinet. A reshuffle of cabinet portfolios was due and Dundas felt his prospects were good. An interfering clerk of deliveries, who might discover something embarrassing, was intolerable and would need dealing with. Dundas considered the problem. Baillie had been careful to document his actions and notify the board. Getting rid of him risked raising questions Dundas would prefer not to answer. Lucrative contracts negotiated by Dundas, on behalf of the board, would be at risk, to say nothing of his prospects for advancement. Henry Dundas needed to discuss the problem with the only man he could trust, his friend Isaac Thomas. The conversation would, however, have to wait until Dundas had an opportunity to visit Merthyr.

Meir stared at the newspaper. She could see the centre of the page but the rest was obscured by a dark cloud, as if she was peering through a black ring. She held the page at arm's length and concentrated on reading the words but her eyes would not focus. She had been seeing dark areas in her peripheral vision for a while but this was worse. Meir polished her spectacles with her apron and looked at the paper again. It made no difference; she still could not decipher the print. The horror of what was happening overwhelmed her.

'You're shaking. What's the matter, Meir?' asked Eira.

'There's something wrong with my eyes. I can't see properly,' replied Meir. Eira went across to her friend and looked at her eyes. The pupils were dull and grey, like soot covered windows.

'Tell me what you can see,' ordered Eira.

'It's as if I'm looking through a tunnel and it's slowly getting longer,' answered Meir.

'You should have told me.'

'There's nothing you can do. I'm going blind,' replied Meir.

'I know I can't help but we will find a doctor who can help you,' promised Eira, hugging her friend.

'Tell me when you can see the light,' said the doctor moving the lantern from left to right. He repeated the test, moving the light up and down. Then, he examined her eyes using a magnifying glass, 'Look up, down.'

'What's wrong with her eyes?' asked Eira when she was alone with the doctor.

'They are inflamed and the lenses are infected. That's why her eyes are cloudy,' replied the doctor.

'Is there a cure?'

'How old is Meir Evans?' asked the doctor.

'I think Meir's about fifty.'

'I'm afraid not. Meir has glaucoma. It's a common condition in old people. Her eyesight's probably been failing for years. Soon, she will be completely blind,' replied the doctor.

'There must be something we can do, drops to ease the swelling or stronger spectacles,' pleaded Eira.

'I have read about an operation by a surgeon where a needle is used to drag the cloudy part of the lens to one side,' said the doctor.

'Does the operation work?'

'There are three possible prognoses, the patient either sees again, which I doubt, goes blind immediately or contracts an infection leading to a slow death. In any event, I cannot recommend such an operation,' said the doctor.

'Why not, if there is a chance?'

'Because the surgeon is probably a quack, making money out of desperate people. Even if he weren't, the operation is unsuitable for Meir since her lenses are completely cloudy,' replied the doctor.

When they returned home, Nye questioned Eira, eager to know the outcome.

'What else did the doctor say?' asked Nye when he heard the news.

'He said there is nothing we can do to help Meir but he's wrong. There are plenty of practical things we can do for her,' replied Eira.

'I don't understand. If the doctor says there's nothing that can be done.'

'I mean we can be her eyes. We can read for her, I can help her wash and dress.'

'What about the Star Tavern? She won't be able to manage the place,' said Nye.

'Then, she will come and live with us,' answered Eira, emphatically. Nye was surprised by his wife's determination and tried to dissuade her from taking on the responsibility. She brushed his objections aside and it was agreed; they would ask Meir to live with them. At first Meir refused, saying she needed her independence, but her eyesight continued to deteriorate and a short while later she moved in with the Vaughns.

On the 26th August the French National Assembly issued a 'Declaration of the Rights of Man and of the Citizen' borrowing ideas from the American 'Declaration of Independence'. The declaration was followed by a demand from the assembly for the right to veto King Louis' rule. The king refused to accept either and there was stalemate. Lieutenant Bonaparte had returned to Corsica and joined a partisan group led by the separatist, Pasquale Paoli. Paoli welcomed Bonaparte's military training and promoted him to the rank of Lieutenant Colonel, in charge of a battalion of Corsican republican volunteers. The Bourbon dynasty, rulers of France and its dominions for over two centuries, had many enemies who were sharpening their weapons and waiting for the opportunity to strike.

The seven Lord Commissioners of the Admiralty listened carefully to the report. When it was finished the First Sea Lord summed up, 'Gentlemen, the news from France is grave indeed. On the 6th October a mob stormed the Palace of Versailles. The king and his family are under house arrest.

The National Assembly has confiscated all church lands and is talking of abolishing the nobility.'

'What's our government's position? The French are no friends of ours but the anarchy in France could well spread. Are we to support Louis and help restore order?' asked a commissioner.

'Dundas, you are close to the Prime Minister. What's his view?' asked the First Sea Lord.

'Broadly, Mr. Pitt supports the idea of overthrowing the French monarchy but publicly we must remain neutral for fear of republicanism crossing the channel. It would not do for the lower orders to get above their station. His main concern however is the uncertainty of French foreign policy. No one knows the intentions of the National Assembly. The Prime Minister believes we should reverse our naval decline and bring the fleet back to its war time strength, ready for the unexpected,' replied Dundas.

'Remind us Dundas. What is the fleet's current strength?' asked the First Sea Lord.

'Since the ending of the American war we have decommissioned many ships of the line. As we speak, the Royal Navy has 500 vessels but many of them are laid up or require major refits to be seaworthy. Another problem is manpower. With so many ships idle, the number of sailors in the service has shrunk from 50,000 to just 12,000. Many of our experienced officers are ashore on half pay,' said Dundas.

'They can be recalled to duty and ships can be refitted. Lord Richmond, as Master General of Ordnance, what is your view?' asked the first Sea Lord.

Richmond, who had been listening quietly, considered the question before answering, 'To fight both the French and Spanish, and there is a distinct danger we will have to, the navy needs to be expanded. We need more ships of the line.

116

A fleet of 500, even if seaworthy and fully crewed is not enough.'

'I agree with you. In your opinion, how many ships would protect our foreign interests and ensure victory?'

'The threat is real. We must double the size of the fleet,' replied Richmond.

'Such an expansion would cost a great deal of money. How the government would fund it is a question that needs to be asked,' said the First Sea Lord.

'We must consider other obstacles to such an expansion,' said Richmond, 'for example, to arm the ships, the Board of Ordnance would need to purchase 50,000 cannons. I doubt if our foundries could cast that many. Another thing, such a fleet would require 150,000 sailors. Where would we find that many able bodied men willing to go to sea?'

'These are all valid issues requiring further examination but first we must get the government's approval and know we have the money. I suggest we adjourn our discussion until we have a decision from the cabinet,' said the First Sea Lord.

Chapter 20

'The expansion of the fleet has been agreed by the cabinet. There is to be a massive ship building program with a lot of ordnance needed but we have a problem,' said Henry Dundas. Isaac Thomas handed his friend a glass of brandy and wondered why Dundas was in Merthyr.

'What sort of problem.'

'The Board of Ordnance has suddenly become cost conscious. It is insisting on competitive tendering for every contract. I can help you win the business but you'll have to lower your prices,' replied Dundas.

'Lower my prices. That would reduce the profit. How much lower?' asked Isaac.

'Enough to undercut Castle Iron Works.'

'But I don't know their prices,' said Isaac.

'I'll be opening the quotations before the board sees them. I will tell you what they quote,' replied Dundas.

'That would work but our arrangement would need to change. Your fee comes out of the profit,' said Isaac.

'Profit is your problem. My commission isn't negotiable. We have a good relationship and I would hate to look for an alternative partner. Isaac, with the navy expanding, there is a fortune to be made but we must be careful. I'll have to let other foundries win some business or the board will get suspicious,' said Dundas. Isaac Thomas nodded, knowing Dundas had the advantage.

Henry Dundas visited Castle Iron Works, the following morning, to advise the directors the company was now a fully approved supplier for naval ordnance and would, in future, receive tender documents from his office.

'These are exciting times. The navy is expanding. We will be buying a lot of guns in the coming years,' explained Dundas. The meeting was affable but Nye felt uneasy. He didn't like Henry Dundas and didn't trust him. The admiralty treasurer was too friendly. Nye's suspicions were confirmed towards the end of the meeting.

'If there is anything I can do to help you win the business, please ask,' said Dundas.

'What sort of things are you suggesting?' asked Nye.

'For a small consideration, let's call it a consultancy fee, I can give you some guidance regarding your prices. If your price is lower than it needs be you can increase it and we all benefit. If it's a bit high, you will know to lower it and win the contract,' said Dundas. Nye studied his visitor and remembered Sir Henry Strachey's words, 'If there is corruption at the Board of Ordnance give me proof and I will expose the culprits.'

'Your offer is an interesting one, Mr. Dundas. My partners and I will need to discuss it,' said Nye and concluded the meeting.

'What do you make of that?' asked Nye after Dundas' carriage had left.

'I've been doing some sums. To arm the number of ships he's talking about they need a thousand cannons a week for the next ten years,' said Will Jones.

'Is that possible?' asked Benjamin Griffiths.

'If every foundry in the land worked day and night it might be,' replied Will.

'What do you think of Dundas?' asked Nye.

'The man's a crook,' replied Will Jones.

'A crook who might be useful,' added Benjamin.

'You're not seriously suggesting we pay him?' asked Nye.

'Why not? It would give us an advantage,' said Benjamin.

'It might give us an advantage but bribery is fraud,' replied Nye.

'Sometimes in business you need to be pragmatic. A few guineas, to oil the wheels of commerce doesn't harm anyone,' argued Benjamin. The discussion went full circle until the partners agreed to do nothing, for now and wait to see how things developed.

That evening, during dinner, Nye described the meeting with Dundas to Eira and asked for her opinion. She agreed it was wrong to pay the man and the correct course of action was to expose him.

'Dundas has probably said the same thing to other iron masters but we don't have any proof. How can we expose him?' answered Nye.

'Can't Thomas Baillie help you?' said Eira.

'Baillie's the Clerk of Deliveries. He works for Dundas. How can he help?'

119

'I don't know,' replied Eira.

'You mentioned Sir Henry Strachey. Tell him what has happened and let him deal with Dundas,' suggested Eira.

'That's good advice Eira. Thank you,' said Nye and decided to write a carefully worded letter to the Secretary of State.

Nye wrote several drafts before he was satisfied with the letter.

'Tell me what you think,' he said, passing the letter to Ben. Benjamin Griffiths read it aloud.

'Dear Secretary of State

Thank you for your advice regarding my company's approach to the Board of Ordnance. Your opinion of Captain Baillie as an honest servant of the board proved sound and I commend him to you most strongly. We have been advised Castle Iron Works is now an approved supplier. The news that a major expansion of the navy is to be undertaken presents a valuable opportunity to iron foundries across the realm and is one we wish to exploit to the full in a spirit of fair competition. In the last week my company has been approached by an officer of the board and offered, in return for a fee, the chance to compare and revise tender documents to our advantage. I believe similar offers have been made to other iron masters. My view is business should be won on merit rather than deceit or fraud. Since the offer was verbal, and can easily be denied, I am unable to provide evidence or a name, aware that, without necessary proof, there is risk of a libel action. The ordnance contracts involve large sums of money and the purpose of my correspondence is to ask the tendering be scrutinized for fairness. The quality of our cannons have been tested satisfactorily in the Admiralty

Proving Houses and you can be assured of my intention to offer the best prices possible.

Your humble servant

Nye Vaughn'

'Are you sure this is the right course of action?' asked Ben.

'What else can we do?'

'Pay Dundas and keep our mouths shut,' replied Ben. Nye kept the letter until the next day when, still of the same frame of mind, he posted it.

When Sir Henry Strachey received the letter, he immediately forwarded it to Lord Richmond. The Master General of Ordnance reacted swiftly, ordering all tender documents be locked away on arrival and made Captain Baillie responsible for ensuring they remained secure until opened in the presence of the board.

Meir's eyesight continued to deteriorate and she spent her time sitting quietly by the window, staring across the valley. Meir couldn't see the trees or the mountain beyond. Her world was black but her memory provided vivid images to fill the darkness. Some were of recent events like the carnival on St David's Day when they picnicked by the river. Others were more distant, from her childhood. Meir saw her mother dressed in a wrap-around pinafore cutting wafer thin slices of bread, holding the loaf against her chest. She could smell the bread and feel her mother's warm embrace. She remembered her son, laughing, full of life and hope for the future. Meir was content retreating into the past; it was a safe place, a haven where bad memories were banished. When she returned from her daydreams, Meir was part of a family that loved and cared for her. Rhys and Bryn sat on her lap to listen to Aunty Meir's stories. They were too young to understand and soon grew bored. When they wriggled she didn't scold them. One evening, after putting the boys to bed, Eira returned to the sitting room. Meir was in her usual seat, by the window.

'Shall I read to you?' asked Eira. Meir didn't answer. Her eyes were open but the memories filling her darkness had faded, never to return.

Chapter 21

Thomas Dadford looked down the valley towards Abercynon to the range pole and checked his theodolite for a second time. He waved his chain man to move left. For the measurement to be accurate, the gunter's chain had to be straight. When it was, Dadford waved a green flag and lifted the telescope to his eye. The chain man in the distance was signalling.

'Eleven chains at 163 degrees and 10 ½ degrees declination,' announced Dadford to his assistant, who repeated the figures and noted them on the plan table.

'It's a steep incline,' commented the assistant. The observation amused Dadford. The incline he was referring to was the side of a mountain and it wasn't the only obstacle in their way. They still had to cross the River Taff. Thomas Dadford had never seen such extreme conditions although he was an experienced civil engineer and leading canal builder. Dadford made a mental calculation. To get past Abercynon they would need fourteen or fifteen locks and an aqueduct.

Dadford looked at his watch, 'It's getting late and that's the last check we need to do. Pack up,' he ordered. Dadford's three month survey of land between Merthyr and Cardiff was complete. All that remained was to present a report to his employers and submit his account.

'Now you have surveyed the route, what is your opinion of the project?' asked Nye Vaughn. Thomas Dadford smiled. He was often asked this question by clients and wondered what answer they preferred. Some wanted the truth; the canal would be difficult and costly to build and should only be undertaken if there was a sound financial advantage. Other clients, like his last employer, Lord Dudley, had shown little interest in the technical aspects of his proposed canal and even less in its cost. Lord Dudley's lack of attention revealed itself spectacularly, during the construction of his canal, when he was shocked to discover the cost of tunnelling 4,000 yards through a hill. Dadford looked around the room. 'These men were different,' he decided, 'They wanted to hear the truth.'

'What I am proposing is a 25 mile canal linking your foundry at Merthyr to the docks at Cardiff. In the design, I have included branch canals linking other foundries and works within four miles to provide extra traffic and income. There are some serious engineering concerns, particularly the area of Abercynon and the sea locks at Cardiff which add a considerable amount to the cost. My initial estimate is that it will cost in excess of £100,000 to purchase the land and construct the canal. If you wish to proceed, the next step is to find a sponsor to take an act through Parliament, giving you the power to compulsorily purchase the land,' said Dadford. The partners asked some questions, thanked Dadford for his diligence and retired to discuss the matter in private.

'£100,000. We don't have that sort of money. Nye, you were mad to commission Dadford's report without consulting the rest of us,' said Will.

'Tell me Will. What's the most expensive cost we have?' asked Nye.

'I don't know,' replied Will.

'Tell him, Ben.'

'The freight charges,' said Benjamin.

'That's right. It costs us more to drag large cannons to Cardiff than it does to cast them. A canal, which we control, would virtually eliminate that cost and mine owners will pay handsomely to ship their coal from the valleys to Cardiff. We can undercut every other foundry and make a handsome profit. The navy contracts will be ours for the taking,' explained Nye.

'It's a pipe dream. Where will the money to build a canal come from?' asked Will.

'We could incorporate another company and invite investors to buy shares,' suggested Benjamin.

'Paxton and some of his friends are interested. I've also spoken to Lord Cardiff. He's prepared to sponsor a bill in Parliament in return for a commercial advantage,' added Nye.

'What commercial advantage?' asked Benjamin.

'Cardiff wants discounted shipping rates for using the canal. He plans to buy coal at the pit head and keep the saving made by moving the coal himself,' said Nye.

'So he gets all the advantages of the canal without investing a penny,' said Benjamin.

Nye nodded, 'There is something else. Dadford's scheme includes a branch canal leading from Isaac Thomas' foundry. I want it removed from the plan. Thomas' ironworks must never have access to our canal.'

The discovery that he couldn't examine quotations before they went before the Board of Ordnance annoyed Henry Dundas but he decided to say nothing to Isaac Thomas. The iron master would stop paying his commissions if he knew he

124

was getting nothing in return. Dundas had no time to dwell on the change of policy; there was too much to do. The admiralty offices, which since the American War had been contracting, had exploded into action. Keels for new 100 gun first rate ships of the line were laid down. HMS Queen Charlotte, was hurriedly completed at Chatham. Plans for bigger, 120 gun, ships were brought forward. Other ships of the line were ordered to expand the battle fleet. Bucklers Hard, the birthplace of the Agamemnon, Swiftsure and Euryalus was alive with carpenters.

Relays of oarsmen towed completed hulls along the River Beaulieu and across the Solent to Portsmouth dockyard. The rowers could not stop to rest; the huge hulls towering above them had no anchors. In Portsmouth, the ships were fitted with masts, rigging, weapons and provisions. Captured Spanish and French warships were repaired, renamed and commissioned as Royal Navy vessels. Naval dockyards at Chatham, Portsmouth, Plymouth and Glasgow bustled with tradesmen. Overseas dockyards in Malta, Bermuda and Halifax added to the fleet. Retired naval officers were recalled and given new commissions. To crew the ships, the king's authority was invoked to impress sailors into the Royal Navy. Merchant ships, approaching their home port after long voyages, were boarded and crew members taken to be pressed. Gangs of press men roamed the taverns, searching for able bodied men to seize. Wives wondered why their husbands vanished, leaving them destitute. Orders for heavy cannons were arriving regularly in the foundries at Merthyr. The preparations for war had begun.

An act of Parliament, authorizing the construction of a canal from Merthyr to Cardiff, was passed on the 9th June 1890. Work began immediately, supervised by Thomas Dadford. The public offering of shares in the canal was a success and the construction fully funded. Nye Vaughn, who argued the canal was his idea, was given a substantial shareholding and he borrowed heavily to buy more stock, making himself the largest shareholder.

Isaac Thomas' initial reaction to the canal was favourable and he bought shares in the venture only to discover the directors were cancelling the branch canal from his works. The financial risk of isolation of his foundry was obvious; he would be at a serious competitive disadvantage. Another danger emerged for Thomas' foundry when the first section of the canal, joining Merthyr to Newbridge, was filled with water. Taking water from the River Taff lowered its level, threatening the supply to Thomas' works. Without water power the furnace bellows would not operate. Isaac was also growing concerned about Henry Dundas and wondered how much help he was really getting in return for the payments he was making to the Admiralty Treasurer. The level of orders had increased but why was Dundas giving valuable work to Vaughn? He was considering what to do when a visitor arrived. It was Evan Jenkins, the land agent who had been promised money, to swindle his master.

'An unexpected pleasure, Mr. Jenkins. What can I do for you?' asked Isaac. Jenkins was in no mood for pleasantries.

'You owe me and I want paying.'

'I owe you? I owe you nothing,' replied Isaac.

'You promised me a shilling for every ton of ore taken from the Tredegar Estate,' snapped Jenkins.

'You misunderstood. That was my first offer but you preferred to have £100 and that's what I gave you. My debt to you is settled in full,' said Isaac. Jenkins knew he was being lied to but was at a loss for a suitable response to the deceit.

'I'll go to his lordship and tell him,' he blustered.

'Go where you please. It makes little difference to me. My contract with Sir Charles Morgan is in writing and is secure but, if you do, your job and your reputation will be, well, finished,' replied Isaac. Evan Jenkins' bravado evaporated. He knew Isaac Thomas was right.

'There is a way you can still make money. Sit down and I'll explain how,' said Isaac. Jenkins hesitated and then sat down. He would listen to Isaac Thomas to discover how to recoup his loss or take his revenge.

'The new canal passes through the Tredegar Estate. You're the land agent. What has been the reaction of the farmers?' asked Isaac.

'Not good. I'm dealing with the evictions. There's a lot of resentment,' replied Jenkins.

'It's only a thin strip of land. Why are there evictions?'

'His lordship is using the canal as an excuse to remove the tenants. He wants the land for grazing sheep,' said Jenkins.

'Is there likely to be any trouble?'

'I don't think so. What sort of trouble?' asked Jenkins.

'A disgruntled tenant, thrown off his land, might take his revenge by sabotaging the canal. Do you know anyone like that?'

'Maybe I do,' replied Jenkins, cautiously.

'If the canal was abandoned because of local opposition it would be a great shame,' suggested Isaac. Evan Jenkins' struggled to understand where the conversation was leading.

'I've some sympathy for evicted tenants and would like to help them. Perhaps you would act on my behalf.'

'In what capacity?' asked Jenkins.

'By managing a fund to sustain those distressed by the canal's arrival,' replied Isaac.

'Distressed enough to stop the canal's construction, is that what you mean?'

'How you apply the fund is a matter for yourself. I'm prepared to be generous, with additional money, particularly if there's a lot of distress. Shall we discuss how much the fund might need to begin its charitable work?' said Isaac.

Chapter 22

On the 28th February 1791 four hundred French noblemen armed themselves and gathered at the Tuileries in Paris, planning to help the king escape. The Marquis de Lafayette ordered the National Guard to arrest the nobles and disarm them. To avoid bloodshed, the king instructed the nobles to put down their weapons. The 'Day of Daggers' as the confrontation was known, ended peacefully but most of the nobles involved were expelled from France. Later, the National Guard fired on an anti monarchy riot killing fifty. Elsewhere, Emperor Leopold II demanded the royal houses of Europe join together to defend King Louis. When news of the revolution reached the Caribbean, slaves rose up in French colonies and slaughtered their owners.

In Corsica, the partisan's campaign against French rule erupted with Bonaparte fighting alongside his fellow countrymen. Corsican loyalties divided between nationalists, republicans and royalists and the outcome was indecisive. Frustrated with the confusion, Bonaparte returned to France where, despite fighting against the French, he was promoted to the rank of Captain in his old regiment. The French Revolution was about to enter a new, blood soaked phase.

'Have you seen this?' asked Eira. Nye took the newspaper from her and studied the picture for a moment.
'What is it?' he asked.
'They call it Madame Guillotine. It's a machine the French have invented for cutting heads off,' replied Eira.

Nye read the article:

'On the 20th March 1792, the French National Council voted in favour of adopting the guillotine as France's official means of execution. The machine, invented by the physician, Joseph Guillotin, is designed to behead without inflicting pain on the condemned person and is said to be modelled on the Halifax Gibbet, a similar decapitating machine in use in the North of England since the 13th Century. The Guillotine was used for the first time on the 25th April, to execute the highwayman, Nicholas Pelletier. According to reports, death was instant, causing the watching crowd to complain it was too quick and call for the return of the hangman's rope.'

'A machine for cutting heads off. It's barbaric,' said Nye and thought of the unfortunate woman executed in London for coining.

'I heard they held up the poor man's severed head and his eyes looked around at the crowd,' said Eira. Nye was about to return the paper to his wife when a second, smaller article caught his attention.

'Do you remember the dinner we went to when Sir Charles Morgan gave a speech, warning France would invade the Netherlands?' asked Nye.

'Yes. It was a nice evening,' replied Eira.

'He was right. It says here that France has declared war on Austria, occupied Belgium and ordered troops into the Low Countries. The war in Europe has begun,' said Nye.

'Thank goodness we aren't involved,' said Eira

The opening of the Merthyr to Cardiff canal was a festive occasion. A crowd gathered on the jetty beside Castle Iron Works, at 10 o'clock, to listen to the speeches. Lord Cardiff spoke at length, praising the engineering skill of Thomas Dadford and complimenting him for the way he overcame considerable difficulties to build the 25 mile canal. Other speakers talked of the benefits to the economy which would follow from increased trade. Sir Charles Morgan reminded those present of the importance of building up the fleet. There were gasps when he announced that an alliance of Austria and Prussia had invaded France. When he added, King Louis XVI had been charged with collaborating with the enemies of France there were cheers, followed by silence.

'Come, Ladies and Gentlemen. Louis isn't our friend but we mustn't cheer his downfall for fear of what'll replace him,' said Sir Charles. The speeches ended with loud applause and a band began to play.

'Are you ready for a boat trip, Mr. Paxton?' asked Nye.

'I warn you I'm a poor sailor. I suffer from the mal de mer,' replied William Paxton.

'What's that?'

'Seasickness,' answered Paxton.

'The conditions are calm today,' said Nye.

'I understand Dadford has submitted another bill,' said Paxton.

'He has, for £17,000 and the Cardiff sea lock isn't finished yet. We're well over budget,' replied Nye.

'The man has inflated his prices,' said Paxton.

'Dadford says the extra cost was unavoidable and he can account for it.'

'Do you believe him?' asked Paxton. The conversation was interrupted before Nye could reply. The dignitaries were moving. They walked slowly along the jetty and boarded two barges. The boats had been garlanded with flowers and gaily coloured flags. A ribbon was stretched across the canal. Rhys and Bryn were dressed in sailor suits and the family took their place in the bow of the first boat waving to spectators lining the bank. When the embarking passengers had settled, Eira cut the ribbon to the cheers of the crowd. A carthorse started to walked along the towpath and as the rope tightened the barge moved slowly forward.

'I told you the conditions were calm,' called Nye, to his friend and smiled. The barges travelled at a sedate speed to Abercanaid where they moored and the passengers disembarked for lunch at the Duffryn Arms.

During the meal, Sir Charles Morgan spoke briefly to Nye and said, 'I am proposing to sink a coal mine at Abercanaid. The canal,' he added, 'will need a dock and turning basin, near the village.'

'I am sure they wouldn't be difficult to construct. I will ask Thomas Dadford's opinion on the idea,' promised Nye.

'Are you pleased with the canal?' asked Eira as they rode home in the carriage.

'It changes everything. Once the sea lock is finished and we can float our barges alongside waiting ships, no foundry in the land will have such an advantage. I know the canal will make money, a lot of money. The Vaughns are about to become very rich,' replied Nye and tousled Rhys' hair.

'I'm already rich. I have you. I have two wonderful sons and there is something else,' said Eira and hugged her sons.

'What else could there possibly be to make us any happier?' asked Nye.

'I am with child. We are going to have another baby,' answered Eira.

The following evening, Bryn complained he had a sore throat. By morning, his temperature was 101°F, his tongue was swollen and he couldn't swallow. His cheeks were crimson and his lips a sickly yellow. A rash appeared on his neck during the afternoon. Nye, who had gone to the foundry, was summoned and arrived at the same time as the doctor.

'How old is Bryn, Mrs. Vaughn,' asked the doctor as he examined the little boy.

'He'll be five in October,' replied Eira. The doctor ran his fingers through Byrn's hair, muttered then inspected his armpits and groin.

'Has he been outside in the cold or with strangers recently,' asked the doctor.

'Yes, he was on the canal with us,' replied Eira.

'Of course, the opening ceremony,' said the doctor.

'What's wrong with him?' asked Nye.

'Can you turn over? I want to look at your back, there's a good boy,' said the doctor. The doctor beckoned Eira and Nye to follow him onto the landing. He shut the bedroom door and turned to face them. Eira was weeping.

'You know what it is, don't you,' said the doctor, quietly.

'Just tell us, doctor,' said Nye.

'It's scarlet fever, isn't it? My sister died of it when she was eight,' whispered Eira between sobs.

'I'm afraid it is,' replied the doctor.

'Is he going to die?' demanded Nye.

'Keep your voice down, Mr. Vaughn or your son will hear. He might die, but the rash has not spread to his body so there is hope,' said the doctor.

'What can we do?' asked Eira drying her eyes.

'There are pustules on his head. We mush shave him and bathe the scalp with cold salt water. I will apply leeches to his temples to reduce the swelling,' said the doctor.

Bryn screamed when the leeches fastened themselves. After he had been bled, Nye wrapped Bryn in a blanket and held him tight while Eira shaved his head. Then she washed it with salt water. He cried again as the salt soaked into the sores.

'Bathe his neck with hot flannels. They will ease the inflammation. Keep him covered and the bedroom warm.

Here is a draft of calomel and senna for you to administer with a little tepid milk. It will purge his bowels and remove some of the poison. Scarlet fever is infectious. No one else must enter this room. I suggest you hang a curtain soaked in a solution of copper sulphate across the doorway to contain the disease. I will call again in the morning,' said the doctor and went downstairs. Nye stopped him in the hallway.

'Tell me the truth, what's going to happen to Bryn?' asked Nye.

'If the rash spreads over his body there is a strong possibility your son will be taken from you. If it doesn't, he may recover,' said the doctor.

'How long does it take?'

'If he is going to survive the fever will lessen within five days,' replied the doctor and left. Nye sat on the stairs with his head down. He didn't notice Eira coming until she sat down beside him.

'Bryn isn't going to die. I'm not going to let him. We aren't going to let him,' she said and held Nye's hand.

Eira continued to bathe Bryn as the doctor instructed. At four in the morning Nye ordered her to bed and took over, changing the warm flannels every few minutes. The doctor arrived at nine o'clock to check on the patient.

'There is no change in his condition but we must bleed him again,' announced the doctor.

'No. You aren't doing that to my son again. The leeches terrified him,' said Eira.

'But bleeding relieves the pressure on the sores,' said the doctor.

'I don't believe you,' whispered Eira.

'Very well but it's against my advice,' said the doctor.

Eira and Nye sat with Bryn throughout the next two nights. They were dozing on the third night of their vigil when he stirred and asked for a drink, the fever had broken.

'He's going to live,' whispered Nye.

It was still early and Nye was washing when a messenger arrived from the foundry.

'The section of canal between Ynysfach and Glyndyrus is dry. Part of the bank has collapsed,' said the messenger. Nye ordered a horse to be saddled, dressed hurriedly and rode to the works. Will Jones was waiting for him and the two men followed the towpath south. Everything appeared normal until they reached the second lock at Ynysfach. Beyond the lock, the canal was empty. Continuing along the path, they passed a barge lying in the mud. Further on they reached Thomas Dadford with some labourers. Beside then there was a large breach in the canal bank. The adjacent field, below the level of the canal, was underwater.

'What happened?' shouted Nye, angrily.

'I don't know. The bank appears to have given way, allowing the water to escape,' replied Dadford.

'Can you repair it?' demanded Nye.

'Of course I can repair it,' answered Dadford, angrily.

'How long will it take to have the canal working again?' demanded Nye.

'About a week,' snapped Dadford.

'We can't wait a week,' shouted Nye, turned his horse and cantered back towards the foundry.

'I can't perform miracles,' yelled Dadford, at the disappearing horseman. Will Jones dismounted and approached Dadford.

'You're going to have to do something quickly Dadford. We have a shipment of 30 cannons for HMS Victory's refit which must be in Cardiff by Thursday. That's four days away,' Said Will.

134

'Send them by wagon,' replied Dadford.

'We can't move them in that time, the guns weigh 120 tons,' explained Will.

Dadford and his men worked through the day, frantically trying to mend the breach. Labourers dug pits and barrowed earth to fill the hole. Men gathered rocks to strengthen the repair. Others fetched wagons loaded with clay. At dusk, foundry workers arrived to relieve the exhausted navigators and the work continued. As dawn approached, Dadford declared the clay lining was thick enough to seal the repair and ordered the sluices opened. Twelve hours later, the canal had filled and four barges loaded with HMS Victory's new cannons began their journey. They reached Cardiff on Wednesday evening, in time to be transferred to the vessel sailing for Portsmouth the following afternoon.

Chapter 23

The summer of 1792 was particularly dry and the level of the River Taff fell to its lowest level. Water taken from the river, to feed the canal, lowered the level further and threatened to stop the waterwheels driving the bellows at Thomas' foundry. Isaac issued a writ claiming his right to the water supply. Facing a wait of months while a court considered the case, Isaac decided to take direct action. His foundry-men marched to the weir, diverting the water from the river, and destroyed it. It was a blatant and very public act of vandalism. Nye Vaughn responded by sending workmen to rebuild the weir and mounting a guard to protect it from further attacks. Then, another section of canal failed and Dadford was summoned from Cardiff, where he was working on the sea lock, to make emergency repairs.

The engineer arrived at Castle Iron Works two days later, demanding a meeting with Nye.

'I want payment of the outstanding £17,000 before my men do any more work. They have to be paid and I'm incurring more expense every day,' said Dadford.

'I'm not paying your account until all the damage, is repaired. Then, we will discuss it,' replied Nye.

'There's nothing to discuss and you have no right to withhold payment.'

'I have every right. The canal you have built is second-rate. It leaks like a sieve.'

'I assure you there's nothing second-rate about my workmanship. Are you going to pay me?' demanded Dadford. Nye shook his head.

'Very well, good day to you Mr. Vaughn,' said Dadford, stood up and put on his coat.

'Where are you going? We still need to settle this,' said Nye.

'I'm going to lay my men off. Our relationship is ended. You insult me and I will have nothing more to do with your canal,' snapped Dadford.

'Sit down Dadford,' said Nye sharply, 'We haven't finished. If my comment offends you personally I apologise. Let us both calm down and find a way to resolve our differences. I have a proposal to make. I will pay you £5,000 today if you finish the repairs. That will ease your cash flow. Before the balance is paid, I suggest we commission an independent expert to inspect the canal and tell us his findings. Is that acceptable to you?'

'Pay me half the money and I will complete the repairs. As for an inspection, I suggest the civil engineer Roger Whitworth. He has a reputation for accuracy and integrity,' replied Dadford.

'Then we are agreed. I am glad for another reason,' said Nye.

136

'And what is that?' asked Dadford.

'If you walked away, you would have been arrested and sued for breach of contract,' said Nye.

'Arresting me would have been a mistake. I promise you, no canal engineer would come within a hundred miles of your canal,' replied Dadford.

'It seems we both need each other,' said Nye and smiled.

'The repair is already finished. The canal will be navigable by tomorrow night,' said Dadford.

'Here will do, it's quiet,' said Evan Jenkins. His men started to dig. Darkness concealed them from prying eyes. When the trench was half way across the towpath they stopped to rest.

'It needs to be deeper. Let's get finished and go home,' said Evans. The men went back to work. Suddenly, water from the canal broke into the trench and the men jumped clear. The flow of water increased as its force enlarged the channel. In minutes the small trench had grown as thousands of gallons of water poured through the gap. The men gathered their tools and went home. In the morning, when the breach was discovered, it was fifteen feet across and all traces of digging had been washed away.

Thomas Dadford believed sabotage was causing the damage and stationed sentries along the canal. The following night, his suspicions were confirmed by a sentry reporting seeing men digging by the canal. When the sentry shouted a challenge, the men threw down their tools and fled, leaving a half dug trench. Realising the risk of capture was growing, Jenkins' accomplices refused to help him any further.

Robert Whitworth was surprised to receive a request to review Dadford's work. Whitworth, who was in his sixties, was the leading canal builder of his day. As well as serving as Surveyor to the Navigation Committee, he was currently retained as the consultant engineer for the Leeds to Liverpool Canal. Despite his busy schedule, Whitworth made time to travel to South Wales and inspect the canal built by Dadford.

'I've walked the entire length and am satisfied with Dadford's design. He has brought the canal through mountainous scenery with wonderful ingenuity. The materials and workmanship are of a high standard and apart from some minor criticisms I will not fault his work,' said Whitworth, completing his report. Dadford was vindicated.

On the 3rd September 1792, news reached Paris that the Prussian army had taken Verdun and was advancing on the French capital to restore the king to his throne and put an end to anarchy. Weapons looted from royal arsenals were hurriedly distributed and orders issued to enlist an army of 60,000 men to defend Paris. As the men assembled, a rumour spread that prisoners were planning to escape and help the Prussians. The undisciplined French troops refused to leave Paris while traitors remained behind. The first prisoners massacred were 24 priests being transported to prison. The mob then went from prison to prison searching for enemies of the state to kill. During the massacre nearly 1400 were executed including priests, politicians and aristocrats. The bodies were piled high in a street near the River Seine. Included among them was Princess Marie Louise of Savoy, governess to the royal children. As predicted by Sir Charles Morgan, the French invasion of the Low Countries threatened British interests and British support was offered to the Prussian campaign. Aware that army officers were being executed for expressing political views, Napoleon Bonaparte kept quiet. He said and did nothing controversial. Captain Bonaparte would wait for a safer time to offer an opinion, until after the king was restored or the republicans had won. Having slaughtered hundreds of prisoners the French army marched to meet the Prussians at Valmy.

The French force, half of which were untrained volunteers, included 40 cannon with experienced gun crews. The French were outnumbered but accurate French artillery fire decimated the Prussians. Withering case shot, fired at waist height, tore through ranks of men cutting them down. The Prussians turned and fled leaving the French Citizen Army of the Revolution to claim victory. Two days after the battle, the French monarchy was abolished and the country declared a republic. In future King Louis XVI was to be referred to simply as Citizen Louis Capet. Bonaparte was not on the battlefield at Valmy, on the 20th September, but the battle's outcome decided his future loyalty.

Evan Jenkins cut the moorings and pushed the barge away from the bank with a branch. He watched the barge drift to the centre of the pool. When he was satisfied it was in the right position, Jenkins ran up the slope and opened the lock gates. Then, he hurried to the far end of the lock, picked up the sluice key and shuffled across the gate, his leather boots slipping on the greasy wood. Jenkins fitted the key and tried to turn it. Water pressure, behind the gate, held the sluice tight. He tried again, this time with both hands. The key began to turn. As he raised the gate water poured into the lock. When the sluice was fully open, he moved across to the other gate. The key turned more easily this time and Jenkins spun it as quickly as possible. The sluice reached the top of its travel and stopped suddenly, throwing Jenkins off balance. He lost his footing, slipped and fell backwards into the lock, hitting the water with a force that winded him. Freezing water from the open sluices cascaded down on him. The current carried the struggling man past the lower gates into the pool. The barge was also moving downstream. The barge had gathered speed when it reached the next lock. The collision smashed the gates open. The boats momentum increased as it filled with water. The next set of gates was also destroyed. By now, the barge was settling in the water. The bow hit the side of the canal and the current turned the barge sideways, wedging it across the canal. Sentries, hearing the noise, rushed to the spot but there was no sign of the vandals.

Evan Jenkins' mutilated body was discovered, trapped beneath the hull, when the boat was raised. An enquiry into his death recorded the cause as drowning but beyond that the jury was divided. Some jurors argued he was responsible for his own death while others maintained he had been murdered after confronting the ruffians who wrecked the lock gates. Going through his pockets, before giving his clothes away, Jenkins' widow was astonished and delighted to discover seventy pounds in the pocket of her dead husband's Sunday coat.

At the end of September, heavy rain raised the level of the River Taff, reducing the threat to Thomas' foundry. During the winter months, there was nothing to impede the output of iron from Merthyr Tydfil and the foundries continued to expand. By the end of the year, six hundred men worked for Nye Vaughn's companies. Discovering that Thomas had secured exclusive mineral rights for Glamorganshire from Sir Charles Morgan, Nye searched to the west and leased land from Lord Dynevor to ensure a continuing supply of coal and iron ore. The canal drove down costs and the iron masters reaped the profits. When the water dispute between Vaughn and Thomas reached court the Admiralty intervened. The First Sea Lord made it clear nothing was to stand in the way of rearming the Royal Navy; a compromise had to be found, one which kept both foundries working at full capacity. An ingenious solution was provided by Thomas Dadford who devised a way to reduce the flow of water through the canal by diverting the outflow from the third lock back to the channel supplying Thomas' foundry. Nye and Isaac were no longer on speaking terms and the final negotiations were conducted through lawyers.

The compromise settled one dispute but there was another commercial impediment the Admiralty wanted removed, to reduce cost. The Admiralty insisted that Thomas' foundry was given access to the canal, a demand which Nye Vaughn initially refused to agree to. Eventually, threatened with losing business from his biggest customer, he relented while consoling himself by charging his competitor a higher tariff than other canal users.

By December, Bryn had recovered fully from his illness except for a red mark on his forehead. As Christmas approached, both boys were getting excited. Nye had promised to take his sons to a magic show on Christmas Eve. Eira, whose pregnancy was nearing full term, stayed at home. When they arrived, the hall was full. Every seat was taken. Nye picked up Rhys and Bryn and sat them on a windowsill, from where they had a better view. The illusionist began his act by walking onto stage and tapping the floor with his walking cane. There were gasps when the cane became a rope. He cut the rope into four pieces which he tied together. When he made the rope vanish and the cane reappear, the audience clapped. The show continued with more illusions.

'Ladies and Gentlemen, we now come to the last part of the evening and I must ask for absolute silence,' announced the illusionist. The audience waited quietly as the stage lights were extinguished. A large white screen was carried onto the stage. It shimmered in the dim light.

'What you are about to witness are some of the greatest wonders of the universe, which will be revealed to you using the science of the phantasmagoria. This machine, Ladies and Gentlemen, created by the renowned inventor Etienne Roberts, is an apparatus capable of showing your innermost dreams. Used by an expert, such as myself, it can produce visions of the future and transport us to distant lands. What is more, and for such purposes we must be very careful, the phantasmagoria makes it possible to see our departed loved ones. Before we begin, I must warn you, great science brings danger. We must take care; the phantasmagoria is powerful enough to summon up phantoms and evil ghosts. That is why the machine is called a phantasmagoria. Indeed, the inventor, Monsieur Roberts once had the misfortune to summon Satan himself. His audience were lucky to escape with their lives,' declared the illusionist. A child, in the audience began, to cry.

'Don't be scared. It's only pretend,' whispered Nye to his sons.

There was a clash of cymbals and a beam of light, from the back of the hall, illuminated the screen with a blurred image. The picture slowly came into focus and the audience saw a woman dressed in a blue dress sitting on a donkey. The illusionist began a commentary and a man with his head covered appeared to walk across the screen. Everyone in the hall knew the story of the nativity and each slide was greeted enthusiastically. The final tableau of the holy family in the stable was cheered. When it faded away it was replaced with a grinning face of an old man whose eyes looked from side to side across the auditorium, the audience stood up and clapped.

'Who's that old man smiling at us?' asked Rhys.

142

'That's Old Father Christmas. He's the spirit of Christmas,' said Nye.

'Is he a ghost?' asked Bryn.

'He's a kindly ghost who makes sure we have enough to eat and drink each Christmas. Do you think he enjoyed the show?' asked Nye, as they were leaving.

'He looked scary,' replied Rhys.

When they got home, the house was busy. Eira was in labour and the doctor was attending her. Servants rushed about with hot water, towels and clean linen. Nye put the boys to bed and waited nervously in the parlour. He heard the cry of a newborn baby, ran upstairs and knocked on the bedroom door. The baby's crying had stopped. The doctor emerged and quickly closed the door behind him. As it shut, Nye glimpsed the midwife wrapping a small parcel beside the bed.

'What time is it?' asked the doctor. He looked tired.

'One and a half hours past midnight,' replied Nye. The doctor nodded.

Nye couldn't contain himself, 'Tell me doctor. Do I have another son?'

'No,' replied the doctor, 'Allow us a few minutes to make Mrs Vaughn comfortable then you can go in to see her and meet your new daughter.'

'Is she all right?'

'Your wife is tired but in good health and your new baby, born on Christmas morning, is perfect. Congratulations,' said the doctor.

'If it was a girl, Eira wanted to call her Cerys,' said Nye.

'It's a nice name, comes from the Welsh for love,' said the doctor.

'She will be loved as we might have loved her sister,' replied Nye, remembering the tiny coffin he lowered into the ground six years before.

Chapter 24

On the 21st January 1793, Citizen Louis Capet was taken to the Place de la Revolution. He mounted the scaffold and said, 'I pardon those who are the cause of my misfortunes,' adding, 'I am innocent of any crime but prepared to die.' Before Louis could continue with his prepared speech, General Santerre, commander of the National Guard ordered a drum roll, whereupon Louis was laid on the guillotine and immediately beheaded. As the head dropped into the basket, members of the crowd rushed forward and dipped their handkerchiefs in the blood dripping from the scaffold. In the king's defence, the executioner, Charles Henri Sanson, stated that Citizen Capet had died bravely.

Eight days later, the French Republic declared war on Great Britain. The declaration was followed by a royalist rebellion in South-western France forcing the National Assembly to concentrate on securing its authority within the country. In June, Napoleon Bonaparte published a pamphlet supporting the republic and sent a copy to the republican leader, Robespierre. It was an astute political move, which raised Bonaparte's profile, winning him promotion and command of the artillery besieging the city of Toulon where 13,000 British troops were supporting Royalist rebels. Toulon was a strategic naval base and its capture was essential. The survival of the republic was at stake. Bonaparte requisitioned more than 100 cannons from different garrisons which he positioned to dominate the harbour defences and town. After a series of fierce battles, the British Commander, Admiral Hood ordered the destruction of all French munitions and the British sailed away leaving the royalists to the mercy of the Republican army. More than 700 were bayoneted or shot as they surrendered. During the battle, Bonaparte who was now a Colonel was shot in the thigh by a British sergeant. The French had retaken Toulon, ended a royalist rebellion and given the British a thrashing. It was a stunning victory for the Republic. Bonaparte's strategy was described by one senior officer, as genius and he was promoted to the rank of Brigadier General. Bonaparte was twenty four years old.

'We have had an invitation to visit Middleton Hall to stay with the Paxtons,' said Eira and handed Nye a letter from Anne Paxton. Nye read the contents and returned the letter.

'I don't have time. There is too much to do,' said Nye.

'Nonsense, you haven't had a day away from the foundry since Christmas. When you aren't there you work in your study at home. A break will do us good,' replied Eira. Nye looked up from his papers and looked at his wife. She was as beautiful as the day they married. Perhaps he was neglecting her. Castle Iron works would manage without him for a few days.

'All right, we'll go. Are you sure the nanny can manage with us away?' he asked.

'She doesn't need too. She's coming with us and so are the children,' said Eira emphatically. Nye recognised the tone of voice and resigned himself to the expedition.

It was October but the weather was warmer than usual for the time of year as the landau, pulled by two greys, arrived in Llandovery. The coachman stopped on King's Road, dismounted, opened the door and offered his arm to Eira. Eira and Nye stepped down from the carriage and waited for the calash, containing the children and their nanny to catch up. When the little carriage came into view, Eira waved. The boys, who were perched beside the driver on the high seat, waved back. Rhys stood up and was promptly scolded by nanny and told to sit or he would fall off the carriage and bump his head. The family took lunch at the Castle Hotel before continuing their journey.

'What happened to the luggage wagon? I can't see it,' said Eira as they emerged from the hotel.

'I sent it on ahead. We can soon catch up,' replied Nye.

'How far is Middleton Hall from here?'

'It's about sixteen miles. We'll be there in time for tea,' answered Nye.

'We're going through Llangadog. Will we visit your father?' He's never seen his grandchildren,' said Eira as the carriage departed. Nye didn't answer.

'We really should. You can't hold grudges forever, he's your father,' pleaded Eira. Nye was getting angry, not with Eira as he knew she was right but with himself, for being stubborn and a fool. And yet, even as Nye admitted his stupidity to himself, he still could not bring himself to face his father. Thirteen years had passed since his mother's death but he remembered everything as if it was yesterday.

'You must confront your demon or it'll haunt you forever. We can do it together,' said Eira.

Nye shouted to the coachman, 'When we get to the square in Llangadog, turn left, along the mountain road. We're calling at Beilli Farm.'

The track leading to Beilli Farm was shorter than Nye remembered. He recognised the stone barn. It had a new roof. As the landau approached the gate, a boy ran across the farmyard and disappeared into the house. Nye stepped down and held the gate open, allowing the coach to go through. A grey haired woman was standing in the doorway of the farmhouse. She watched as the coach turned and stopped in the yard. The calash pulled in behind. Nye walked across the yard. The house had recently been lime washed and there were new doors on the cowshed.

'Hello Nye,' said the woman. Nye looked at her and the boy standing beside her.

'You don't remember me, do you?' she said.

'Are you Jean?' Before she could answer two men came into the yard.

'Who are you and what are you doing on my farm?' shouted one of them. Nye recognised the voice and turned. His father was standing by the carriage. The features were the same but his pallor and the way he stooped aged him. Father and son stared at each other. Eira stepped down from the carriage and held Nye's arm.

'Hello father. This is my wife, Eira,' said Nye.

'It's good to see you, Nye,' said his father and hugged him, 'You already know Jean. She's Mrs Vaughn now. This is our son. His sisters are at school. Richard, come and say hello to your brother.' The boy came forward sheepishly and shook Nye's hand. The second man introduced himself as Jean's brother, Dan. Richard took Rhys and Bryn to see a newborn calf and the adults went into the house. Richard's sisters arrived from school and were excited to find a baby in the house. Nye and his father went for a walk.

'I'm sorry for the way I treated your mother. I was scared and didn't know what to do. I loved her so much,' said his father.

'It's done and in the past,' replied Nye. The two men stopped and leaned on a gate.

'You didn't put a marker on mother's grave,' said Nye.

'I had no money.'

'I've paid for one,' said Nye.

'I know. I see it when we take flowers.'

'What of the present? You seem content.'

'Jean's a good wife and her brother a hard worker. Between us we've made a good life,' said Nye's father.

'It's strange to discover I have a brother and two sisters,' said Nye.

'It's good to see you. You've done well for yourself,' said Nye's father. They talked until Nye looked at his watch. It was getting late.

'We need to be going,' said Nye and they walked back to the farmhouse.

'Was it the right thing to do?' asked Eira, as they drove down the track.

'Yes, thank you for making me come. Instead of demons I discovered a brother,' replied Nye.

'And two lovely sisters. Jean's nice. I like her. How old is Richard?' asked Eira.

'Jean told me he was twelve.'

'Did you notice how much he looks like you?' said Eira and smiled at her husband.

William and Anne Paxton greeted the Vaughns warmly when they arrived at Middleton Hall. The luggage had arrived earlier and was already in their rooms. Anne took Eira to show her the nursery.

'Five children to look after and another on the way, Anne you must be exhausted,' said Eira.

'William insists on the staff taking care of the children. He tells me it's not my responsibility and I confess the arrival of the twins rather proved his point,' replied Anne.

'We have a nanny but I like to look after the children myself,' said Eira as they went downstairs.

'Two nannies and a nursery maid look after ours,' said Anne.

'You have a lovely house.'

'This is the old hall. William's having a new mansion built. I expect he's told Nye about it,' said Anne.

The following morning Paxton's friend, Captain Williams, arrived and the party spent a day in the grounds of Middleton Hall. Paxton showed them the foundations for his new mansion and took his visitors on a carriage tour of the estate. In the evening, after the ladies had withdrawn leaving the men to enjoy their brandy and cigars, Captain Williams shared the latest news from France. A reign of terror had started. Mass executions had been ordered for everyone accused of opposing the revolution. Nobles and clergymen were being arrested and summarily killed. False accusations were used to send old enemies to the guillotine. Thousands were being killed and the streets of Paris, he reported, ran red with blood.

'That is sad news. God help us if the revolution spreads to this country,' said Nye.

'It could never happen. We have law and order and are a disciplined, civilised race,' said Paxton.

'That may be but there are already mutterings for a revolution. I recently read a vitriolic republican pamphlet by Thomas Paine called 'Rights of Man' and there are calls for all men to have the right to vote. The aristocracy have good reason to be fearful,' said Captain Williams.

'Thomas Paine's a traitor and should be hung from the nearest available tree,' snorted Paxton.

'I'm afraid there's more bad news from France. Queen Marie Antoinette was convicted of incest with her eight year old son and executed a few days ago. Apparently, she apologised for standing on the executioner's foot. They tossed her body in an unmarked grave,' said Captain Williams.

'Incest, with an eight year old boy is an outrageous charge. The French are a disagreeable lot, make no mistake,' said Paxton.

'What happened to her son, the Dauphin?' asked Nye.

'There are rumours that he's been quietly killed,' answered Captain Williams.

'Let's change the subject. I have some more uplifting news,' said Nye.

'Then please us by sharing it,' said Captain Williams.

'Captain Baillie, who you remember is the Clerk of Deliveries at the Board of Ordnance, visited me last week and told me Admiral Hood is being given command of a battle fleet being prepared to sail to the Mediterranean. His orders are to seize Corsica from the French. Baillie says, after the thrashing Hood got at Toulon he's ready for a fight,' said Nye.

'That is good news. When are they sailing?' asked Paxton.

'In the new year as soon as the ships are ready and the winter storms permit. The foundry is working night and day to supply the ordnance,' replied Nye.

'It will need to be a sizeable fleet to take Corsica. Do you know how many ships we're sending?' asked Paxton.

'Not in detail but I know of one, HMS Agamemnon, she's a 64 gunner. I received a letter from her captain, thanking Castle Iron Works for delivering new 24 pounders. Captain Nelson wrote saying he was pleased with the cannons and promised to sink at least one Frenchman with them for us,' said Nye.

'Captain Nelson, I've never heard of him,' said Paxton.

'Baillie told me it's a new commission. Nelson's been on the reserve list for several years but was considered to be an exceptional captain during the American War,' said Nye.

Chapter 25

Nye Vaughn wondered why a representative of the American Secretary for War wanted to see him. After the War of Independence, America sold its only warship and, with no navy, had no use for naval guns. The visitor was shown into his office.

'Thank you for seeing me at short notice, Mr. Vaughn,' said the American.

'Forgive me for asking, Mr. Price, but you sound like a Welshman?' said Nye.

'My grandparents emigrated from Pembroke in 1720s,' said the American.

'Welcome home. What can I do for you?' asked Nye.

'The United States of America has decided to build a navy,' said Mr. Price.

'Is America planning another war?'

'No. None of us want that. Our problem is piracy. After we became independent, your Royal Navy stopped protecting American merchant vessels in the Mediterranean. Eleven have been taken by Barbary Corsairs in the last year. The pirates looted the ships and sold the crew into slavery. In January Congress authorised the building of six frigates to deal with the pirates and clean them out of Algiers. I'm here to do business with you, to purchase the ordnance we require,' said Mr. Price. Nye sat back in his chair. His visitor smiled.

'What do you need?'

'Officially, they will be rated as 38 gunners,' replied Price.

'With a main armament of 24 pounders?' asked Nye.

'Each frigate will carry thirty 24 pounders, twenty two 32 pounders, twelve carronades and four 9 pounder chase guns,' replied the American.

'That's not the armament of a frigate. It's enough cannon for a ship in the line of battle,' said Nye.

'They aren't going to be ordinary frigates, Mr. Vaughn, but they will have a frigate's speed.'

'And the firepower of a three deck man of war,' added Nye.

'We need the first consignment for the USS Constitution. Deliver the guns to Cardiff and I will arrange their shipment to Boston, Massachusetts. I will write with the other delivery instructions when I know them,' said the American.

The British fleet arrived off the coast of Corsica on 12th July 1794 and began a bombardment of French fortifications, defending the Corsican town of Calvi. Nelson played a leading role in the attack, bringing ships guns ashore and moving them to high ground to fire into the town. As he was directing a forward battery, an incoming salvo sprayed debris in his face blinding his right eye. Nelson's eye was bandaged and, despite losing the eye, he led an attack capturing French positions. Running short of munitions and food, the French surrendered on the 10th August. The French garrison had resisted for forty days, during which the British fleet fired 24,000 cannon balls into their positions. Because of the bravery shown by the French, Admiral Hood, allowed them to retain their weapons and leave the island with full military honours. Corsica was declared to be part of the Kingdom of Great Britain and the Corsican partisan, Pasquale Paoli, installed as president of the new protectorate.

The battles of Valmy, when French cannon routed the Prussians, Toulon, where Bonaparte used massed artillery to drive out the British and the siege of Calvi, where British naval guns smashed French positions, demonstrated the effectiveness of concentrated bombardments. Military planners across Europe were devising new strategies to defeat their enemies. Valmy, Toulon and Calvi were the opening skirmishes of a war that was about to erupt, a war where men would die in their thousands.

General Bonaparte stood on the quarterdeck of the Sans Culotte watching, with professional interest, the gun crews being drilled.

'It's a fine ship, Admiral Martin,' said the general.

'118 guns, she's the most powerful ship in the French Navy,' replied Martin. Bonaparte scanned the horizon. The admiral's huge flagship was escorted by a squadron of warships and Bonaparte felt confident.

'How soon will we reach Corsica?' asked Bonaparte.

'If the wind holds, we will be there in two days,' replied the admiral and beckoned his flag officer.

'Signal the Serieues to put on more sail. She's falling behind,' ordered the admiral. Bonaparte watched the warship set its topsails.

'Sail on the larboard bow,' shouted a lookout. Admiral Martin studied the sail, on the horizon through his telescope.

'It's a frigate. She'll be signalling our position to the British fleet,' said Martin.

'How do you know? They may be leagues away.' asked Bonaparte.

'The British use frigates like eyes, to see over the horizon,' explained the admiral, 'Signal the troop ships to fall back.' More sails appeared on the horizon.

'Are we going to fight?' asked Bonaparte.

Admiral Martin studied his young passenger for a moment. He disliked Bonaparte, regarding the man as an arrogant upstart who used friends in high office, like Robespierre, to advance himself. Pierre Martin was a career sailor with thirty years sea going experience. He had fought in the American wars and been wounded in action. The 'boy general' on Martin's ship did not impress him.

'Order the fleet to turn north. We are returning to France,' commanded the admiral.

'Admiral, my orders are to retake Corsica and yours are to deliver my army!' shouted Bonaparte. Admiral Martin nodded and pointed to the sailors scrambling up the rigging.

'Do you see those men, preparing to turn the ship through the wind? If I ordered them to fight, they would, and they would die bravely for France. Then, your army would be unprotected, at the mercy of the British gunners. I have five warships to protect a flotilla of unarmed transports. The British have twice, possibly three times as many. We are outnumbered and outgunned. If there is a battle today, your army will be annihilated like rats in a barrel. We are returning to France. You can die a glorious death another day,' said the admiral.

The admiral's words infuriated Bonaparte. To turn and run, in the face of the enemy, was cowardly but it was the admiral's fleet and his decision. Napoleon Bonaparte leaned against the taffrail of the French flagship, watching the pursuing British vessels, and vowed never to rely on a French admiral for a victory.

Delyth Thomas' banishment to Leominster was a shock to her. She had always thought of her husband as pliable and never expected to be dumped so deceitfully. Isaacs' excitement, planning the trip to Birmingham, had fooled Delyth completely and she concluded he was a cruel, ungrateful man. Delyth fumed and vowed to take her revenge. To do so she needed money but the problem was she had none. Aunt Lily was her usual acerbic self. Lily tried to make allowances for her niece but they were both selfish women and, being similar, repelled each other. As the months passed Delyth schemed and, necessity being the mother of invention, adapted her temperament to her new situation. At first, it was difficult to ignore her aunt's barbed criticisms and rudeness. Replying in kind was easy but

154

Delyth learned to keep her tongue in check. When Aunt Lily was unpleasant or insulting, Delyth simply talked about something else. Slowly, the two women came to a tacit understanding. Aunt Lily could be as rude as she pleased and Delyth would not get upset. One afternoon, when they had been getting along tolerably well, Delyth broached a sensitive subject.

'What's going to happen to me in the future?' she asked.

'What do you mean?'

'I mean, my husband doesn't provide for me. I only have a roof over my head because of your generosity. Where will I go if something happens to you? Will I be homeless?' asked Delyth. Aunt Lily considered her niece's question impertinent.

'Are you expecting me to die soon? If so, you will be disappointed. I have no intention of dying in the foreseeable future,' replied Aunt Lily.

'Of course not, Aunt Lily, I pray you live for many years to come but it frightens me to think of being thrown on the streets.'

'You won't be homeless, Delyth. Your husband has a duty to provide for you,' said Aunt Lily.

'Isaac hates me. He would let me starve. Would you look after me?'

'If I'm dead it would be rather difficult, don't you think?' snapped Aunt Lily, growing tired of the conversation. Delyth knew she had said enough and changed the subject.

Aunt Lily surprised Delyth a few days later by asking her niece to sit down and listen to something important.

'I have been thinking about our conversation and what might happen to you. I know I am sometimes unpleasant. It isn't deliberate. I suppose I've been on my own too long, it makes one selfish. It's probably why Charles never visits me. Delyth, I value your company and am fond of you, like a daughter.' Aunt Lily hesitated. Delyth leaned forward, gently

155

held her aunt's hands and nodded slowly, willing her to continue.

'I've instructed my solicitor to write a codicil, amending my will to give you financial security,' said Aunt Lily, 'All I ask, in return, is your love.'

'You are so kind. I will always love you,' said Delyth and hugged her aunt.

Part 3 1795 - 1805

Chapter 26

The foundries of Merthyr grew quickly during 1795. Business was good and the town expanded. Rows of terraced cottages spread along the valley as the furnaces worked day and night to keep up with demand. Soot filled the air and covered the ground. When rain washed the streets, filthy water poured into the Taff, turning it black. Tramways, bringing materials to the ironworks, spread like giant spiders' webs. Men, woken at 5am by the knocker-up's pole, trudged to work while others wearily made their way home. Castle Iron Works was the biggest in the town. By the end of the year, over 1200 men worked for Nye Vaughn. They raised their caps when he passed. Some admired him, others resented his success but most of all, they feared him. Nye Vaughn, Iron Master, had become a powerful man.

'Gentlemen, welcome to the first Annual General Meeting of the Glamorganshire Canal Navigation Company,' shouted Lord Cardiff. The crowded room fell silent.

'The first item on the agenda is the election of officers. If there are no objections, I propose the existing board of directors remain in place, that is Mr. Nye Vaughn as Managing Director, Mr. Benjamin Griffiths as Finance Director and myself as Chairman. Will someone second the proposal?' A hand went up in the audience.

'Thank you Mr. Paxton. Our next item of business is to approve the excellent accounts prepared by Mr. Griffiths. Has everyone seen them? There was a murmur of agreement. Can I have a proposer?' asked Lord Cardiff.

'I will,' cried a voice.

'Thank you Sir. Who will second the motion?' A hand was raised.

'Our final agenda item is the distribution of profit. You will see from the notes, your board recommends a dividend of 8% of issued share capital. Are you willing to propose the dividend Mr. Paxton?' William Paxton nodded.

'Just a minute,' called a voice from the back of the room.

'Does someone have a question?' asked Lord Cardiff. Isaac Thomas stood up.

'I have several questions, Lord Cardiff,' said Isaac. Lord Cardiff turned to Nye Vaughn and whispered, 'He's going to cause trouble.' Nye shrugged.

'If they are relevant to the dividend we will hear them Mr. Thomas,' said Lord Cardiff.

'As a shareholder I challenge the 8% dividend. The company has been extremely profitable and has generated a return much higher than 8%. I propose a dividend of 20% be paid to the shareholders,' said Isaac. There were shouts of agreement. Lord Cardiff looked at Nye questioningly.

'Perhaps I can explain why we are suggesting 8%. When Parliament passed the Glamorganshire Canal Act it limited the dividend to a maximum of 8% to discourage profiteering. Much as I agree with Mr. Thomas that it would be preferable to increase the amount, we are not allowed to pay any more,' said Nye.

'Thank you Mr. Vaughn. Is there a second for the motion?' asked Cardiff. Several hands went up.

'The motion is carried. That gentlemen, concludes our business. The meeting is closed,' declared Lord Cardiff.

'I haven't finished,' shouted Isaac Thomas.

'The meeting has ended,' repeated Cardiff, firmly.

'By what right do you use the canal while paying nothing, Lord Cardiff?' yelled Isaac. Lord Cardiff jumped up angrily.

'My trading arrangements are none of your business,' he shouted.

'I'm a shareholder. That gives me the right to demand an answer,' replied Isaac. There were shouts of, 'Answer the question.' Nye Vaughn got to his feet.

'Gentlemen, calm yourselves. When Lord Cardiff agreed to sponsor the parliamentary bill for us it was in return for free use on the canal. That was the agreement,' said Nye.

'Free use for life, what a bargain! Why were the shareholders never told? I've another question. Explain to us your own excuse for not paying, Vaughn? How is it, you're the biggest user of the canal but you never pay a penny in tariffs? demanded Isaac. The room was silent as the shareholders waited for Nye's answer.

'Because it is my canal, I'm the biggest shareholder, it was my idea, I built it and I run it,' bellowed Nye, defiantly.

'You run it for your own benefit. You're a crook,' yelled Isaac.

'Thomas, if you're unhappy, I suggest you sell your shares. Plenty here will buy them, including me,' said William Paxton.

'This isn't over,' shouted Isaac and stormed out.

'You warned he might cause trouble but I didn't expect such a personal attack,' said Lord Cardiff.

'He's my brother- in-law. We don't get on,' replied Nye.

'Not the sort of relative I would want. What did he mean by, this isn't over?'

'There's not much he can do so I have no idea what he meant,' said Nye.

'It was a threat. You need to watch him,' warned Lord Cardiff.

Nye didn't forget his promise to build Eira a new house. The house, which resembled a castle, stood on a hill overlooking the foundry. The lake below the house, created to supply the foundry with waterpower, was landscaped. They took up residence during September 1795 and invited friends to stay

159

to celebrate the completion of the house. To entertain his guests, Nye staged a naval battle on the lake. Sailing boats, armed with saluting guns firing blanks, served as British and French warships. A French boat capsized as it was being boarded and the crews had to swim to the shore. In the evening, conversation turned to the real war.

'I've been told there was another royalist uprising in Paris which ended with a massacre,' said Nye.

'Why do the royalists keep fighting? They don't have a king to put on the throne. Don't they know the Dauphin's dead?' said Captain Williams.

'What happened?' asked William Paxton.

'Bonaparte was ordered to fight the rebels. He ordered forty cannons to be brought into Paris, corralled the royalists in narrow streets and opened fire with grape shot. They say the cannons kept firing for two hours. The royalists didn't stand a chance. Bonaparte's a hero in France,' said Nye.

'He sounds more like a butcher than a hero,' commented Benjamin Griffiths.

'Do we have news of our forces?' asked Paxton.

'There has been a battle in the Bay of Biscay. The Queen Charlotte suffered considerable damage. It's been called Cornwallis's retreat because he sailed close to the French and had to withdraw rather sharply,' said Captain Williams.

'I hear the Spanish have made peace with France. If they join forces our Mediterranean fleet will be in trouble,' said Nye. Eira entered the room with her sons. The men stood to greet her.

'Are you talking war again? The boys have come to say goodnight,' said Eira. The boys went to their father and kissed him.

'Did you enjoy the battle, today?' asked Nye.

160

'It was good. I liked when the men fell in the water. I'm going to be a sailor and fight the French, when I grow up,' replied Rhys.

'The war will be over long before then. Goodnight boys,' said Nye and hugged his sons.

'They're fine boys,' said Captain Williams after Rhys and Bryn went to bed.

'Rhys is spirited but Bryn is very quiet. He rarely speaks,' said Nye.

'How old is he?' asked Captain Williams.

'Bryn is nine,' answered Nye.

'He'll grow out of it. Do you remember Henry Dundas?' asked Paxton.

'The Admiralty Treasurer? He once asked me for a bribe,' replied Nye.

'The Prime Minister has made him Minister of War. It's a disaster. They say Dundas is so profoundly ignorant of war he's not even conscious of his own ignorance,' said Paxton.

'I hear you are entering politics Mr. Paxton,' said Benjamin Griffiths.

'It's true. I've been adopted by the Whigs to be their candidate for Carmarthenshire,' replied Paxton.

'The sitting member is a popular local man. How will you beat him?' asked Griffiths.

'I'll give the voters free dinners, beer and promise to pay for a bridge over the River Towy. That's my strategy for winning,' said Paxton.

'So it's true then. All politicians are corrupt,' said Nye. Paxton grinned and the men laughed.

Chapter 27

Aunt Lily sat by her dressing table, watching Delyth's reflection in the mirror. Her niece untied the old woman's tresses allowing her hair to fall down her back. The long grey strands were tired and dry. Delyth began to brush them gently.

'Do you see this necklace?' asked Aunt Lily. Delyth had seen the necklace before, when she had secretly explored Aunt Lily's jewel box one afternoon.

'It's beautiful,' said Delyth.

'Try it on,' said Aunt Lily and passed Delyth the necklace. Delyth held it up to her neck and admired herself in the mirror.

'The stones are rubies. My husband gave it to me as a wedding present. I have a matching brooch and tiara,' said Aunt Lily. Delyth knew about the brooch and the tiara; she had already tried them on.

'You're very fortunate to have such wonderful things,' said Delyth.

'Fortunate! They're trinkets.'

'He must have loved you very much,' said Delyth.

'Love. He never loved anyone except himself. My husband was a liar and womaniser, just like his brother,' said Aunt Lily.

'I never knew my father. He died when I was young. What was he like? asked Delyth.

'He was good looking. I wanted to marry your father but he never asked me. He used me and passed me on to his brother. It was a game they played only I ended up marrying one of them and having Charles,' said Aunt Lily.

'Aunt Lily, are you saying Charles might be my brother?' asked Delyth.

'He could be. He's as selfish as your father,' replied Aunt Lily. Delyth finished brushing the old woman's hair and helped her into bed.

'You remember you said, you would take care of me in the future? Did you change your will?' asked Delyth. Aunt Lily took hold of Delyth's hand and squeezed it.

'Don't worry, everything will be alright,' said Aunt Delyth and shut her eyes.

Delyth gently removed her hand from her aunt's grip and covered her with the blanket. Aunt Lily's mouth was slightly open. Delyth watched her rhythmic breathing and thought how ridiculous the old woman looked. The servants were at the far end of the house. It would be easy. No one would hear if the old lady struggled. Delyth took hold of a pillow and was about to put it over Aunt Lily's head when there was a commotion outside. A horse whinnied and a man shouted. The old woman stirred and opened her eyes.

'What are you doing? What's that noise?' asked Aunt Lily.

'I was making you comfortable. I'll have a look,' said Delyth and hurried to the window. Aunt Lily's son, Charles, was standing in the courtyard. He looked up at the window and waved to Delyth. Aunt Lily had gone back to sleep. Delyth went downstairs to greet Charles.

'It's good to see you again, Cousin,' said Delyth. Charles was removing his coat in the hallway.

'How's mother, still in rude health?' asked Charles and threw his hat aside.

'Rude as ever but otherwise well, for her age,' replied Delyth.

'She seems to want to live forever.'

'Old ladies do.'

'Pity. They should depart when they're no longer useful.'

'You're in a bad mood. Have you come for money?' asked Delyth. Charles snorted, went to the dining room, poured a sherry and drained the glass.

'She keeps me short on purpose; thinks I can't manage my own affairs,' said Charles and refilled the glass.

'I would help but I don't have any money.'

'Then we are both beggars,' said Charles.

Aunt Lily was in a dangerous mood the following morning. She shouted at the maid serving breakfast, reducing the girl to tears. When Charles appeared and tried to ingratiate himself she belittled him and made unpleasant remarks about his lack of character. Delyth kept quiet during the exchange, wondering how to turn the confrontation to her advantage. Suddenly, Aunt Lily rang her bell and ordered her servant to wheel her bathchair into the morning room. Charles followed and shut the door. Delyth listened to the muffled voices.

'No, Charles. I told you last time,' said Aunt Lily.

'For God's sake, it's only fifty pounds. I'll pay it back.'

'Like all the other money you were going to pay back.' Aunt Lily's voice was strident.

'I won't ask ever again, I promise,' pleaded Charles.

'The answer is still no,' shouted Aunt Lily. The door flew open and Charles stormed past Delyth.

Delyth found Charles sitting on a garden bench. He was angry. She sat down beside him.

'The selfish old woman won't even advance me fifty pounds,' said Charles.

'I heard. Why is she so vindictive to you?'

'She's always been like that, even when my father was alive. She was just as nasty to him,' replied Charles.

'It would be awful if she had an accident,' said Delyth.

'What sort of accident?' asked Charles. Then he saw Delyth smile and understood.

'Is it true? Have the Spanish joined France?' asked Nye.

Thomas Baillie nodded, 'The alliance treaty was signed in August. We're now fighting France and Spain which is why
164

the Master General of Ordnance has sent me to Merthyr. There are rumours there is to be an invasion so the War Office has decided to build defensive Martello Towers around the coast. To give us time, the Mediterranean fleet has been recalled to blockade Spanish ports.'

'What about Corsica?' asked Nye.

'Defending Britain is our priority. The French can have Corsica,' replied Baillie.

'You said Martello Towers. What are they?'

'Tower Mortella is a Corsican fort. Its walls withstood a prolonged bombardment from two of our warships. We've copied the design. The plan is to build a hundred Martello Towers and make Great Britain impregnable,' replied Baillie and handed Nye a sheaf of papers. Nye flipped through the pages. It was a schedule of works for the construction of the forts with details of ordnance and delivery dates. Nye passed the papers to Will Jones.

'The batteries are heavier than anything we have ever cast,' said Will.

'I did say impregnable. Gentlemen, time is against us and the safety of the realm is at risk. Can you deliver on those dates?' asked Baillie.

'The foundry is already working day and night. We will need another furnace and more men,' said Will.

'My partner is always cautious what he promises but you can rely on us. The guns will be ready when you need them,' promised Nye.

'Good. I will send you the full specifications and contracts as soon as I get back to London,' said Baillie.

Chapter 28

In February 1797 a Spanish battle fleet sailed from Cartagena with orders to join the French fleet at Brest. As dawn broke on the 14th Admiral John Jervis, commander of the British squadron blockading Spanish ports was aboard his flagship HMS Victory. When he was told the sails of an enemy ship had been sighted he ordered his squadron of fifteen ships to prepare for action in line of battle and sail towards the enemy's position.

'There are now eight enemy sail of the line, Sir John,' reported the officer of the deck.

'Very well, Sir,' replied the Admiral.

'There are now twenty sail of the line, Sir John.'

'Very well, Sir,' replied the Admiral.

'There are now twenty five sail of the line, Sir John.'

'Very well, Sir,' replied Sir John.

'There are now twenty seven sail of the line, Sir John.'

'Enough Sir, no more of that, the die is cast and if there are fifty enemy sail I will go through them,' said the Admiral.

The British squadron was outnumbered two to one and the Spanish fleet included the Santisima Trinidad, with 130 guns, the biggest warship in the world. The Battle of Cape St. Vincent started conventionally with the opposing lines of battle passing each other, exchanging broadsides. Horatio Nelson, who now held the rank of commodore, was aboard HMS Captain, a 74 gunner. HMS Captain was near the rear of the British line and Nelson realised the Spanish fleet would escape unless he turned his ship to break the Spanish line of sail. He ordered the Captain to leave the British line of battle and cut across the Spanish ships to disrupt them. Doing so was to disobey Admiral Jervis' orders. Nelson risked court martial. Bringing his ship about brought it under attack from several Spanish ships including the Santisima Trinidad. Nelson's ship was raked with shot losing its foretopmast and steering gear. HMS Captain was practically un-sailable. The confusion caused by Nelson's manoeuvre caused two Spanish ships to collide and become locked together with tangled rigging. Nelson managed to bring the Captain alongside and lead a party of marines onto the San Nicholas, a 74 gunner, whose officers surrendered after their captain was shot. The marines then crossed to the second ship, the San Jose, a 112 gunner, and captured it. The Spanish fleet was in disorder and the Santisima Trinidad struck her colours. Later, the Spanish flagship escaped from the British and limped back to Spain. Admiral Jervis had won a stunning victory thanks to Nelson's inventiveness and Spanish confusion. After the battle, the admiral invited Nelson to come aboard his flagship and praised him for using his initiative.

When news of the Spanish defeat reached Merthyr Tydfil church bells rang in celebration. The story of Nelson's courage and audacity grew with each retelling, how he boarded the enemy ship and fought her captain with his sword, killing the Spaniard with a thrust to the heart.

'Was there treasure on the Spanish ships?' asked Rhys.

'No but Nelson and his crew will be paid prize money for capturing an enemy ship,' replied Nye.

'Is the war over?' asked Bryn.

'Not yet but it soon will be,' said Nye. Eira put down her sewing and looked at the boys. They were growing up quickly.

'Will father be in the war?' asked Cerys. Eira smiled at her daughter and shook her head. Suddenly, there was furious banging on the front door followed by a commotion in the hallway. Benjamin Griffiths burst into the room. He looked flustered.

'Have you heard?' asked the out of breath visitor.

'Heard what?' asked Nye.

'The French have invaded Wales. They landed an army at Fishguard yesterday,' said Benjamin.

'Sit down, catch your breath then tell us what you know,' said Nye.

'Nye, I'm going to take the children for a walk,' said Eira and shepherded them from the room.

'A French warship sailed into Fishguard Bay yesterday morning but withdrew when the fort fired on it. At first, it was thought to be a lone vessel but a French fleet had landed men and arms further along the coast. Some say it's the Black Legion led by Bonaparte himself,' said Benjamin and wiped his brow.

'But Bonaparte's fighting in Italy,' said Nye.

'They say, there are thousands of French soldiers advancing inland, burning farms and killing as they go,' said Benjamin.

'We must think of the foundry. If the French capture the guns we have it would be a disaster,' said Nye.

'Should we spike them?'

'Not yet. The French may not get this far. Arm the men with whatever you can find. We don't have much gunpowder for the cannons but there are small arms we can use. Prepare some barricades to slow the French down. I'll join you shortly,' said Nye. After Benjamin had gone, Nye went outside to find Eira and the children.

The arrival of French troops in Wales worried Nye. If they got as far as Merthyr he knew there would be fighting. He told Eira to pack some things and take the children to London where Paxton's partner, Charles Cockerell, would look after them. She refused to go. Seeing that his wife would not be persuaded Nye gave up and went to the foundry where a messenger had just arrived on horseback from Fishguard.

He told how a French ship had sailed into Fishguard flying a Union Jack. The soldiers at the fort were not fooled by the flag and fired a single shot at the Frenchman who sailed away, unaware that the fort only had three cannon balls in its magazine. Unwilling to risk an opposed landing in Fishguard the French began to land soldiers in a small bay further along the coast. Alerted by a farmer, a small militia, led by a young squire, set off from Fishguard to intercept the French, followed by curious townsfolk. When the French Admiral saw the militia approaching along the cliff path, he mistook the long line of spectators with their red cloaks and black hats for British Army soldiers. Thinking he saw a battalion of redcoat soldiers he ordered the fleet to withdraw, leaving 1400 French soldiers on the beach. Cannons and a considerable number of weapons including 50 tons of cartridges had been landed and the French troops appeared to be ready to fight. The young squire, who's men were armed with a few rusty flintlocks and farm implements, realised he was outclassed and retreated to Fishguard to report what he had seen and wait for reinforcements.

Nye believed the French would return and land more men. If they did and were not confronted there was a danger the French might move east. In case they came to Merthyr, Nye ordered his workers to prepare gunpowder charges ready to be placed in the furnaces. He wasn't going to leave a working cannon factory to the French.

Elsewhere, events were moving quickly. The Pembrokeshire Yeomanry were assembled for a funeral at Stackpole when news of the invasion reached them. Lord Cawdor, a captain in the Yeomanry, ordered his men to march north to Haverfordwest where his force of 250 was joined by 150 sailors armed with nine cannons they had brought ashore. Cawdor arrived in Fishguard, assumed overall command and set up his headquarters at the Royal Oak Hotel.

The commander of the French force was an Irishman called Tate. Tate fought for the Americans during the War of Independence and hated the English. He believed the Welsh felt the same and would rise up to fight alongside his men to defeat the English. It was a foolish notion. The French had already killed a number of farmers and antagonised the local population. Tate's force included 600 well trained members of the notorious Black Legion, sent by Bonaparte, but the rest were released convicts and royalists who had little enthusiasm for fighting.

Tate moved inland, looting farms as he went. Discovering a large cache of wine, salvaged from a wrecked Portuguese merchant ship, the soldiers began to drink and discipline deteriorated. Tate considered his position. Believing he was facing a large army and that many of his own men would not fight, Tate decided to negotiate a conditional surrender and sent two officers to Fishguard under a flag of truce.

The two Frenchmen were escorted to the Royal Oak where Lord Cawdor listened politely to their terms. He knew the French force was considerably larger than his own but decided to bluff. Cawdor dismissed the French demands and said he planned to attack in force the following morning when no quarter would be given to the invaders. It was late when the French officers returned to Tate with the news. Groups of Frenchmen were sheltering from the cold night air in farm buildings. Some had commandeered the church at Llanwnda and were burning the pews for warmth. Knowing the French fleet had sailed away, abandoning the men to an uncertain fate, the French soldiers were ready to give up. Most were drunk and incapable.

The next day, the 24th February 1797, Lord Cawdor assembled his men on Goodwick Sands and waited. At 2 o'clock French drummers led Tate's troops onto the beach where they surrendered. By 4 o'clock their weapons had been collected and the prisoners were marched through

Fishguard into captivity. Deserters and laggards, recovering from their hangovers, were captured by indignant locals.

The immediate threat from invasion was over. Tate and most of his men were prisoners. Further reports followed. One told of Jemima Nicholas, a stout farmer's daughter who armed herself with a pitchfork, rounded up twelve French deserters and locked them in St. Mary's Church. After the invasion, Merthyr returned to normal and cannon production was speeded up to arm the Martello Towers being built to defend the coastline.

The undertaker lifted Aunt Lily's frail body into the coffin and straightened her shroud. The old woman's mouth was open and her face was contorted, as if she had died of fear. The undertaker closed her eyelids, placing a penny on each and tightened the bandage around her head to pull the mouth shut. No one, he was told, wished to pay their last respects so he put the lid on the coffin and screwed it down. The old woman had been found dead on the floor of her bedroom. She had, apparently, fallen from her bed in the night. The doctor declared, she had died from a visitation by God, who had taken her because her time had come. Her funeral was attended by Charles, Delyth and the household staff. Aunt Lily's gardener, Tom, brought a bunch of lilies to the graveyard. His were the only flowers. After she was interred the mourners returned to the house. There was no wake, Charles didn't want a fuss. The staff returned to the kitchen and raised a quiet glass to their dead mistress. Charles and Delyth went into the parlour.

'I'm glad that's over,' said Charles.

'Did you see the flowers from the gardener? They looked pathetic,' said Delyth.

'You are a heartless woman. He meant well. I'll see the solicitor tomorrow. He needs to sort the probate out quickly. I've some debts that won't wait,' said Charles.

'I'm coming with you. Don't forget Aunt Lily promised she would look after me so I have an interest in her will,' replied Delyth.

Aunt Lily's solicitor offered his condolences, invited Charles and Delyth to make themselves comfortable and opened the file on his desk. He had been the family lawyer for many years and had dealt with Aunt Lily's husband's estate when he died. Charles was impatient and the solicitor suspected that he was going to be upset when he learned the state of Lily's affairs. Contrary to everyone's belief, Aunt Lily had few assets. The house and grounds had been left in trust to Charles, when his father died. According to the laws of entailment Aunt Lily could never inherit from her husband, the estate had to pass to the eldest son. The trust, drawn up by the solicitor, included the provisos that Aunt Lily could live there for the rest of her natural life and only on her death did the house become Charles'. In order to support Aunt Lily, the trustees, namely the solicitor and his partner, mortgaged the property and, on Aunt Lily's death, the solicitor was sorry to say, it reverted to the creditors.

'What does that mean? Tell me in plain English,' snapped Charles.

'It means your mother's spent your inheritance. There's no money for you. It's all gone,' replied the solicitor. Charles turned white.

'What about me. Aunt Lily said she'd look after me. She added a codicil to her will. She told me,' said Delyth. The solicitor nodded.

'Your Aunt did leave a will dealing with her personal effects and there is a codicil in your favour Mrs. Thomas.

She's left her jewellery to you,' said the solicitor, 'and I have to tell you her jewels are worth a great deal of money.'

Charles felt sick as he watched the auditor making an inventory of the contents of the house. The servants had been dismissed and Delyth seemed to have forgotten the plans she and Charles had made. Charles didn't know what to do. He had no money, not even the monthly allowance his mother used to send. He couldn't return to London. His creditors would commit him to debtor's prison. Charles regretted listening to Delyth. It had all sounded so simple.

'Smother her with a pillow,' said Delyth, but it didn't happen like that. When Charles went to his mother's room she was awake. He tried to smother her but the old woman fought like a tiger. Then, she fell out of bed and he landed on top of her. He was fumbling to get up when she let out a long deep sigh and was still. The look of terror on his mother's dead face horrified Charles and he was weeping when Delyth arrived.

'It's perfect. Everyone will think she fell out of bed,' said Delyth and tidied the bed. Charles had killed his mother for nothing.

Delyth instructed the solicitor to have her jewels valued and to arrange their sale. Anticipating a good price the solicitor advanced her a loan and she began to plan her future.

'Here you are, Charles. Pay your gambling debts,' said Delyth and offered her cousin £50. Charles took the money, ungraciously.

'Now you're rich, what are you going to do?' asked Charles.

'I'm going to Merthyr. I have some business with my husband, you remember, the man who sacked you. Come with me,' said Delyth and smiled.

The Annual General Meeting of the canal company, where it was revealed that Nye Vaughn was taking unfair advantage, using the canal for free, while overcharging other users, caused resentment. His angry outburst surprised the shareholders and, fuelled by Isaac Thomas' constant complaining, they began to wonder if Nye was the most suitable person to manage the canal. Users wanted their tariffs lowered but Nye dismissed their demands saying they could always move their goods by road. It was an arrogant stance and angered the canal users. Isaac Thomas invited some of the iron masters and mine owners to a secret meeting where he outlined a plan to destroy Vaughn's transport monopoly. What Isaac proposed would eliminate Vaughn's inflated carriage charges. His idea was received enthusiastically. Isaac began to buy plots of land between Merthyr and Cardiff. He leased others from sympathetic owners. Sir Charles Morgan contributed a long strip of land through his Tredegar estate and lent money to the scheme. Nye Vaughn heard of Thomas' unusual land purchases but dismissed them as unimportant.

Chapter 29

In July 1797 Horatio Nelson, now a Rear Admiral, led an expedition to the Canary Islands with orders to take the town of Santa Cruz de Tenerife and seize Spanish treasure ships on their way from South America. Nelson's fleet included four hundred cannons and four thousand men. The Spanish had a strong garrison at Santa Cruz and their commander, General Guitierez, was prepared for an attack. He had reinforced the town defences with double rows of cannon, armed the populace and devised an effective plan of defence. Nelson's strategy was to land a thousand men, during the night and capture the town. Heavy Spanish cannon fire decimated the landing troops, forcing them to retreat. The British warships were unable to get close enough to offer supporting fire while the shore batteries, with their longer range, continued to bombard the attacking vessels.

Seeing how precarious the British position was, Nelson led a second landing himself and was wounded in the right arm. The admiral was rowed back to his ship where the arm was quickly amputated and thrown into the sea. The Royal Navy had suffered a crushing defeat, losing several ships and hundreds of men. After the battle, the Spanish general offered Nelson two schooners to transport his wounded men back to Britain. The admiral responded by sending a round of cheese with a letter of thanks for Guitierez's chivalry. Nelson returned to Britain and spent the next year recuperating from his wound.

Meanwhile, Napoleon Bonaparte, commander of France's Army of Italy, was striking at the heart of the Austrian Empire. After a series of bloody battles, when Bonaparte's army of 50,000 men was within one hundred miles of Vienna, the Austrians sued for peace. Bonaparte had built an unstoppable war machine which crushed all who opposed it. The victorious general returned to Paris to plan his next campaign. His first scheme was to invade Great Britain but there was a second easier prize; the conquest of Egypt. The general lost confidence in the French navy after the retreat from Corsica and believed it was unsafe to attempt to cross the English Channel for the present. Egypt, he reasoned, was the route to India where British influence could be destroyed. If Bonaparte turned the Indian princes against the British they would be driven out of India. The British Isles, Bonaparte decided, could be dealt with later.

Eira received her visitors in the parlour. Jean Vaughn had never been in a big house and Eira could see she was uncomfortable. Her brother, Dan, stood awkwardly by the doorway with his cap in his hand.

'What a lovely surprise. It's good to see you both. How are you? How's the family?' asked Eira.

'The children are well but I come with sad news. Nye's father's been injured. He was kicked by a stallion. It broke his back,' said Jean and began to cry. Eira comforted her.

'I'm so sorry. When did it happen?' asked Eira.

'Last week. He's been asking for Nye,' replied Jean.

'Who's looking after him?' said Eira.

'We left Richard with him,' said Jean.

'Richard's just a boy,' said Eira.

'He's almost full grown. He knows what to do,' replied Jean.

'I couldn't let mum come alone. It isn't safe,' said Dan.

Eira took Jean and her brother to find Nye. He was in the foundry office. Hearing his father was seriously ill, Nye ordered a carriage and they hurried to Beili Farm. Richard heard them coming and opened the gate leading to the farmyard. Nye jumped from the carriage before it stopped and rushed up the narrow stairway to the tiny bedroom. His father was in bed, staring at the ceiling. At first he didn't recognise his son.

'How are you father?' asked Nye. The old man knew the voice and smiled.

'Not good. I can't move my legs,' said Nye's father.

'What happened?'

'The stallion was covering a mare. I turned away for a moment and the horse kicked me with both legs. He won't do it again. Dan shot him,' whispered Nye's father. Nye sat with his father until Jean brought some soup and tried to feed him. The old man had a mouthful, pushed the bowl away and shut his eyes.

The Vaughn family gathered in the kitchen. The girls were crying. Eira had helped Jean lay the table for supper but no one was hungry. Richard and Dan went to tend the animals. Jean sat in the fireside chair with her hands in her lap. She looked small and vulnerable. Nye thought of his own mother in the same chair and the memory blurred with the present.

'His back won't mend. My husband's a cripple. That's what the doctor said,' mumbled Jean.

'We can care for him,' said Eira.

'He's given up. Says it hurts all the time. He wants to die,' said Jean. Nye went back to his father. The old man was awake and lucid. The family could hear them talking quietly. Nye came downstairs after an hour and said his father was asleep. Jean had made up a straw mattress in the corner of the kitchen and the family tried to settle for the night. Eira had never slept on straw and Nye was restless. They dozed in the fireside chairs until the early hours of the morning. Nye dreamt someone was creeping down the stairs. They gently touched his arm and he woke. Jean was standing beside the chair.

'I'm sorry Nye. Your father's passed on,' she whispered.

The staircase was too narrow for a coffin and the old man was brought down to the kitchen wrapped in a blanket where he was placed on the kitchen table to be washed and laid out by two ladies from the village. Nye was surprised by the number of mourners who crowded into the kitchen to view his father's body. Eira and Jean, dressed in black, served tea and biscuits to the visitors. Some were sombre. Others smiled and shared a joke with the corpse as they said goodbye. Nye saw a woman, he didn't know, put a rose in the coffin. Nye's father was carried to the church on a neighbour's wagon and he was buried beside his first wife. When a mourner whispered there was room for the second Mrs. Vaughn on the other side, Jean overheard, lost her self control and began to sob.

It was late when the family returned to Beili Farm. Nye helped feed the animals and secure them for the night. It felt strange to be herding geese into their pens and collecting eggs after so many years. While the men worked outside the women prepared supper. It was a simple meal of bread, ham and tea.

'Eira and I return to Merthyr tomorrow,' said Nye.

'You can't just leave. What will you do about the farm?' asked Jean.

'I don't understand,' said Nye.

'You're his eldest son and your father didn't make a will. The farm belongs to you now. It's what he would have wanted,' said Jean. Nye hadn't considered who would inherit but Jean was right. If he wanted it, the farm was his. Eira looked imploringly at her husband and was about to offer her opinion when Nye held up both hands and declared, that he had given up farming seventeen years before and had no desire to return to it. What's more, he would transfer ownership of the farm to his younger brother, Richard, in five years time, when he came of age. Hearing he would own a farm, Richard grinned. Jean, who had believed they would soon be homeless, hugged Nye and said she loved him. Nye had made peace with his father and re-established contact with his family. Despite his father's passing, he felt calm. An unhappy, fearful day was over and the relief was felt by everyone in the kitchen.

Isaac Thomas learned of Aunt Lily's death when her solicitor wrote to say, Delyth's maintenance cheques should no

178

longer be paid to Aunt Lily but direct to Delyth who had moved back to Merthyr. The solicitor included Delyth's new address. It was a fashionable house in Trefechan. Isaac couldn't understand how his wife could afford such a property and decided to call on her. A housemaid opened the door and, after a few moments, showed him into a comfortable sitting room where Delyth was seated. Her cousin, Charles, was stood behind her with his hand on her shoulder. Isaac hadn't expected Charles to be there and seeing the embezzler again unsettled him.

'Isaac, it's been a long time. How kind of you to call,' said Delyth.

'What are you doing in Merthyr?' he asked.

'I live here,' replied Delyth.

'No. I mean why have you come back? What do you want?' asked Isaac.

'I've come back for what you owe me.'

'I owe you nothing,' snapped Isaac.

'My lawyer tells me you have a legal duty to support me and, I promise, you will. I made you a rich man, Isaac and how did you thank me? You discarded me and left me at Aunt Lily's. That wasn't nice. I want half the foundry put in Charles' name. If you don't I will take everything you have,' said Delyth.

'Our solicitors can discuss the terms of your allowance. Good day,' snapped Isaac.

'He has no idea what we're doing, does he Charles?' said Delyth, after her husband left.

Chapter 30

Napoleon Bonaparte's invasion army of twenty five thousand men landed in Alexandria on the 1st July 1798. The Mamluk rulers of Egypt hurriedly gathered a similar sized force and the two armies met near the Pyramids of Giza. Bonaparte's men formed hollow squares which the Mamluk cavalry could not penetrate while cannon fire, from within the squares, decimated the Egyptians ranks, killing more than two thousand. The French losses during the battle were twenty nine men.

The British were aware of French ambitions in Egypt and Admiral Nelson, having recovered somewhat from losing his arm, was hurriedly despatched to the Mediterranean with orders to find and destroy the French fleet. He found the French and engaged them on the 1st August. During the Battle of the Nile Nelson destroyed all but two of the French ships of the line. The turning point of the battle came when the French flag ship 'San-Culotte' which had been renamed 'The Orient' came under fire from five British warships and her magazine exploded, blowing the ship to pieces. Part of the Orient's mainmast was salvaged and used to make a commemorative coffin, which was presented to Nelson after the battle. Nelson returned to Britain a hero and was elevated to the peerage as Baron Nelson of the Nile.

Sinking the French fleet trapped Bonaparte's army in Egypt without a reliable supply line. The French were facing constant uprisings and Bonaparte became increasingly brutal. Following an attack on Jaffa, he ordered fourteen hundred prisoners to be bayoneted to death. When an outbreak of bubonic plague swept through his troops he had the sick men poisoned so they didn't slow the army down. On the 24th August 1799, Bonaparte abandoned his Army of Egypt to an uncertain fate and slipped quietly back to France.

'When do we have to start paying income tax?' asked Nye.
'Straight away. William Pitt says it's to pay for the war. The Prime Minister claims the tax will raise ten million

pounds,' replied Benjamin. The two men studied the treasury document.

'Ten percent of my income, I call that robbery,' said Nye.

'The men in the foundry won't be happy and it'll mean more book keeping,' said Benjamin. Will Jones came into the office brandishing a pistol.

'Have a look at this gun and tell me what's odd about it,' he said and offered the pistol to Nye. Nye examined the pistol and noticed the barrel could be detached from the breech.

'That's odd, why does it do that?' he asked. Will showed them how the pistol could be loaded through the breech and how the barrel had grooves in it to spin the bullet, making it a more accurate weapon.

'It's a Queen Anne pistol. Do you see? If we built a breech loading cannon with a rifled barrel it would be faster and easier to load and more accurate to use,' explained Will. The partners examined the pistol again, debated its advantages and decided to approach the Board of Ordnance and ask if it was interested in Will's idea.

When Nye returned home that evening he found Eira in an agitated state. Rhys had refused to apologise for being rude to his mother and they had argued.

'Where is he? I'll speak to him,' said Nye.

'I don't know. He stormed out when I told him to go to his room. He said he hates me,' said Eira.

'He's a thirteen year old boy. Boys say stupid things at that age. He'll come home soon,' said Nye and comforted his wife. Rhys didn't come home that evening. Nye searched for him the following day but there was no sign of the boy and his parents began to worry.

The magistrate listened to Delyth with incredulity. He knew Isaac Thomas and found her claims improbable. Delyth wept as she told how Isaac forced her to befriend the solicitor Marcus Jacobs to discover the contents of his fathers' will. The magistrate remembered the Jacobs case well and had helped get his death sentence commuted to transportation to New South Wales. When Delyth told him the solicitor had changed the will to Isaac's advantage, he began to listen more carefully. Jacobs had been convicted of forgery and theft of documents. Delyth's next accusation was more serious. She said she had, for some time, suspected her husband of murdering his own father. When the magistrate asked what evidence Delyth had to support her allegation she admitted there was little hard evidence but pointed to the circumstances. Isaacs' father, she said, had told her he was leaving the foundry in a trust. Eira would say the same thing if asked. What's more, during the reading of the will, Eira claimed it had been altered by the solicitor and she had proof but the proof had mysteriously vanished from her bedroom.

'Isaac was the main beneficiary and killed his father to inherit the foundry. He admitted it to me,' said Delyth.

'These are serious allegations Mrs Thomas. Why didn't you speak up at the time?' asked the magistrate.

'My husband's a violent man. He had his brother-in-law beaten half dead. He had the solicitor's offices burnt down and has kept me a prisoner in Leominster until my jailer died recently. I'm afraid of him,' said Delyth. The magistrate considered what he'd heard. Delyth was convincing but nothing she said would convict a man of murder.

'You realise, as a wife you cannot give evidence against your husband in a court of law. Unless someone else has evidence there is nothing I can do and you need to think very carefully before making such allegations against your husband,' said the magistrate.

'Speak to Eira Vaughn or her husband Nye or my cousin Charles. They'll tell you I'm not lying and how devious Isaac is,' said Delyth.

'Your cousin Charles, what does he know?'

'He worked for Isaac until he discovered the truth. He confronted Isaac who accused him of stealing money from the foundry, sacked him and threatened to ruin his reputation if he spoke out,' said Delyth.

'I need to hear what your cousin has to say,' said the magistrate.

Rhys Vaughn was angry when he left the house. Why did his mother treat him like a child? Others of his age were working for a living instead of doing lessons. They were treated like men, not being made to learn the subjunctives of French verbs.

'Why learn an enemy's language,' he asked himself? It was a stupid idea. He was never going to speak French. Better to learn how to sail a ship and fight the French. Rhys dreamed of a new life and the sea was calling. He walked along the Heads of the Valley Road towards Hirwaun where a wagon driver, with a load of timber, offered him a lift. The driver asked where Rhys was going and, learning his passenger intended to go to sea, suggested Swansea as the port where a bright young man, looking for adventure, might find a berth. Rhys spent the night at the wagon driver's cottage and arrived in Swansea the following day. He walked down the road past copper works belching foul smoke. The river was a strange yellow colour, dead trees lined the bank and the smell of arsenic made Rhys wretch. He followed the river to the docks. Merchant ships lined the quays. Anthracite bound for London was being loaded aboard colliers. Copper sheets, to clad new warships, were stacked on wooden bearers waiting to be transported to the navy dockyards.

Copper ore imported from Cornwall and North Wales was being hauled to the smelting works. Stacks of slate and lead covered the quays. Barrels of salt and bales of wool filled the warehouses. Oakum lay in bundles, ready for loading. The strange sounds and smells intoxicated Rhys. He picked his way along the quay, clambering over mooring ropes, unsure what to do.

'Are you looking for a berth?' Rhys turned around. A squat man wearing a sailor's coat was standing behind him. He was carrying a cudgel and a short cutlass hung from his belt.

'I'm not sure,' replied Rhys nervously.

'If you are, I can help. How old are you?' asked the sailor.

'I'm sixteen,' lied Rhys.

'That's a shame. You look older. If you told me you were eighteen I'd take you to my lieutenant. He's looking for stout lads like you.'

'I made a mistake. I am eighteen,' said Rhys.

'Good. Come on,' said the sailor and set off along the quay.

Rhys followed the sailor to The Compass Tavern, hidden in an alleyway off Goat Street. The bar was dark and filled with smoke. A barmaid was serving a group of sailors.

'Who's this?' demanded a lieutenant standing by the bar.

'Says he's eighteen. What's your name, boy?' asked the sailor.

'Rhys Vaughn,' replied Rhys awkwardly. The alien surroundings were making him uncomfortable. The lieutenant smiled and beckoned. Rhys approached the bar.

'I'm recruiting men who want to see the world. Do you want to see the world, Rhys?' asked the lieutenant. Rhys nodded.

'Good man,' said the lieutenant and handed him a glass, 'It's rum, a sailor's drink.' Rhys sniffed the drink and put it on the bar.

'No thank you. I'll be going now,' he said. Suddenly, vice like hands seized Rhys from behind and he was bundled from the bar into the cellar. Rhys kicked and shouted as they shackled his legs to a ring on the floor.

'Shut your mouth,' yelled a sailor and punched Rhys. The sailors shut the door leaving Rhys alone in the dark cellar. He sat on the cold stone floor and gently touched his nose with his fingers. It felt like a bloody pulp.

Time passed slowly in the darkness and Rhys was relieved when the door opened and the lieutenant returned.

'Have you calmed down?' asked the lieutenant.

'You have no right to do this,' said Rhys.

'I have every right. I'm Lieutenant Voss. I hold a commission in the Royal Navy and my orders are to impress seamen for service,' replied the lieutenant. The sailors dragged another pressed man down the cellar stairs and chained him alongside Rhys.

'I've just landed from New York. I was walking home when they took me. I haven't seen my wife for two years. She doesn't even know I'm in Swansea and we're being shipped out tomorrow,' said Rhys' companion when they were alone.

'What'll happen to us?' asked Rhys.

'We'll be marched to the docks in chains and put aboard a cutter to join a transport ship taking us to the fleet. If you try and escape the marines will shoot you down.' Rhys and his sailor companion continued to talk. When Rhys admitted he was only thirteen the sailor told him it was unlawful to press anyone under eighteen years of age.

Five more men were dragged into the cellar during the night, two so drunk they slept while they were chained up. In the morning, when the lieutenant returned Rhys announced, he was thirteen.

'If you are thirteen, prove it and I will set you free,' replied the lieutenant. Rhys had no proof and made no answer.

'I'm not unreasonable. While I have a job to do, I understand some of you have no desire to spend the next ten years at sea and want to go home. I will release any man who can buy his freedom,' said Lieutenant Voss. The shackled men sat in silence. Any money they possessed had already been stolen by the press gang. The lieutenant smiled. The ruse sometimes worked; revealing a few hidden gold coins to be pilfered before the pressed men were marched to the waiting boat.

'I can pay, that is, my family are rich. They will pay,' said Rhys.

'Get them out,' ordered the lieutenant.

The press gang hauled its prisoners up to the street and headed towards the docks. The chains rattled as they dragged over the cobbles and onlookers watched the pitiful group being led away. A group of red coated marines, with fixed bayonets, was waiting on the quay. As the pressed men were unchained, they were taken aboard a cutter. When it was Rhys' turn, Lieutenant Voss stopped him.
'Not this one. I need to check his age. If he's old enough, you'll have him next trip,' said the lieutenant to the captain of marines.

Rhys was escorted back to the Compass Tavern and returned to the cellar. A short while later the barmaid came down to the cellar. She was carrying a candle, bread and cheese and some water. She gave the food to Rhys.

'Why are you back here?' she asked.

186

'I don't know,' replied Rhys as he ate. When the food was gone, the barmaid returned to the bar leaving the candle behind. The candle had burnt out when two of the press men arrived. They unchained Rhys and took him upstairs to a room where Lieutenant Voss was waiting.

'Tell me about your family,' instructed Voss. Rhys told his captor about his family. Voss appeared friendly and asked questions about his father's business then, he produced a pen and writing paper.

'You're going to write to your dear mother and father. I'll tell you what to say,' said the lieutenant and handed the pen to Rhys. After Rhys had finished writing he was abruptly returned to the cellar.

'Are we going to let him go?' asked the sailor who first lured Rhys to the Compass Tavern.

'We can't, unless you want to swing on a gibbet,' replied Voss.

'So we kill him then?' said the sailor.

'Not unless we have to,' replied the lieutenant.

The pressed men who had been marched through the streets in chains, were rowed out to a waiting supply ship to join others on their way to serve in the fleet. The tender left Swansea with her cargo of pressed men and was caught by bad weather driving it against the cliffs at Pwlldu Head. The ship stuck fast, wedged between rocks. Some crewmen managed to clamber along the bowsprit and onto the shore. Later, farmer John Morris was roused from his bed by someone banging his door. It was the master and first mate of the tender. They asked where they were, said little of the disaster or the sixty eight people trapped on board, grabbed a lantern and vanished into the night. In the morning the wreck was discovered by locals. Most of the unfortunate souls on board were dead, drowned in the hold as the rising tide flooded the vessel. The dead were buried in a mass grave nearby. At his court martial, the master of the tender blamed the pilot for the wreck and was acquitted of all charges. No mention of the sixty eight dead prisoners was made during his trial.

Chapter 31

As 1799 drew to a close the French Government was in trouble. The continuing war with its military setbacks and increasing royalist insurrection was bankrupting the French economy. French politician Emmanuel Sieyes approached Bonaparte and asked for his military backing to seize power. Bonaparte agreed but used Sieyes as a smokescreen to stage a Coup d'état of his own. Napoleon Bonaparte appointed himself First Consul on the 9th November, replacing the French Republic with a military dictatorship. He styled himself on the Roman Emperor Caesar and assumed absolute power. At last, the general was unfettered to pursue his military ambitions whatever the cost.

Isaac Thomas was furious when he heard Delyth's allegation that he had killed his own father.

'She's insane. What evidence has she offered for such a vile claim?' asked Isaac.

'Very little apart from the circumstances and your sisters claim that the will was altered. I have pointed out to Mrs Thomas that any evidence she offers would be inadmissible. She cannot give evidence against her own husband,' replied the magistrate, 'Her cousin Charles is another matter. His testimony could be very damming for you.'

'Charles is a thief and a liar,' said Isaac.

'That may be so but you say you have kept no record of the theft and the book keeper who discovered his crime is dead. Charles is a convincing fellow. A jury might be persuaded his evidence is true,' said the magistrate. The prospect of being put on trial for the murder of his father, horrified Isaac but what could he do? Thinking back to his father's death another possibility occurred to him; had Delyth killed his father? He knew she was an evil woman with a twisted mind but a murderer? Isaac shuddered.

'What do you intend to do?' he asked the magistrate.

'Your wife is spreading malicious rumours, destroying your reputation. Isaac, we went to school together. I know you didn't kill your father but mud sticks. I'll ignore her allegations, they're groundless, but you need to silence her before she does more damage,' said the magistrate.

The housemaid placed the letter on a silver tray, carried it to the sitting room and offered it to Eira. Eira saw the envelope, recognised Rhys' handwriting and tore it open to read the contents.

Dear Mother and Father,

I am in good health and have been told I will remain safe if you comply with these instructions. Men have taken me prisoner planning to sell me to a press gang for a bounty. They are willing to release me unharmed in return for a reward of £500. Father must bring the money to Swansea on Tuesday next. He is to come alone on the morning coach and go straight to the Six Bells Inn on Union Street. The landlord will have further instructions. Father will be watched. If Father is followed or has company with him my throat will be cut and my body thrown into the river on the ebb tide. If there are constables near the Six Bells you will never see me again. I want to come home safely. Please do as they say.

Your obedient son, Rhys.

'Tell the footman he must run to the foundry and get my husband, quickly!' ordered Eira. Nye hurried home when he heard the news. Eira had been crying but had regained her composure. She handed him the letter.

'How must Rhys have felt writing about how he was going to be killed? What are we going to do?' asked Eira as she dabbed her eyes.

'I'm going to Swansea on Tuesday to find him,' said Nye angrily.

'Are you going to pay them?'

'I don't know. They can still kill him when they have the money.'

'But they're sure to kill him if we don't pay. We must pay,' shrieked Eira. Nye held Eira's shoulders and looked into her eyes.

'Eira, I will find Rhys and get him back safely. I promise,' said Nye with as much conviction as he could. They held each other close until the tears stopped.

'It's Thursday, I must go. There are things to do,' said Nye and stood up.

'If they harm our son, find them and kill them all,' said Eira. Nye nodded.

Captain Williams willingly agreed to help Nye and rode to Swansea the following morning. He returned on Saturday and went straight to Nye's home.

'There are four press gangs working in Swansea and they're all pretty violent. Some pay bounties for an able bodied sailor but only a small amount. Rhys isn't an able bodied mariner. He's a landsman and wouldn't be worth a bounty to them. Most of the men taken are seized for nothing. The worst is the gang that operates from the Compass Inn but I don't know if they have Rhys,' said the captain.

'What about the Six Bells?' asked Nye.

'It's a vermin ridden drinking house frequented by sailors. There's a brothel upstairs which is always busy. The landlord is a retired seaman. They say, he pays the press gangs to leave him in peace,' explained the captain.

'So you think one of the press gangs has Rhys so we should be able to find him?'

'I'm sure of it but we have to be careful. They're capable of killing him,' replied Captain Williams.

Nye was up early on Tuesday morning. He shaved, dressed and took the bag containing the ransom money to the coach stop at the George Hotel. It was a cold December morning and the horses, which were already harnessed to the stage coach, were steaming and pawing the ground, eager to start. Nye was glad of his long coat and stamped his feet to keep warm. There were four other passengers waiting to board the coach to Swansea. Nye studied them, wondering if one was there to watch him. The journey was uneventful. Nye sat, with the bag on his lap, avoiding conversing with the other occupants of the coach. He arrived in Swansea late in the afternoon and asked for directions to the Six Bells on Union Street. Captain Williams was right. The Six Bells was disreputable, a place decent citizens should avoid. Nye went inside and asked for the landlord.

'Who wants him?' asked the barman suspiciously.

'My name's Vaughn. He has a message for me,' replied Nye. The barman disappeared into a back room to fetch the publican who emerged moments later. The landlord was a heavy set man with hands like buckets. His face was large but his eyes were small and gimlet like. The landlord put his hands on the counter and leaned forward. His breath smelt of rum.

'I was told to ask for you,' said Nye quietly. The landlord studied the bag at Nye's side.

'You on your own?' he asked. Nye nodded. The landlord grinned, revealing tobacco stained teeth. Nye stiffened. Two men were standing close behind him. Cutlasses hung from their belts. So they would take the money here. Nye heard pistols being cocked.

'You gentlemen, by Mr. Vaughn, will live longer if you step back,' said Captain Williams. Nye turned as the men backed away and saw Captain Williams, dressed in an old fisherman's coat, seated in the corner of the room. The captain walked to the bar with the guns levelled at the landlord.

'Now my fat friend, where is the boy?' demanded Captain Williams.

'You won't be in time,' said the landlord.

'We aren't joking,' said the captain. The landlord remained silent. Captain Williams turned and fire one of the pistols. The room filled with smoke and a man screamed. One of Nye's attackers fell to the floor.

'You're next. Where's the boy?' hissed Williams.

'The Compass Inn. He's in the cellar,' replied the landlord.

Nye and his companion ran to the Compass Inn. Lieutenant Voss looked surprised when they burst in.

'Where's my son?' demanded Nye.

'I don't know what you're talking about,' replied Voss. Nye hit him in the stomach and Voss fell forward. Nye hit him a second time with an uppercut to the jaw. The lieutenant crumpled to the ground.

'Where's the cellar?' shouted Captain Williams to the barmaid. She pointed to the cellar door.

'He isn't there. They're taking him to the dock,' she said.

Nye caught up with the press gang as the prisoners were being loaded aboard the cutter. The marines barred his way. He could see Rhys in the bow of the boat and shouted his name. The boat pushed away from the jetty and the crew began to row.

'My son's on that boat you must stop it,' shouted Nye. The marines ignored him. Captain Williams, who had stopped to check the cellar and reload, arrived.

'Where's your captain?' he barked.

'I daresay he's in the tavern enjoying a glass of wine,' replied the marine corporal, truculently.

'If you value your stripes, you'll fetch him, now!' ordered Captain Williams. The corporal recognised an order backed with a threat and hurried to fetch his officer.

The captain of marines sauntered across the quay to find out what was going on. As he listened to Nye's story his manner changed. He sent four men to the Compass Inn to arrest Lieutenant Voss and commandeered a jolly boat to row to the fleet tender, lying offshore. The pressed men were already in the hold when Nye, Captain Williams and the Marine Captain boarded. Nye identified himself to the tender's master and gave his word that Rhys was only thirteen.

'We can't take him if he's under eighteen. Release the boy and bring him here,' ordered the ships master. Father and son were reunited and rowed ashore together with Captain Williams. They returned to Merthyr the next morning.

An admiralty letter arrived, three weeks later, apologising to the Vaughn family for any distress caused by the incident and to inform them Lieutenant Voss had been court marshalled, stripped of his rank, given fifty lashes and dishonourably discharged from the service. His accomplices in the press gang had also been flogged and returned to sea as junior deck hands. A hurriedly scrawled footnote added, 'You might like to know that following Voss' discharge, he was arrested and pressed back into the navy as an ordinary seaman.'

Chapter 32

The prison van made its way slowly up the hill. The driver cracked his whip and shouted at the labouring horses, urging them on. Charles called his cousin Delyth to the window and they watched as the strange vehicle approached. It stopped outside the house. The driver stepped down and opened the doors at the back. Three men emerged. The party came up the path to the front door and rang the bell. When the maid opened the door they brushed her aside and came into the sitting room.

'How dare you. What do you want?' demanded Delyth.

'Are you Mrs Delyth Thomas wife of Mr. Isaac Thomas?' asked the driver. His tone was abrupt and businesslike.

'I am. By what right do you barge into my house?' said Delyth.

'Take her,' said the driver. His companions grabbed hold of Delyth and dragged her towards the door. Delyth struggled but the men were strong.

'You can't do that. Let her go,' shouted Charles and tried to intervene.

'Stand aside,' ordered the driver. Charles got hold of Delyth's arm and attempted to pull her back. Suddenly, the driver spun around and hit him with a cosh.

The maid was bending over Charles shaking him. His head throbbed and he struggled to gather his thoughts.

'Where's Delyth?' he asked.

'The men took her,' replied the maid. Charles sat up and wondered what he should do. The maid told him the men had left without saying another word but Delyth had yelled, 'Get the magistrate,' as they shut her in the prison van. Charles

194

went out of the house and stumbled down the hill. The magistrate's house was more than a mile away. By the time Charles got to the magistrate's house the fog in his head had cleared, leaving a throbbing ache. The magistrate was out and not expected to return for some hours. Charles returned home. He needed to think.

In the evening, Charles went back to the magistrate's house and was admitted to the drawing room where he was asked to wait while the magistrate finished his dinner. Charles wandered around the room looking at the ornaments and pictures. After a few minutes the magistrate arrived. He invited Charles to sit down and state his business. Charles described the abduction of his cousin and asked what the magistrate proposed to do.

'I'm aware of today's events. Your cousin, Mrs Thomas, has been taken to a place of safety for her own protection. I signed the warrant on behalf of her husband. He came to me with evidence that she is insane,' replied the magistrate.

'What evidence?' demanded Charles.

'Mr. Thomas was concerned for his wife's sanity and asked two doctors to examine her. They did so and both swore affidavits confirming she is a lunatic. I'm very sorry but it was done for her own good,' explained the magistrate.

'No one's examined Delyth. I would know. Where's she been taken?' asked Charles.

'I'm afraid I have no idea. You'll have to ask Mr. Thomas. He made the necessary arrangements to take care of his wife. Now you must excuse me, I have an excellent apple crumble that's getting cold,' said the magistrate.

Charles left the magistrate and went straight to Isaac Thomas' home. He angrily confronted Isaac and demanded to know where Delyth was.

'I'm glad you've come. We need to talk,' said Isaac and invited Charles into his study. Isaac poured two large brandies and pointed to a chair beside the fire. The fire was roaring and the room was warm.

'Take your coat off and sit down.'

Charles sat down warily. Isaac took the opposite chair and raised his glass.

'Tell me something Charles. Where did Delyth's money come from? asked Isaac.

'My mother left Delyth her jewellery,' replied Charles.

'What did you get?'

'Nothing. My father's estate was worthless,' replied Charles.

'And your mother's will. Did she leave you anything?'

'Not a farthing.'

'Was her will changed, after Delyth came to live with your mother?' asked Isaac.

'Yes. There was a codicil in Delyth's favour,' replied Charles. Isaac nodded. Charles wondered where the questioning was leading.

'I expect Delyth has told you, I altered my father's will and murdered him. She's told everyone else,' said Isaac. Charles nodded and sipped his brandy.

'It's completely ridiculous of course. How did your mother die?'

'She fell out of bed. The doctor said it was her time and she was visited by God,' replied Charles. Isaac watched his visitor's face turn red.

'I think Delyth's mad enough to start saying you killed your mother to get her fortune,' said Isaac.

'But I didn't get any money,' said Charles. He was starting to tremble.

'She'd say your plan went wrong and send you to the gallows. That's why I've committed her. To protect us all,' said Isaac.

196

'What should I do?' asked Charles.

'Do you know where the money is?'

'Yes. It's in a strong box in Delyth's bedroom,' said Charles.

'The jewellery was your mother's and the money should be yours. If I were you, I'd take what's rightfully yours and leave Merthyr. You could go anywhere,' said Isaac and offered his visitor another drink.

Charles didn't get home that evening. He was walking along a dark alley when a thug attacked him from behind and pushed him into the river. Charles couldn't identify his attacker. The man's face was covered with a scarf. A passing miner heard Charles' cries for help and pulled him out of the water. When Charles got back to Delyth's house, he went up to her bedroom and discovered the strongbox had been forced. All her money was gone.

As the end of 1799 approached, the Vaughns decided to have a party. Eira took charge of the planning and marshalled the forces she needed to make it a spectacular occasion. There were several reasons to celebrate. King George had been on the throne for forty years, making him one of the longest reigning monarchs in British history, the new-year was the beginning of a new century, the French had been thrashed by Nelson and Castle Iron Works was more prosperous than ever. Tuesday the 31st December was selected as the most suitable day. Huge tents were erected in Bryant Field. Workmen dug fire-pits and filled them with ash logs. A special brew of dark winter beer was ordered from Merthyr Brewery. A band practiced popular tunes for the party including the new Scottish song written by Robert Burns 'Auld Lang Syne'. The evening before the party, three bullocks were placed on spits over the roasting pits and the fires lit. The beasts were basted and turned through the night. There was a hard frost on the ground in morning and the sky was clear. It was a perfect winter's day.

The celebrations started with games for the children. There were running races, pin the tail on the dragon, tag and jelly throwing. A conjuror performed in one of the tents. The fancy dress competition was won by a worker's daughter dressed as a Red Indian. On the far side of the field, men were playing a competitive game of Welsh Quoits. The beer tent, near the bandstand, was filled to capacity. Bryant's Field was alive with people enjoying themselves. Nye cut the first beef at noon and the partners of Castle Iron Works worked hard to serve the long queue that formed for lunch.

There were recitals in the afternoon and the poem 'The boy stood on the burning deck,' written to celebrate the destruction on the French flagship Orient, during The Battle of the Nile received the loudest cheers. More games followed. Nye and Eira withdrew and entertained special friends at a private dinner before returning to Bryant's Field to light a huge bonfire. Midnight and the beginning of the 19th Century, was marked with a firework display which lit up the town.

Chapter 33

Isaac Thomas' land acquisition continued during 1800 and Nye was becoming suspicious of his intentions. Will Jones suggested Thomas planned to build a second canal but it seemed an absurd idea. Even if he had a corridor of land all the way to Cardiff he would still need Parliamentary Approval and Nye was confident his friends would block any attempt to get it. When Nye learned that Isaac was offering to buy a farm at Coedpenmaen he made a counter offer. Isaac immediately raised his price and a bidding war began. Isaac Thomas eventually acquired the farm but the price he paid was exorbitant. It was becoming increasingly clear Isaac was desperate to find a new route to Cardiff.

'Bonaparte has crossed the Alps with an army and invaded Italy,' announced Benjamin Griffiths.

'Didn't the Roman general, Hannibal, do that with an army of elephants?' asked Nye.

'You can laugh but it's serious. He's proclaimed himself the King of Italy. The man's a megalomaniac,' said Benjamin.

'And he's outlawed the French system of measuring to introduce a new system of measurement with multiples of ten. It's called a metric system. It'll never be accepted,' said Nye.

'You're in a strange mood this morning,' said Benjamin.

'I've discovered Isaac Thomas' scheme. He's building a tramway to Cardiff. They've started laying the tracks,' said Nye.

An extensive network of tramways already existed, to move raw materials around Merthyr but a twenty nine mile long one had never been attempted before. If he succeeded, Isaac Thomas would threaten the canal's monopoly and could challenge the profitability of Castle Iron Works. Nye consulted the engineers who built his tramways and was reassured that, although the track might get laid, it would be impossible to move the volumes needed to make it viable. The horses would not be able to pull the loads required and the cables from a steam winding engine, the very latest technology, would never reach such a distance. Nye and his partners need have no fear.

'Such a long tramway is impractical,' declared the engineers.

Rhys' narrow escape from the press gang had knocked his confidence for a while but he had learned and matured as a result of the experience. He still wanted to join the navy but no longer as an ordinary seaman. Eira tried to dissuade him but his mind was set. During a family discussion about his future, Rhys promised his father to study hard and wait until he was old enough to join as a midshipman. In return Nye promised to use his influence at the Admiralty to help Rhys with his ambition. Eira was unhappy with the arrangement. She didn't want to lose her son but was consoled when Nye told her the war with France would be over years before Rhys went to sea.

Bryn had other ambitions. The sea held no fascination for him. Bryn wanted to be an engineer. The foundry with its possibilities to make machines excited him. Nye had given Bryn a book of engineering plans for his birthday and Bryn spent hours studying it. He began to copy the drawings and invent his own machines. Bryn sometimes went to the works with his father and would wander around the workshops asking the men questions. On one occasion, he got too near a ladle of molten metal and a man had to grab him and throw him clear. Bryn landed in an undignified heap in the sand but it didn't dent his enthusiasm.

Thomas Baillie visited Castle Iron Works in September 1800. He was in his seventy third year and his health was deteriorating. Baillie would have retired already but for the war and the Board of Ordnance needed him to continue his work. He thanked Nye Vaughn for the foundry's efforts and told him, the Admiralty was pleased. Regarding Nye's proposal to produce a breech loading cannon with a rifled barrel, the Board of Ordnance had considered the idea and rejected it. Rifling and an opening breech would, they believed, make the weapon too complicated to use on a moving gun deck and liable to failure. The Admiralty preferred the proven designs already in use.

'There is a personal matter I would like to ask your advice about,' said Nye. The two men had become friends over the years and Nye knew he would get an honest answer.

'Ask away,' said Captain Baillie.

'My Son, Rhys, wants to go to sea. What's the best way for him to proceed?' asked Nye.

'How old is he?' asked Baillie.

'He'll be fifteen this year.'

'He's old enough to be a midshipman but he'll need a sponsor; someone who'll introduce him to the Admiralty and vouch for his character as a suitable candidate,' replied Baillie.

'Would you sponsor him?' asked Nye. Captain Baillie shook his head.

'I still have enemies at the Admiralty. If I sponsored your son he would be refused,' said Baillie, 'but I can think of a far more capable sponsor to advance your son's career.'

'Who are you speaking of?' asked Nye.

'The plans haven't been made yet but Admiral Nelson has expressed the desire to visit Castle Iron Works and see where his cannons are made. Would you be willing to entertain a visit?' asked Captain Baillie.

'Lord Nelson of the Nile wants to visit Merthyr? Of course we'll entertain him,' answered Nye.

'I'll pass your agreement on to the Admiralty and I believe, if you ask him, he'll support your son's application,' replied Baillie. Nye was grinning.

'You smile. Is it because of the admiral's visit or the help he might give your son?'

'Both,' replied Nye.

'The situation in Europe is getting worse. To stop supplies reaching the French from America we're now blockading France, Spain and the Low Countries. Orders have been sent to the fleet to intercept and search merchant ships regardless of their flag. When they find cargo destined for France it is to be seized. It's a provocation which, I believe, will bring other countries into the war. That's why the Prime Minister introduced income tax; to continue building up the navy and pay for the war,' said Baillie.

'Does Mr. Pitt expect to fight all of Europe?' asked Nye.

'If we must,' replied Baillie. The two men reflected on the enormity of a war with the rest of Europe.

'Enough of war. I have given my advice and now I want yours,' said Captain Baillie, 'I have evidence the Secretary for War, Henry Dundas, is misappropriating admiralty funds. He's a dangerous man with powerful allies. What should I do?' Nye remembered his conversation with Sir Henry Strachey, the Secretary of State, relating how Baillie's promising naval career had been destroyed for exposing fraud at Greenwich Hospital. He could see that his friend was uncomfortable.

'I've had dealings with Dundas. He's a crook. Is Sir Henry Strachey still a Secretary of State?' asked Nye.

'Not any more. I believe he's been appointed Master of the Royal Household,' answered Captain Baillie.

'Take your evidence to him. He'll know how to deal with Dundas,' said Nye.

Napoleon Bonaparte's foray across the Alps created a new threat to British interests in the Mediterranean. Anticipating Bonaparte's intentions, Nelson's plans were changed and he sailed for Southern Italy to defend the King of Naples against the threatened French invasion. The visit to Merthyr would have to wait. Bonaparte's army advanced south through Italy towards Naples and Nelson decided to withdraw, taking with him the Royal Family, the British Ambassador William Hamilton and his young wife Emma. Nelson and the Hamiltons left the fleet at Florence and returned to Britain overland. On Nelson's arrival in the United Kingdom he was told to prepare for an expedition to the Baltic. Annoyed by British interference of their shipping, Denmark, Norway, Prussia, Sweden and Russia formed an alliance and declared they would break the British blockade. The Russian Tsar, Paul, formerly an ally of Britain had fermented the trouble and led the alliance. Captain Baillie's fear that the war would spread had been proved right.

On the 31st January 1801, Emma Hamilton gave birth to a girl she name Horatia. Nelson didn't acknowledge Horatia as his daughter but his affair with Emma was common knowledge and he lived openly with the Hamiltons. Shortly after the birth, Nelson sailed from Yarmouth as second in command of a hastily assembled fleet to confront the new threat in the Baltic; an alliance of 123 enemy ships of the line.

In February, Eira and Nye travelled by private coach to London. Nye had business to conduct with the Board of Ordnance and the trip combined work with pleasure. They spent an evening at Covent Garden watching a performance of Shakespeare's Richard III with John Kemble playing the king. Kemble's oratory electrified the auditorium and he received four curtain calls at the end of the play. The following evening they went to Drury Lane to see Sheridan's School for Scandal starring Sarah Siddons. During the interval there was gossip regarding King George's mental health. The Vaughns listened to an account of a recent visit the king made to the same theatre when a member of the audience tried to shoot him. King George appeared unconcerned after being shot at and ordered the play to continue. As the actors resumed their places on the stage, the king fell asleep and onlookers muttered he was mad. Before Nye or Eira could comment on the story, the bell rang, summoning the audience for the second act.

The Vaughn's last night in London was spent at a dinner hosted by William Paxton and his wife. Paxton booked a private room at Almacks, a club noted as a meeting place for the well to do. The lively conversation included the war, the king's health, Nelson's love child and politics. The news that William Pitt had resigned as Prime Minister the same morning had surprised everyone.

'Why did he resign?' asked Eira.

'His policy of blockade and expanding the war with France is unpopular,' replied a diner.

'And expensive. Income tax, that's what finished him,' said another.

'Paxton, are you going to stand if there's a general election?' asked Nye.

'My name's already gone forward as the Whig candidate for Carmarthenshire,' replied William Paxton.

'Let's hope Nelson has a speedy victory against the Dutch and her allies. Then we won't need an election,' said Anne Paxton.

'Nelson isn't in command. Admiral Parker leads the fleet,' said her husband.

The British fleet attacked Copenhagen on the 1st April 1801. Admiral Sir Hyde Parker ordered Nelson to take part of the fleet across shallows to bombard the Danish ships. The Agememnon was the first ship to run aground on a mudflat. Two more followed. Undeterred Nelson began the bombardment but the return fire was intense and he was soon in difficulty. Watching the attack, Parker realised Nelson was in trouble and signalled for him to withdraw. When the signal was drawn to Nelson's attention he put his telescope up to his blind eye and said,

'To leave off action? Well, damn me if I do! You know, I have only one eye. I have a right to be blind sometimes. I really do not see the signal!' Then, he continued with the attack. Before long, accurate fire from the British ships began to silence the Danish guns. Several Danish ships struck their colours and Nelson sent a message ashore calling for the Danes to surrender or he would destroy the town. Crown Prince Frederik, who had been watching the battle from the shore agreed to a ceasefire to allow the wounded to be attended to. Nelson went ashore to negotiate an end to the fighting, unaware that Tsar Paul of Russia had been assassinated and the alliance was on the point of disintegrating. Nelson had a two hour meeting with the Crown Prince which ended when Nelson threatened to bombard the town. While the men were negotiating the British fleet had moved closer inshore and Copenhagen would have been destroyed had Prince Frederik not capitulated and signed an armistice. The Battle of Copenhagen was won. During a banquet to celebrate the armistice Nelson confided to Prince Frederik that the battle had been the most severe he had ever experienced.

After the battle, Admiral Sir Hyde Parker was recalled and ordered to hand his command over to Nelson. The victory was Nelson's and he returned to a country wanting to honour a hero. Nelson was rewarded with ennoblement and became Viscount Nelson of the Nile. Subduing the Baltic Alliance had removed one threat but another, more alarming, danger was becoming apparent. Bonaparte had returned from Italy and was massing an invasion army by the English Channel. Nelson was despatched to the South Coast to command the Channel Fleet; the last line of defence.

Nye Vaughn heard the shouting, from his office and went to the foundry to find out what was causing the commotion. Men had thrown down their tools and were shaking hands. Others were laughing and hugging. A furnace man was dancing a jig on the furnace top and singing a sea shanty.

'What's going on?' shouted Nye.

'It's all over Mr. Vaughn. The war has ended,' replied a grinning labourer.

As soon as he was appointed as the new Prime Minister, Henry Addington approached Bonaparte, offering to negotiate terms for peace. The bargaining continued until October 1801 when a peace treaty was signed at Amiens on the 22nd. The peace came at a price for Britain including the loss of its Mediterranean possessions. Giving up Malta and other important naval bases was accepted in return for concessions from the French. Although a treaty had been signed and was being celebrated in every town in the United Kingdom, there were still a great many unresolved disputes with the French and negotiations continued to find ways to cement the peace.

Having ended the war and riding a wave of popularity, the Prime Minister called a general election for August 1802. William Paxton stood for the Carmarthenshire constituency. Paxton's campaign was a lively affair. James Williams, the sitting MP, was a popular local man and Paxton had never fought an election before. He did however have a lot of money and was determined to buy the votes he needed. Paxton kept a record of his expenditure showing he bought voters 11,000 breakfasts, 40,000 dinners, 25,000 gallons of beer and 11,000 bottles of spirit. Paxton's total expenditure on his campaign was £15,690. He lost to Williams by forty six votes. The Prime Minister, Henry Addington, was returned to office with an increased majority.

On the 16th August 1802 an open landau, pulled by two greys, was seen approaching Merthyr. A troop of cavalry accompanied the carriage. More coaches followed behind. Men ran forward, unhitched the horses and pulled the landau through the flag lined streets. Crowds cheered and waved as the carriage passed under triumphal laurel arches. Ear piercing whistles, from the crowd, filled the air. There were shouts of 'bravo' and 'well done.' Vice Admiral the Right Honourable Viscount Nelson of the Nile sat upright on the back seat. Lady Emma Hamilton and her husband William sat opposite. Nelson waved, acknowledging the cheering crowd. As the carriage passed Castle Iron Works Nye Vaughn couldn't contain himself and shouted,

'It's Nelson. Cheer you buggers.' The men didn't need encouraging and were still cheering when the carriage had disappeared from sight.

'Where's the admiral lodging?' asked Nye.

'The Star Inn. I hear Miss Jenkins has considerably improved Meir's old tavern,' replied Will Jones.

'Meir would be proud to know an admiral was staying there,' said Nye and smiled at his partner.

Admiral Nelson visited Castle Iron Works, the following morning, to inspect the foundry and watch a cannon being cast. During Nelson's tour, the Hamiltons called on Eira and took coffee in a summerhouse beside the lake. A cannon was fired near the lime kilns, to salute Nelson's arrival. As the gun discharged, it recoiled hitting a boy and killing him. When she heard of the accident, Lady Hamilton insisted on giving the dead boy's family eight guineas to pay for a proper funeral. A reception was held in the afternoon and Nelson was invited to make a speech to the crowd which had gathered outside the civic hall.

Nelson appeared on the balcony to loud cheers and urged the people to calm themselves. The admiral spoke clearly and the speech was heard in silence. Nelson ended with his view of duty,

207

'To obey orders is all perfection. To serve my King and destroy the French, I consider as the greatest order of all, from which little ones spring; and if one of these militate against it (for who can tell exactly at a distance), I go back and obey the great order and object, to down – down with the damned French villains! My blood boils at the name of a Frenchman! Down, down with the French! ... is my constant prayer.' The crowd cheered.

In the evening, the Mayor of Merthyr held a grand ball with Nelson as the guest of honour. During the dancing, Nye approached the admiral and asked for his help to enrol Rhys as a midshipman.

'We depart for Ross on Wye at ten o'clock tomorrow. Bring your son to my lodgings at nine o'clock and I will speak with him,' replied Nelson.

Nelson had just finished breakfast when they arrived. He looked Rhys up and down and asked him why he wanted to go to sea.

'To fight the French and defend the King's realm,' replied Rhys.

'The war with France is over. Our government says there's no longer any need to fight them,' said Nelson.

'My Lord, you said down with the French and they are villains, so we must fight them again,' said Rhys. Nelson smiled.

'I think your son would make a good politician, Mr. Vaughn. I will sponsor his application to the admiralty. Rhys, I'll give you the same advice I give to the midshipmen under my command. Firstly you must always implicitly obey orders, without attempting to form any opinion of your own regarding their propriety. Secondly, you must consider every man your enemy who speaks ill of your king; and thirdly you must hate a Frenchman as you hate the devil.' Nelson stood up and offered his left hand to Nye.

'He's a stout young man. I believe he'll do well in the service and be a credit to you,' said the admiral and went outside to the waiting carriage.

Chapter 34

Shortly after Nelson's visit to Merthyr, Isaac Thomas called a meeting, to make a public announcement. The civic hall was filled to capacity when Nye and Benjamin arrived. They stood at the back of the hall. Isaac Thomas was on a platform at the front of the hall with a stocky man Nye didn't recognise. Isaac called for quiet.

'Gentlemen, thank you for coming this evening. As you know the transportation of goods from Merthyr is controlled by the owners of the canal and the canal is run for the benefit of one foundry, owned by Mr. Vaughn. He treats it as if it were his personal property.'

There were cries of 'shame' from the audience.

'It's a monopoly that's inequitable and morally wrong and I'm going to break it,' said Isaac, 'I am going to build a tramway from Merthyr to Cardiff.'

'It won't work,' whispered Nye to his companion.

'How are you going to haul the trucks? It's too far for horses.' asked a man.

'We aren't going to use horses. We're going to use steam engines. Mr. Trevithick will explain,' said Isaac and invited the man sharing the platform with him to continue.

'Good evening, my name's Richard Trevithick. I'm a mine engineer from Cornwall and I build steam engines to pump water from the mines. Mr. Thomas has asked me to look at how to use steam to power the tramway. My initial idea was to put a series of winding engines along the tramway and use cables to drag the trucks along but with nearly thirty miles of

209

track the number and cost of the engines is impractical so I had to find another way. My solution is a radical one, something that's never been done before. I propose to make the steam engine smaller, put it on wheels and use steam power to propel it along the track together with the trucks. I shall call the moving engine a locomotive,' said Trevithick.

'I'll wager it won't work,' shouted Nye from the audience.

'What are you doing?' whispered Benjamin.

'A steam engine must weigh twenty or thirty tons. The track isn't strong enough to support so much weight and no engine in the world is powerful enough to move such a heavy object,' whispered Nye.

'Vaughn, have you the stomach to put real money on the wager?' called Isaac.

'How much of the tramway is built?' shouted Nye.

'We're as far as Abercynon, nearly ten miles,' replied Isaac.

'I offer a bet of one hundred guineas that Mr. Trevithick's engine cannot haul ten tons of iron from Merthyr to Abercynon and return with the empty carriages,' said Nye.

'A hundred guineas is a paltry sum. I will wager five hundred guineas that it will,' replied Isaac.

'Five hundred guineas? I accept. When will the challenge be tested?' said Nye.

'I'm afraid, Gentlemen, you will have a wait. The locomotive hasn't been built yet,' said Trevithick.

'This is madness, Nye. Trevithick has a reputation. He could well succeed,' said Benjamin.

'I'm confident he won't. Anyway the bet is made,' replied Nye.

Rhys Vaughn received a 'letter of service' from the admiralty in November 1802 ordering him to travel to Chatham and report to HMS Conqueror, a third rate ship of the line with 74 guns. Rhys would join the ship as the captain's servant, the first step in his naval career.

'How long will you be the captain's servant?' asked Eira.

'It'll be two years before I'm considered for promotion to midshipman but I have a good berth. The Conqueror is a new ship. She was only launched last year,' replied Rhys.

'I know, we supplied the cannons,' said Nye.

'When will you come home?' asked Cerys.

'I don't know. Perhaps next year,' replied Rhys and kissed his sister.

'Goodbye Rhys,' said Bryn.

'Look after yourself and write often,' said Eira and hugged her son. Nye shook his son's hand.

'I'm proud of you Rhys. Remember Nelson's advice and obey orders without hesitation,' said Nye and released his grip. Rhys climbed aboard the coach and it set off. Eira was weeping as the coach disappeared from view.

'He'll be alright. We're at peace,' said Nye. Eira didn't answer.

'I heard today that, a French woman called Madame Tussaud has opened a wax works in London. She's exhibiting models of royalists executed on the guillotine,' said Nye as they returned home. 'She copied the heads after they were cut off.'

'What a horrible idea,' said Eira wiping her eyes.

Thomas Baillie visited Sir Henry Strachey at Buckingham Palace on the12th December. Sir Henry was admiring an oil painting.

'It's a view of Venice showing the Campanile and the Doges Palace. The king has a large collection of Canaletto's paintings,' said Sir Henry. The two men discussed the translucent quality of the picture.

'There is a matter of some delicacy I wish to discuss,' said Baillie. Sir Henry took his visitor to a small office where they could talk in private. Baillie showed Sir Henry the evidence he had collected, revealing fraud at the Admiralty. Sir Henry questioned Baillie and told him to leave the papers so that he could examine them further.

'Are you well Captain Baillie? You look pale and seem short of breath,' said Sir Henry.

'It's nothing but a chill. I'll soon get over it,' replied the captain. Thomas Baillie died, peacefully in his bed, three days later. He was seventy two years old.

Sir Henry Strachey showed Baillie's evidence to Prime Minister Addington who saw an opportunity to attack a political enemy and immediately appointed a Commission of Enquiry to investigate Henry Dundas. The War Secretary had already been dismissed by Pitt's replacement and the enquiry threatened him with disgrace and political ruin, but Dundas was a fighter and had powerful allies, including his friend William Pitt.

Addington's peace with France was coming under increasing pressure. The French and British distrusted each other. Bonaparte's expansionist policy was continuing in Europe and he sent a fleet to America to reclaim French Louisiana which it had relinquished as part of the Treaty of Amiens. The United States was unprepared for war and negotiated to buy Louisiana, from the French for 3 cents an acre amounting to $15m. Bonaparte was also pushing east toward Russia. Responding to the continuing threat, Addington maintained the British army at its war time strength of 180,000 men and continued to expand the Royal Navy. When Addington changed his mind and refused to withdraw the navy from Malta, Bonaparte accused the British of perfidy.

On the 17th May 1803, HMS Conqueror intercepted a French merchant ship, sailing in the English Channel and hailed its captain to heave to. Rhys Vaughn was in the boarding party that rowed across to seize the ship. The French captain protested but, faced with armed marines, resistance was futile. The ship was sailed to Portsmouth where the crew were told they were prisoners of war and led away to join crews of other French ships captured the same day. Britain declared war on France the following morning. Britain's pre-emptive action, seizing French ships, infuriated Bonaparte who ordered the arrest of every Englishman in France and vowed to cross the Channel with an army to teach Perfidious Albion a lesson.

A letter arrived written by Rhys aboard HMS Conqueror, towards the end of August. It was dated 16th June 1803.

'My Dear Mother and Father,
I am well and confess that life at sea suits me. We are now at war with France and have been ordered to blockade the port of Toulon to stop the French ships from going to sea. Captain Butler, who speaks freely in my presence, says 'we must keep the French bottled up' and the fleet is spread along the Spanish and French coasts waiting for the enemy to emerge and offer battle. As well as serving the captain's needs, I am charged with learning ships duties and have been taught to load and fire a cannon from father's foundry, a fact I have not shared with shipmates for fear of being mocked. We practice almost daily and can fire and reload in less than two minutes. When we clear for action my job is to empty the captain's cabin, load his furniture into a boat, towed behind the ship and man a stern gun. Last time we exercised, I almost dropped his dining chair into the sea.

The crew are in good spirit although there are some malcontents, mainly pressed men. The captain treats them fairly but discipline is strict when needed. Last week a man was flogged for failing to obey an order. He deserved the punishment and the spectacle, witnessed by the ships company, was a necessary reminder.

I pray your lives in Merthyr are satisfactory, that Cerys is continuing her lessons and my brother is still dreaming of building engines. I have heard talk that steam engines will replace sails, one day, but think it unlikely. Nothing is as powerful as the wind. Tell father, Merthyr cannons are well liked by the men and to make more so we can defeat the French once and for all time. Everyone aboard wants Nelson to be given command of the Mediterranean fleet and join us at Toulon. If he does, we are assured of victory.

I will write again soon.

Your loving son, Rhys.'

Rhys didn't tell his family that the press gang officer who took him prisoner in Swansea was aboard. Lieutenant Voss was now an ordinary seaman berthed on the lower gun deck of the Conqueror. Nelson arrived at Toulon aboard his flagship HMS Victory in July 1803, a month before Rhys' letter reached Merthyr.

In August a squadron of American frigates led by the USS Constitution arrived in the Mediterranean with orders to deal with the Barbary Coast pirates. On the night of the 14th the Constitution's lookouts saw an unidentified sail and quietly went alongside with its gun ports open. Edward Preble, the captain of the Constitution hailed the ship and asked it to identify itself. The ship he approached replied demanding he identify himself first.

'Identify yourself or I will put a shot into your hull,' answered Preble, curtly.

'This is his Britannic Majesty's Ship Donegal of 84 guns. If you give me a shot I'll give you a broadside,' replied the commander of the strange ship, Preble had apparently surprised a British ship of the line and was outgunned. Undaunted, Preble ordered his gun crews to prepare to fire. Fortunately, a British lieutenant then boarded the American ship and apologised on behalf of his captain for not answering the American's hail in courteous manner. The apology defused the tense situation with both ships ready to fire. The Lieutenant then revealed his ship was HMS Maidstone a frigate with inferior firepower than the Constitution.

Major Henry Shrapnel of the Royal Artillery visited Castle Iron Works in November to discuss the manufacture of a new kind of shell the army was adopting. The ammunition, invented by Shrapnel, was a cannon ball, filled with lead shot which exploded in mid air. The shrapnel shell, as it was known, had proved to be effective and was to be manufactured in quantity. Shrapnel dined with the Vaughns during his stay in Merthyr.

'I understand you have a son in the navy,' said Shrapnel after the meal.

'He's in the Mediterranean fleet, on the Conqueror,' replied Nye.

'A fine ship, I saw her launched at Harwich. The navy is doing an excellent job, keeping the French at bay,' said Shrapnel.

'In your opinion, how will the war end, Major Shrapnel?' asked Eira.

'That's a very astute question Mrs Vaughn. We are fighting a military genius who is also a despot and ambitious. Sitting on our island hoping the navy will keep us safe will not defeat Bonaparte. At some point we will have to engage the French on land and crush them,' explained the major.

'You mean invade France. Surely that would be madness,' said Eira.

'Madam, Napoleon Bonaparte rules most of Europe. His Grande Armée is the finest fighting machine in the world. Until we destroy it and him there will be no peace,' said Shrapnel.

Chapter 35

The Royal Navy maintained a continuous blockade of French and Spanish ports to prevent the enemy moving their ships to the English Channel where Bonaparte's army was waiting for transport. Bonaparte confronted his admirals and ordered them to devise a plan which would gain control of the English Channel for six hours. With a fair wind, it was all the time needed to cross.

Rhys' next letter arrived in February 1804.

'My Dear Mother and Father,
I write to you this new-year's day to wish you a prosperous year. The boredom of blockade is interrupted by the possibility of action at last. Conqueror is ordered to leave Toulon and accompany HMS Superb to Algeria. The Dey of Algiers, who is the ruler, is a pirate and has seized Maltese ships bringing supplies to the fleet. We are to recover them and demand an apology from the Dey. Captain Butler says the intention is to anchor close in and bombard the prince's palace if he does not comply. A Mr. Falcon, King George's envoy, will go ashore to explain his majesty's displeasure.

When Captain Butler was ordered to attend Lord Nelson to receive his instructions I was in the jolly boat which rowed him across. The Victory is a magnificent ship and we are glad to have Nelson as our Admiral.

Father will remember Lieutenant Voss, the rogue who imprisoned me in Swansea. Voss was serving on the Conqueror as an able seaman. He told shipmates he would do for me. When I learned of Voss' threat, I confronted him below decks and told him I would thrash him. The coward apologised but was not to be trusted. Since then, the man has vanished. I believe Voss had other enemies onboard and is now at the bottom of the sea. Good riddance I say.

Your letters of August and October last were delivered by a supply boat just before Christmas. I approve of Bryn's ambition to join Boulton and Watt's foundry in Birmingham and study engineering. Bryn will be pleased to learn the navy has commissioned its first steam tug. I pray father wins his wager with Mr. Thomas. It will be a spectacle worth seeing. I am sorry to hear of Aunt Jean's passing. I liked her and remember our visits to the farm at Llangadog with fondness. With his mother gone, Uncle Richard will need to find himself a wife.

My studies are continuing well and I believe Captain Butler will recommend me for promotion next year. From captain's servant to midshipman means more responsibility and I will be ready for it. Hug my sister for me.

Your loving son, Rhys.'

On the 21st February 1804 a large crowd gathered to watch Richard Trevithick's locomotive emerge from its shed at Thomas' foundry. The engine belched smoke as it trundled across the points and stopped. Trevithick signalled from his position behind the engine and the points were changed. The Cornishman cracked open the steam valve, there was a loud hiss and the engine slowly backed along the track towards five waiting trucks.

'Ten tons of iron we agreed,' said Nye.

'The iron's already loaded and I'm going to add some more weight,' replied Isaac and waved to his workmen. Seventy men clambered aboard the loaded trucks.

'Mr. Thomas seems very confident, father,' said Bryn.

'The thing has to get to Abercynon without breaking down. It's a long way,' replied Nye, 'Why are they putting sand on the rails?'

'To give the engine traction,' replied Bryn.

'Are you ready to lose your money Vaughn?' called Isaac. A stranger approached Nye.

'Mr. Vaughn, my name is Davies Giddy. I'm an engineer employed by the government. You're a brave man to wager 500 guineas,' said the stranger.

'So you think it'll work Mr. Giddy? What is your interest here?' asked Nye.

'I helped Trevithick with some boiler calculations and the government sees possibilities for the invention,' replied Giddy.

'God speed Trevithick,' shouted Isaac as the engine began to move. The crowd cheered.

The train proceeded along the track at a walking pace with spectators accompanying it on foot. Trevithick opened the furnace door and added coal to the fire. Suddenly, there was a loud crack. Trevithick stopped the engine and stepped down to see what had happened. The weight of the engine had snapped a rail. Nye smiled. The engine had gone less than 100 yards.

'I'll have my 500 guineas if you please,' he shouted to Isaac.

'Mr Vaughn, the engine has not broken down and can continue along the damaged rail. Your wager's not won yet,' said Trevithick and returned to his place on the engine.

The trucks passed slowly over the broken rail and the train continued for another mile to where a bridge crossed the track. The locomotive reached the bridge and the tip of its funnel caught the underside of the arch. There was a tearing sound as the impact crushed the funnel and bent it backwards. Trevithick inspected the damage, announced the chimney was still serviceable and the train would proceed. As a precaution, he sent men to Abercynon to measure the height of all the bridges. Trevithick's locomotive hauled its cargo the ten miles in just over four hours despite shattering several more rails during the journey.

'Are you satisfied with the engine?' asked Isaac as the men unloaded the wagons.

Trevithick nodded, 'I am. I needed no extra water for the boiler and she only burnt two hundredweight of coal.'

'I hope you brought the money with you,' said Isaac to Nye.

'I have but it's not yours yet. The engine still has to return the trucks to Merthyr,' replied Nye.

'But the trucks are empty,' replied Isaac.

'They may be empty, Mr. Thomas, but the return journey is uphill,' said Mr. Giddy, 'and that might be a problem.'

Richard Trevithick straightened the funnel as best he could before leaving Abecynon on the return journey to Merthyr. The engine worked well reaching nearly five miles an hour on a level stretch and Isaac Thomas was feeling increasingly confident when, two miles from their destination, a mounting bolt sheared and the boiler started to leak. To save his engine from destroying itself, Trevithick was forced to damp down the fire and stop. Nye declared the locomotive had failed and he was the winner of the wager. Isaac Thomas, however, contended the leak was a minor problem which could be repaired. The repair was completed the following day and the engine completed its journey. Both men claimed victory and the wager went unpaid.

Nye Vaughn's prediction that the engine would be too heavy for the track had proved correct and the locomotive never ran again. Instead, the locomotive's wheels were removed and it was used by Thomas as a stationery engine to power a forging hammer.

Napoleon Bonaparte held up the telescope and focussed on Dover Castle.

'How many men do you have, General Ney?' asked Bonaparte.

'My 6th Army Corp here at Boulogne has more than 100,000 and we have another 100,000 soldiers at other camps along the coast,' replied the general.

'The invasion barges, they are ready?' asked Bonaparte.

'They are First Consul, 2000 of them but the English are attacking. Yesterday they sent two fire ships into the harbour,' replied Admiral Villeneuve.

'Villeneuve, you will devise a plan to take control of the English Channel. Admiral Bruix tells me he can transport our invasion flotilla across in six hours. You must keep the British Navy at bay for six hours so he can sail without hindrance. Is that too much to ask?' said Bonaparte.

'I will engage the British fleet and destroy it,' replied Villeneuve.

'I doubt it but you will give me six hours at the cost of all your ships if necessary,' said Bonaparte. Admiral Villeneuve nodded.

The massing French forces could be seen from the cliffs of Dover. English newspapers printed stories that Bonaparte's army was tunnelling under the English Channel, that invaders would fly to England in a fleet of balloons and published drawings of huge invasion rafts, powered by giant paddle wheels. The increasing threat of invasion was demoralising the population and undermining the authority of the government. Addington panicked and called a general election which removed him from office. The Whig leader, William Pitt returned to power on the 10th May 1804.

On the 4th April Rhys Vaughn arrived in Merthyr having been granted leave of absence from his ship. HMS Conqueror had returned to England and was in Chatham for repairs. Eira arranged a gathering to celebrate her son's return. Richard Vaughn and his sisters came from Llangadog. Invited friends included the Paxtons and Captain Williams. Life at sea had matured Rhys and he had grown in stature. He entertained the family with accounts of his adventures, gave Bryn a curved dagger from North Africa and Cerys a silver locket.

'How does the captain treat you?' asked Nye.

'We have a new captain, Sir Israel Pellew. He's been recalled from retirement. The Conqueror is to sail to Toulon and rejoin the blockade,' replied Rhys.

'When do you return?' asked Eira.

'I leave in two days,' replied Rhys.

'So soon! You've only just got here,' said his mother.

'Tell us Paxton, now you're in parliament, what's the Prime Minister proposing to do about the war?' asked Nye.

'William Pitt's going to win it at any cost. That's his one thought but I fear he will not. Do you remember Henry

Dundas, the crooked admiralty treasurer who proved himself an incompetent Secretary of War? Pitts' enobled him and made him First Lord of the Admiralty. Lord Melville he calls himself now,' said Paxton.

'What about the commission of enquiry into his affairs?' asked Captain Williams.

'It's been quietly forgotten,' answered Paxton.

'Scum, it seems, rises to the top,' said Nye.

'Until it's blown away by an honest wind. Dundas isn't popular. His time will come. For my part on the war, I'm raising a Carmarthenshire Militia. When Bonaparte lands, we will fight,' said Paxton.

'I heard the Duke of Beaufort's Monmouth and Brecon Militia has a fine troop of cavalry. The whole country's arming itself ready for the French,' said Captain Williams.

'They'll never cross the Channel,' said Rhys, 'We have a navy to stop them.'

During the visit Richard asked to speak with Nye in private saying he wanted his brother's advice. Richard began by thanking Nye for the farm which he was pleased to say was doing well. The war had increased food prices and lambs were selling for a premium. He went on to say the owner of the next farm had died and the son wanted to sell. Richard asked if he should borrow money to buy the farm. Nye asked the price and agreed, after some discussion, to lend his brother half the amount needed if Richard could raise the rest. Richard said he would borrow it from the bank and they shook hands on the arrangement.

'There's another matter. I don't know what to do about my sister Bethan. Since our mother died she's changed, become argumentative and difficult,' said Richard.

'Bethan's the elder sister. How old is she now? asked Nye.

'Sixteen and she's walking out with a minister's son from Llandeilo. I don't believe his intentions are honourable. He's a bad one but she won't listen to me,' said Richard.

'What's the boy's name? Asked Nye.

'David Rees, but he isn't a boy; he's twentysix,' said Richard.

'This is something I can't help you with. You need a woman's advice,' said Nye and called Eira to ask her view of Richard's quandary.

Eira listened as Nye explained the issue and suggested that Bethan would benefit by staying with them in Merthyr for a time. Bethan's absence from Llangadog would remove the attention of the minister's son and give her an opportunity to make more suitable friends. Richard agreed to the proposal and went to tell Bethan. When Bethan heard the news, she sulked.

Chapter 36

Rhys returned to his ship and sailed for the Mediterranean. Captain Pellew, an experienced master mariner in his fifties, worked the crew hard. Gun crews practiced loading until the heavy cannons could be loaded and ready to fire within ninety seconds. The ship was repeatedly turned through the wind to train for manoeuvring in battle. Rhys memorised the signals in Popham's book of flags and was appointed to assist the flag officer, when in action. Under Pellew's guidance the crew was trained to a high state of readiness. As the ship became a more effective fighting machine the crew grew in confidence and morale was high. Pellew looked after his men. When, he noticed a Lieutenant of Marines looking unhappy and enquired why the man looked so dejected, the lieutenant pointed to a departing supply ship, carrying mail home and said a letter to his wife had not gone aboard with the other post. Knowing the next supply ship wasn't due for a month, Captain Pellew ordered Rhys to signal the supply ship to return and collect the letter. On the 11th November Pellew promoted Rhys to the rank of Midshipman.

At 9 a.m. on the 2nd December a Papal procession left the Tuileries lead by a bishop. He was riding a mule and holding a crucifix high in the air. When the pageant reached Notre Dame, Pope Pius VII was carried through the cathedral to his throne by the high altar. A short while later a second procession approached the cathedral. Napoleon and Josephine were riding in a carriage drawn by eight bay horses escorted by a regiment of hussars, their green jackets and bright plumes adding a touch a gaiety. Behind the hussars came dragoons with their brass casques over tiger skin helmets and long guns across their saddles. Then came the giant, six feet carabineers, dressed in white with gold breast-plates and tall helmets with red plumes. Four hundred musicians accompanied the parade. An enormous hot air balloon, illuminated with 3000 lights, floated high above the cathedral. Napoleon and his wife stepped down from their carriage and entered the cathedral and the crowd cheered. Attendants vested the couple in satin tunics, embroidered with gold, and cloaked them with crimson velvet, lined with ermine. Three handmaidens carried Josephine's train to the altar as choirs sang the mass. Napoleon's mantle, embroidered with golden bees and weighing more than eighty pounds, was supported by four gentlemen. A gold crown sat on the altar. The coronation service was long and tedious. Napoleon lost interest in the pomp and grew bored. Pope Pius was still blessing the imperial regalia when Bonaparte unexpectedly removed his laurel wreath, picked up the crown, placed it on his own head and declared himself Emperor of France. 'Long live the Emperor.' shouted the congregation. The ceremony, like first Republic of France was over.

Bethan Vaughn's stay at Merthyr was problematic. Her surly behaviour and refusal to join in with the family was irksome but worse was to come. Two weeks after her arrival Bethan's attitude appeared to change. She was more cheerful, answered when spoken to and stopped hiding herself away. It was twelve year old Cerys who drew Eira's attention to what was happening. Cerys told her mother that the silver locket from Rhys was missing. Eira said she must have mislaid the locket and it would turn up. When some silver spoons vanished from the dining room Eira became suspicious. Other trinkets disappeared then Cerys told her mother she heard Bethan moving about during the night. Nye was in London on business. After everyone retired for the night, Eira went downstairs and waited in the dark. The house had been silent for some time when she heard someone shuffling down the back stairs. Eira could hear footsteps on the bare wooden treads. The servant's door at the back of the hall opened. Eira stepped back into the shadows. Bethan emerged, walked quietly to the front door and let herself out.

Eira moved to the sitting room and watched through the window. A man was standing by the yew tree in front of the house. Bethan hurried over to him. They kissed and vanished into the bushes. Two hours passed before Bethan returned to the house. Eira was waiting, in the hallway, when Bethan opened the front door.

'Come in Bethan. We need to talk,' said Eira and led the girl into the sitting room.

To begin with, Bethan denied everything, including meeting a man outside the house, but Eira's questioning was persistent and Bethan's defence crumbled. She confessed to stealing Cerys' locket and the other items. The man outside the house she said was her fiancé David Rees.

'Why did you steal from us?' asked Eira.

'David said he needed money to pay his lodgings. He asked me to,' replied Bethan.

'There's something else you need to tell me, isn't there Bethan?' said Eira.

'No. Nothing.'

'You can't hide it much longer. You're with child,' said Eira. Bethan began to weep.

'Does David know?'

'I told him tonight. He says he'll marry me. What shall I do?' replied Bethan.

'You must bring him to talk to Nye. My husband will help. When are you seeing David next?'

'On Sunday night,' said Bethan.

Nye returned home the following afternoon and Eira told him what had happened.

'Does he agree to marry her?' asked Nye.

'She says he does but I've told her to bring the boy to talk to you. They need our help. If he doesn't marry her she'll be ruined,' said Eira.

'Of course we'll help but I'll have to speak to Richard. He'll be upset when he discovers Bethan is carrying a child,' replied Nye.

There was a thick frost on the ground when Bethan went outside to see her lover and ask him to meet Nye. There was a bright moon and the sky was clear. Nye and Eira turned out the sitting room lamp and watched Bethan. She waited by the yew tree for an hour but David Rees did not keep the assignation. When Nye went outside and brought Bethan indoors, she was frozen.

The next day Bethan went to Rees' lodgings. The landlady fetched him from his room and left them alone in the kitchen.

'Why didn't you come last night?' asked Bethan.

'I wanted to see you. I love you but it's difficult.'

'What's difficult?' said Bethan.

'I can't marry you. I told my father and he said he'll disown me. I have no money. How would we live?' replied Rees. Bethan looked at David Rees and felt contempt for him. What point, now, was there in telling him about Eira's offer to help?

'So you've ruined me and now you're abandoning me,' she spat.

'I'm not abandoning you or ruining you,' said Rees and produced a small bottle. 'I bought it from a physician in Brecon. It's a medicine that will terminate your pregnancy. Do you understand? We will both be free.'

Bethan took the bottle and held it up to the light. It contained a cloudy liquid.

'What's in it?'

'The doctor said, it's a herbal cure, used by women to get rid of unwanted babies. He said to drink it and the baby will be gone within three days,' replied Rees. Bethan put the bottle on the table and moved towards the door.

'I'm sorry I can't marry you Bethan but this is the best thing for us both,' said Rees. Bethan hesitated, went back to the table and swallowed the contents of the bottle.

Bethan was nearly home when the pain started. Eira saw her stagger, called for help and ran out of the house. By the time they got her indoors she was vomiting and had diarrhoea.

'Get the doctor. Hurry,' ordered Eira. Bethan was shouting when the doctor arrived. He examined her and gave her a dose of valerian.

'What's wrong with her?' asked Eira.

'She's got food poisoning. The valerian will calm her but we must purge her. Send a servant to fetch my clyster syringe. I'll wash her bowel and we must make her vomit again,' said the doctor.

'Bethan, have you eaten or drunk anything since you went out this morning?' asked Eira.

'Just some medicine,' replied Bethan.

'What medicine? Tell us quickly,' ordered the doctor.

'David gave it to me to get rid of the baby,' sobbed Bethan.

'Find him and find out what the medicine was,' said the doctor. Eira ran to the foundry and asked Nye to hurry to Rees' lodgings.

Bethan screamed when the enema was injected. Rees' landlady told Nye her tenant had gone taking his things with him. Nye told the woman about Bethan's sudden sickness and she produced a bottle she had found in her rubbish.

'He said he was going home to Llandeilo. I'm glad he's gone. I didn't like him,' said the landlady.

Bethan's condition deteriorated. By the second day she was hallucinating and passing black urine. Richard arrived in the afternoon and the family took turns to sit with Bethan. The doctor examined the bottle, Nye recovered and discovered it contained traces of arsenic. Bethan had been poisoned. The dose was not enough to kill her quickly but its effect was fatal. Her heart stopped three days later.

Nye and Richard rode to the minister's house in Llandeilo and demanded to know where David Rees was. Reverend Rees asked what business they had with his son.

'Your son is a murderer. Where is he?' said Nye.

'Who has he murdered? That's a heinous accusation,' asked the reverend.

'It's a heinous crime. He killed my sister and her unborn child. Where is he?' repeated Nye and raised his fist.

'There's no need for violence. I'll tell you where my son is and I'm sure he's innocent. He's a foolish boy but he isn't a murderer,' said Reverend Rees, 'David left yesterday. He's going to America to start a new life. He told me he got a girl into trouble but he said she lost the baby.'

The brothers caught up with David Rees in Liverpool. He had booked a passage on the Star of the Sea bound for New York. Rees was arrested on board and returned to Merthyr, in chains, to stand trial for the murder of Bethan Vaughn.

On the 29th March 1805 the British blockade of Toulon was disrupted by a storm allowing Admiral Villeneuve's ships to break out. His plan was to sail into the Atlantic, combine with the Spanish fleet and lure the Royal Navy west, to the Caribbean. From there, he planned to race back to destroy any remaining British warships guarding the English coast. With the straits between England and France under French control and the bulk of the Royal Navy still en route from the Caribbean Bonaparte's invasion would proceed. Nelson chased Villeneuve across the Atlantic. On the 11th June Villeneuve turned back and headed east, reaching Cape Finisterre on the 22nd July where he was intercepted by a squadron of fifteen British warships. Villeneuve chased the outnumbered British squadron and then sailed to La-Coruna in northern Spain. The next part of the plan, to join with the Spanish fleet and sail to Boulogne was about to be executed when the French Admiral was misinformed that a large British Fleet blocked the way. Unaware that Nelson's fleet was still a long way off Villeneuve panicked, disobeyed Bonaparte's orders and sailed south to Cadiz.

Bonaparte was furious and wrote, 'Villeneuve does not possess the strength of character to command a frigate. He lacks determination and has no moral courage.' Villeneuve had confirmed Bonaparte's opinion of the French navy and he ordered the admiral to be sacked. A short time later, Nelson arrived at Cadiz and resumed the blockade of the harbour now containing thirty four French and Spanish ships of the line. Believing the enemy was unlikely to come out and fight Nelson ordered the Victory to leave the fleet and sail to England. Nelson and his flagship had been at sea for two years without a break.

Chapter 37

David Rees' trial began on the 6th August. He admitted giving Bethan the medicine but claimed he bought it from a doctor, understanding it was a remedy for an unwanted pregnancy. He said he didn't know what the bottle contained and never intended to harm Bethan. Rees' father pleaded his son was of good character and the jury were moved by his words. Before the jury retired to consider a verdict, the judge reminded them of the facts. David Rees had administered the poison and Bethan Vaughn died as a result of his actions. This was agreed by all but the jury had to decide if it was murder or a terrible accident. Was his flight to Liverpool an attempt to escape justice or a coincidence? If, as the defendant claimed, he didn't know Bethan Vaughn would die it might be the latter. The Vaughn family listened in silence to the judge's summary and Nye began to suspect Rees would cheat the hangman's noose.

The jury was split. Some had no doubts; David Rees was a murderer. Others had been convinced by the boy's father that he was innocent. The argument in the jury room continued for hours until the judge lost patience and ordered the jury to reach a verdict within thirty minutes. The jurors returned.

'How do you find the defendant?' asked the Judge.

'Guilty of murder,' replied the foreman of the jury. The clerk of the court placed a black cap on the judge's head and he pronounced sentence.

'David Rees, you have been found guilty of the murder of Bethan Vaughn. You will be taken hence to the prison in which you were last confined and from there to a place of execution where you will be hanged by the neck until you are dead and thereafter your body buried within the precincts of the prison and may the Lord have mercy upon your soul.'

On the day of his execution David Rees was paraded through Brecon on a small horse drawn cart. ' A crowd of 10,000 had gathered to watch the hanging. He protested his innocence until the trapdoor opened, sending him to his death. After the execution his body was dissected.

News reached Nelson on the 2nd September that the enemy was preparing to break out of Cadiz. He rushed to Portsmouth and HMS Victory departed reaching Cadiz on the 29th. Admiral Villeneuve had received a warning that he was being replaced and was determined to put to sea before the orders reached him. The combined French Spanish fleet of thirty three ships of the line emerged from Cadiz on the 18th October. Captain Blackwood aboard HMS Euryalus was watching the harbour. He sent a signal which was relayed to the British fleet fifty miles further west.

Nelson ordered his battle fleet of twenty seven ships of the line, to shadow the enemy but not engage them. Rhys was on watch aboard HMS Conqueror. He noted the admiral's order in the log and relayed it to Captain Pellew. The British fleet followed for three days until Nelson was ready to attack. On the 21st October at six in the morning Rhys saw new signal flags flying from the Victory's mast.

'Captain Pellew. Victory has signalled, prepare for battle,' shouted Rhys.

'Very well Mr. Vaughn,' replied the captain and altered course. Rhys watched the fleet sail slowly towards the enemy.

'There's another order, Sir. Bear up in succession on the course set by the admiral,' reported Rhys. The ships turned east north east and unfurled more sail. Conqueror was fourth in the line behind Victory. A second line of battle led by Royal Sovereign was to the south. A band was playing Rule Britannia on the Leviathan. Captain Pellew went below to shave and have some breakfast. By nine o'clock the enemy were five miles distant. Captain Pellew toured the ship, dressed in his best uniform, encouraging and reassuring the crew. Gunners stripped to the waist and tied kerchiefs around their heads to protect their ears from the blast of the guns. At eleven o'clock the fleets were three miles apart. Shortly before noon, Nelson signalled, 'England expects that every man will do his duty,' and 17,000 men cheered. Captain Pellew ordered cheese and a ration of rum for the crew. Then, Nelson signalled, 'Engage the enemy more closely.' The signal remained at the masthead until it was shot away. At ten minutes to noon the French ship Fougueux fired a broadside, the opening shots of the Battle of Trafalgar.

A copy of the London Gazette containing an account of the battle reached Merthyr on the 9th November. Admiral Collingwood's report, which was printed in full, described the destruction of the enemy fleet. Collingwood's ship, Royal Sovereign, led the lee attack and was the first British ship to engage the French. The destruction of the enemy's fleet was cause for celebration but it was overshadowed by the loss of Admiral Lord Nelson, shot dead by a French marksman during the battle. Bonaparte's invasion was now impossible; Britain could breathe more easily. After Villeneuve's retreat to Cadiz, Bonaparte had redeployed his invasion army east to invade Russia. Nye and Eira were pleased for the Royal Navy's victory but feared for Rhys. Reports of the battle said, that the Conqueror was in the thick of the action and had captured the French flagship. Admiral Villeneuve had, according to the newspaper report, been taken aboard the Conqueror as the prisoner of Captain Pellew. Was Rhys still alive? Had he been wounded? The Vaughns prayed and waited for news of him.

Part 4 1806 - 1815

Chapter 38

Twenty five years had passed since the young farmer's son walked over the mountain from Llangadog to seek his fortune. Since then, Merthyr Tydfil had changed. The infant iron industry had become a megalith. Four great foundries dominated the town employing several thousand men between them. Many were casual labourers, drifters who came when the price of iron was high and left when demand was low and there was no work. They lived in squalid slums by the River Taff; a place known as China, filled with prostitutes and ragamuffins, where the law of the fist prevailed. Others were skilled iron workers, well paid and looked after by the masters. Their families lived in the company owned terraced houses of Cefn and Georgetown. These were loyal company men who banded together to guard the secrets of their trade, the furnace men, puddlers, cannon borers and forge men. Most of the parishes of Vaynor and Penderyn were owned by the masters. The biggest of the foundries was Castle Iron Works with 25 furnaces, steam driven forges, a foundry, 2 rolling mills and stables for 80 horses. In little more than twenty years Nye Vaughn and his partners had built the biggest industrial complex that the world had ever seen. 60 miles of tramway fed Nye Vaughn's furnaces with coal and iron ore and selling cannons to the navy made him rich while the canal, which was busier than ever, made him richer still.

The Vaughns had moved and were now living in Vaynor Hall, a palladian villa with 36 hearths. The estate included the village of Vaynor, six farms, a deer park and 3,000 acres of high pasture. Vaynor was Nye's rural retreat from the grime of Merthyr, a place where he could relax. Nye had changed. He was heavier and grey hairs revealed his age. The nervous youth had become a self-assured leader, a fair man, quick to make decisions, a man who didn't suffer fools. Some admired him. Others feared his wrath but all the men of Merthyr raised their caps when Mr. Vaughn, the ironmaster, passed.

Isaac Thomas was also making money but, without the profits from the canal, his foundry was smaller and less profitable. Thomas found other ways to augment the profit. His workers were paid with tokens, to be spent in company shops where prices were inflated and credit came at a price. Thomas' workers lived in constant debt to their employer, fearful of the knock of the tally man sent by the master to collect his due. If they didn't pay, the debtor's court, eviction and a jail they called 'the black hole' followed.

Nye Vaughn ripped open the envelope. It looked official; perhaps containing some news of Rhys. Inside was a single piece of card with a black seal. 'Funeral of Lord Nelson. St. Paul's Jan. 9th 1806. Admit the bearer south door. Signed, Bishop of Lincoln – Dean.'

Nye left his carriage at Charing Cross and told the coachman to water and feed the horses. The streets between the Admiralty and St. Paul's were filled with spectators. Every vantage point was taken. It seemed the whole of London wanted to see the funeral cortege of the hero of Trafalgar's, to watch as his funeral car, designed to look like a ship passed by, to tell their children and their grandchildren they were there when the great man was laid to rest. The previous day, Nye had watched Nelson's coffin arriving from Greenwich on the royal barge. He hurried on through the crowd.

Thirty two admirals, a hundred captains, crewmen from Nelson's ship and ten thousand soldiers escorted Admiral Nelson on his last journey. Silent onlookers removed their hats as the procession slowly climbed Ludgate Hill and a sound, like a wave breaking on a shore, rippled through the crowd. It was nearly dark when the coffin was placed beneath the great dome of St. Paul's and the lament of the funeral march died away. High above, one hundred and thirty lanterns pierced the gloom, illuminating the catafalque in a ghostly beam. The black coffin, decorated with ornate golden images of Nelson's life, glittered in the light. Captured enemy flags, once swirling in the whirlwind of battle, hung motionless in silent tribute. Nye Vaughn watched the defeated French Admiral, Villeneuve bow his head as sailors, from HMS Victory carried the coffin to the crypt. They placed the casket in a marble sarcophagus while a herald listed Nelson's titles ending with the words, 'The hero who, in the moment of victory, fell, covered with immortal glory.'

Nye approached several sea captains as they left the cathedral, asking for news of his son but none could help. 'The Conqueror,' they replied, 'was still at sea.' Nelson's funeral had depressed Nye and filled him with a sense of loss. Was he mourning a dead son? He didn't know. Was Rhys lying on the ocean floor or was he crippled, perhaps without a leg or an arm? Nye couldn't say and the pain of not knowing was consuming him. He returned to Merthyr in a pensive mood.

Eira heard the carriage approaching Vaynor Hall and ran outside. She was holding a letter in her hand. She watched as Nye read it.

Dear Mother and Father

By now you will have heard the news of our great victory over the French and Spanish fleets. We chased the enemy across the Atlantic and back before bringing them to battle. Our ship was fourth in the line of attack. We sailed behind the French flagship and fired a broadside through her stern. The shots passed along the length of the ship killing many of her gun crews. Then Captain Pellew took us alongside and a party of marines boarded the enemy whereupon Admiral Villeneuve offered them his sword in surrender. The captain of marines told me he pulled down the enemy's flag and went below. The gun deck was littered with corpses that he had to climb over to reach the powder magazine which he locked, putting the key in his pocket. In all we captured 22 enemy ships. It was a bloody business but God was smiling on the Conqueror and we only had three men killed. After the battle, there was a terrible storm and many of the captured ships were lost. There is some grumbling amongst the crew about losing their prize money but I am just glad to have survived. The sad news of Admiral Nelson's death is almost unbearable. I saw Captian Pellew cry when I gave him the signal. I am well and send the family all my love.

Your obedient son Rhys.

'He's alive,' said Eira with tears in her eyes.

At the end of January, William Paxton called at Castle Iron works. He was returning to Carmarthenshire from London and had important news to share.

'Bonaparte has turned his army east and invaded Austria. He crushed the Russian and Austrian armies at Austerlitz. They say his soldiers slaughtered 30,000 men,' said Paxton.

'The same soldiers that were going to invade us? Thank God we have a navy to keep them from our shores,' replied Nye.

'William Pitt is dead. Some say the stress of war killed him,' said Paxton.

'Was it the stress or the three bottles of port, I heard, he drank every day?' asked Nye.

'There is some good news. Without Pitt's protection, Henry Dundas' enemies have impeached him for misappropriation of public money. The old crook has resigned as First Lord of the Admiralty. He's finished,' said Paxton.

'That is good news. I never liked Dundas. He deserves everything he gets. Will you stay with us at Vaynor this evening? I know Eira would be pleased to see you and we would like to hear more of your plans for Tenby,' said Nye.

'So you've heard about my spa and the hotels?' said Paxton.

'The spa is common knowledge as is the tower you're building at Middleton Hall. It's difficult to spend money and keep it secret,' replied Nye and smiled.

There was another guest at the Vaynor Hall that night, Captain Thomas Foley. Foley was on leave, travelling to his family home Abermarlais near Llangadog. He had stopped at Merthyr to deliver a letter from Rhys. During dinner, the conversation turned to Trafalgar.

'I used to live near Abermarlais. It's a fine Mansion,' said Nye.

'It's been our family home since Henry Tudor gave it to my ancestor Rhys ap Thomas as a reward for his service at Bosworth Field. My father always said Rhys killed Richard III and put the Tudors on the throne,' said Captain Foley.

'Were you at Trafalgar?' asked Eira.

'I was at the Battle of the Nile and had the good fortune to be Nelson's Chief of Staff at Copenhagen but, I'm sorry to say, I missed Trafalgar,' replied Foley.

'When did you see Rhys?' asked Eira.

'The Conqueror was in Gibraltar undergoing repairs when we put in. I had dinner with Captain Pellew and his officers. According to Pellew, your son acquitted himself well during the action and has a good future in the service,' said Foley.

'Now Bonaparte has conquered Austria is he likely to invade us? asked Paxton.

'It's doubtful. We've destroyed his navy and without it he has no way of crossing the channel. Let him stomp across Europe and leave us in peace. That's what I say,' answered Foley.

'According to Major Shrapnel of the Royal Artillery, to end Bonaparte's rampaging we will have to fight a land battle,' said Nye.

'I'm a sailor and know nothing of land warfare but my view is this. With Pitt dead, there's no taste for war in the government. Provided Bonaparte leaves us alone, we'll do nothing to antagonise him,' replied Foley.

'Mr. Paxton, tell us about your tower and the spa at Tenby,' said Eira.

'As you already seem to know, I'm building a tower at Middleton Hall,' said Paxton.

'A tower seems a strange thing to build. What's its purpose?' asked Eira.

'It'll be a place where I can entertain my friends but will also serve as a memorial to Admiral Nelson. I've commissioned stained glass windows commemorating his life. You must come and dine with me when it's finished,' said Paxton.

'And the spa, is that a memorial?' asked Captain Foley.

'No, Captain Foley. The spa is a commercial venture. My plan is for Tenby to be a resort where fashionable people can take the waters and enjoy the recuperative sea air. The spa will open this summer and will, I believe, rival Bath in popularity.'

'It sounds delightful. We shall be your first visitors,' said Eira.

'I shall look forward to your arrival,' replied Paxton.

After their guests had retired Nye and Eira opened Rhys' letter. It was dated 4th January 1806.

Dear Mother and Father

We have been chasing French stragglers from the battle into the Mediterranean and have just returned to Gibraltar for repairs and victuals. Captain Foley has offered to take this letter and deliver it to you, a kindness for which I am grateful. It was Foley who turned the Battle of the Nile to our favour, by sailing around the French van, enabling Nelson to defeat the enemy. They say, Nelson offered him the rank of Captain of the Fleet before Trafalgar but he was unwell and declined, leaving the post open for Captain Hardy.

Last week I undertook my Lieutenant's examination in Admiralty House, Gibraltar and have passed. Your son is now Lieutenant Vaughn. There is talk that Parliament will compensate the crews for lost prize money. If they do I will be rich. After we leave Gibraltar, we are ordered to patrol the Algerian coast where Barbary Pirates are up to their usual tricks.

How is life in Merthyr? Cerys must be a grown woman by now. Is Father still building the biggest cannon foundry in the world? He must be proud to know they were used to defeat a

240

tyrant who is trying to take over the world. I told Captain Pellew about Mr. Jones idea for a breach loading gun and he was interested to learn more. He says new inventions will help make our nation the greatest in the world but machines are useless without determined men to use them. Tell Bryn there is a steam tug in Gibraltar Harbour and it is a fine sight although I know steam will never replace sail for ships of the line. How long is his apprenticeship at Boulton and Watt? Vaynor Hall sounds magnificent. I look forward to seeing it. I think of you often Mother and send you my love.

Your obedient son Rhys.

Chapter 39

John Crichton-Stuart, 2nd Marquess of Bute, greeted Isaac Thomas and offered him a glass of madeira. It was Isaac's first visit to Cardiff Castle. The marquess, descended from an ancient noble family, regarded Thomas as a tradesman but was careful to hide his distain. He needed Isaac Thomas to fulfil a plan that had been developing in his mind for some time. John Crichton-Stuart had watched Merthyr grow with considerable interest and realised the iron industry as an opportunity to make money. The marquess appreciated the dividends from his shares in the Merthyr to Cardiff Canal but he wanted more and Isaac Thomas, he had decided, was the man to get it for him.

'I understand you are considering expanding your foundry but your bankers tell me they are wary of allowing you to over extend yourself,' said the marquess.

'If my bankers told you that, they are impertinent and indiscreet. It's true I would like to expand but profit margins are tight and Castle Iron Works controls the canal,' answered Isaac.

'I can solve your problem with the canal and would like to put up the money required to double the size of your foundry to one that would dwarf Castle Iron,' said the marquess. Isaac sipped his drink and wondered what his host wanted.

'What's the point? There's still the canal. Vaughn fixes the prices to his advantage,' replied Isaac.

'He may control the canal but I own Cardiff Dock and can dictate what he pays to use it.'

Isaac smiled. He was beginning to understand why he had been invited to Cardiff.

'Why do you want to invest in my business?'

'Because your foundry is being squeezed by unfair competition but with my finance and your expertise, we will both get very rich,' explained the marquess. Isaac knew the marquess was right. His business was struggling to compete. If the marquess was able to break Vaughn's transport monopoly and was prepared to provide money to expand the foundry, anything was possible. Best of all, if the docks were closed to Nye Vaughn, he would be finished.

'If I agreed, what would your terms be?' asked Isaac.

'I need to protect my investment. That means I would have a controlling shareholding in the foundry,' replied the marquess. The marquess' audacity surprised Isaac. He was being asked to give away control of his company.

'I appreciate any concerns you may have and I'm happy to give certain guarantees regarding your own future,' added the marquess.

'You're asking me to give you control of my foundry.'

'It's better to have part of something big than all of nothing,' said the marquess.

'What do you mean by that?'

'If I choose to stop Vaughn using my docks because it's to my advantage, what is there to stop me doing the same to you?' said the marquess.

'You're saying, if I don't agree, you'll put me out of business.'

'You make it sound melodramatic,' said the marquess and offered his visitor another glass of madeira. The marquess' threat stung Isaac, who had no intention of relinquishing control of anything. He looked at the marquess and saw a naive, greedy man with a high opinion of himself, a man who was contemptuous of others, a man who might be of some use.

'My Lord, if you believe you can close your docks to my foundry or Castle Iron you're misguided. Firstly, you would face an expensive legal battle which you might lose and secondly, you would certainly lose valuable tariffs from the iron shipments,' said Isaac.

'You may be right but don't underestimate me, Mr. Thomas. I'm not a man to cross,' said the marquess.

'I've no desire to cross you. Quite the opposite, I propose we become allies and work to our mutual advantage. I'm unwilling to give you control of my foundry but there is a way to achieve what we both want. Let me explain,' said Isaac and poured another drink for himself.

Benjamin Griffiths made a note in the ledger, leaned back in his chair and stretched his arms in the air. He had just completed checking Castle Iron Work's monthly accounts. Benjamin smiled to himself. The turnover was up on last year and profit was well above target. Benjamin liked to check the chief clerks work. He didn't need to. Mistakes were rare but it was satisfying to run his practiced eye down and across the columns to make sure they balanced. Benjamin Griffiths removed his spectacles and slowly got up from the desk. The pain in his back and legs was worse than usual. He walked stiffly to the window where he caught sight of his reflection in the glass. For a moment, he didn't recognise the grey haired old man who stared back at him. A thrush, perched on the gutter below the window, attracted his attention. It was singing proudly, calling for a mate or defending its territory, he wasn't sure which. Benjamin marvelled at the brightness of the spots on thrush's body. It was so close. He could almost reach out of the window and touch it. Benjamin stumbled and hit the window, disturbing the bird which flew away. He felt giddy and there was a pain in the centre of his chest, as if it was being crushed by an elephant. In the outer office, the clerks heard a crash and rushed to investigate. They found the Finance Director on the floor. His heart had stopped.

The body was watched for three days in case life returned and, knowing him to have been an honest man, the family refused to let the sin eater enter the house. No one was going to eat a meal from the coffin lid to consume his sins. There was no production at Castle Iron Works or at any of the other foundries on the day of Benjamin Griffith's funeral. The people of Merthyr gathered to show their respect for a man who was liked by all. The church was full and the congregation overflowed into the graveyard where hundreds of mourners stood in silence, unable to hear the readings or the minister's prayers. When the sound of hymns spilled from the church, a few of the mourners in the graveyard joined in. Others, self-conscious and unsure of themselves, stood silent. They watched awkwardly as the family followed Benjamin to his grave, his sobbing widow helped by her daughters.

The next day, there was a meeting in the board room at Castle Iron Works.

'What'll happen to his shares?' asked Will Jones.

'That's a matter for the family to decide. We must give them time to come to terms with what has happened but I believe they will want us to buy them out,' replied Nye.

'They might want to keep the shares. What then?' asked William Paxton.

'Then, they would be entitled to continue sharing in the profit and have the right to appoint a director to the board. If they do, Benjamin's son Alan would be an excellent candidate. He has his father's eye for numbers,' said Nye.

'We can manage with the chief clerk doing Ben's work for the present. I propose we leave matters as they are for a month. Then, if the family have said nothing, we will ask them what they want to do,' suggested Will. There were nods of agreement.

'Have you heard the news from France? Bonaparte has declared a continental blockade against Britain. He says, any country that trades with us will be severely punished,' said Paxton.

'Do we have any customers on the continent?' asked Nye.

'We have several customers in Russia and Portugal. They have placed some orders due for delivery in the next three months,' answered Will.

'We must ask for payment in advance and complete the orders as quickly as possible, before Bonaparte's blockade takes effect,' ordered Nye.

'I have another matter we need to discuss. The puddlers are agitating for more money again. They claim their skills are undervalued but this time someone is organising them and there is talk of them taking action,' said Will.

'What sort of action?' asked Nye.

'I don't know.'

'I won't have anarchy. Pay someone to tell you what's going on; find out who the ringleaders are and make an example of them. When you discover who's responsible for causing trouble, fire them and, if necessary, evict the families,' ordered Nye.

'That's a harsh way to treat a man and his family. It's the sort of thing Isaac Thomas would do,' said Paxton.

'Your comment is unfair. Understand this, there can only be one master here,' answered Nye angrily.

In July, Nye and Eira travelled to Middleton Hall to stay with the Paxtons. In the evening, carriages collected the party from the hall and took them through the park to a wooded hill where the road climbed to the summit and a triangular gothic tower. The tower had roof terraces and crenellated turrets at each corner.

'I employed Scottish stonemasons to build the tower. It reminds me of Edinburgh, where I was born,' said Paxton as they approached. The carriages entered an archway at the bottom of the tower, where the passengers alighted and climbed stairs leading to the second floor.

'This is the panorama room. What do you think of the views?' asked Paxton. The visitors admired the scenery stretching out before them. The River Towy meandering along the valley floor, Carmarthen to the west and, to the east, the ruin of Dryslwyn Castle and the Carmarthenshire Fans beyond.

'The views are spectacular but what's this inscription?' asked Nye.

'It's a Latin dedication to Lord Nelson. There's one in Welsh on that wall and a third, over there, in English,' said Paxton pointing to the far wall. The party descended to the room below where a banquet had been laid out. Liveried servants stood ready to serve. Three fires warmed the room while late evening rays of the sun shone through stained glass windows illuminated with images of Nelson's famous battles.

'It's a magnificent monument to Nelson. You must be proud,' said Eira as a servant poured her wine.

'I am, but there's another reason I built it,' said Paxton.

246

'What was that?' asked Eira.

'To show I didn't bankrupt myself, buying votes, as my opponent claimed,' replied Paxton.

'Why bother. You shouldn't listen to jealous fools,' said Nye. William Paxton was silent for a moment.

'You're right but it's important to me. You see I wasn't always rich. My father was a wine merchant's clerk in Edinburgh and I went to sea as a cabin boy when I was twelve,' explained Paxton.

'Then we both come from humble stock and there's no shame in it,' said Nye.

'Enough of this talk,' said Paxton, 'Tomorrow I'm taking you to Tenby to see my new bath house. Sea bathing is all the rage. There are two pools so ladies and gentlemen can enjoy the water without embarrassment. After we have bathed, I suggest the warm vapour rooms and in the evening we'll attend the theatre.'

'Where will we stay?' asked Eira.

'I have a house there with fine views of the sea,' replied Paxton.

'Did you hear about Admiral Villeneuve? He was released and returned to France where he was found dead in a hotel room. He'd been stabbed six times. The French said he committed suicide because of the shame of defeat,' said Nye.

'Six stab wounds. That sounds like murder to me, Bonaparte's idea of justice,' said Paxton.

The conversation continued as they ate and it was dark when the carriages returned, to Middleton Hall, accompanied by footmen with torches.

The visit to Tenby was a success. William Paxton's dream of turning the town into a holiday resort for the gentry had been organised to the last detail. He provided a new water supply for the town, built lodging houses, billiard rooms and a ballroom for the visitors to enjoy. The Vaughns returned to Merthyr invigorated and unprepared for bad news.

Chapter 40

The letter from Birmingham was abrupt and said little, other than Bryn had been involved in an accident at Boulton and Watt's steam engine factory. 'Come to Soho Foundry as quickly as you are able,' said the footnote. The carriage drove through the night stopping only to change horses. James Watt met them at the foundry's main gate and led the way to a small cottage inside the works. Bryn was asleep in an upstairs room. His face was bandaged.

'What happened?' whispered Nye. James Watt beckoned for Nye to follow him from the room.

'The men were testing a boiler when it exploded. Four of them were standing near it. Two were killed immediately and the third died this morning. Your son is the only survivor,' answered Watt.

'What's wrong with him?' asked Nye.

'The steam stripped his skin away and the doctor says he's in a deep sleep. We've tried but we haven't been able to wake him,' said Watt.

'Does the doctor say he'll recover?

'He doesn't know but he told me to stop trying to wake Bryn. While he's asleep he can't feel the pain.'

'Thank you. Is there somewhere nearby we can stay? My wife will want to be with him,' asked Nye.

'With your permission, we'll move him to my house. It isn't far and there's room for you all,' said Watt. Nye thanked him again and went into the bedroom. Eira was kneeling beside the bed, holding Bryn's hand.

The doctor called at the house every morning and dressed Bryn's face and hands with cotton wadding soaked in carron

248

oil. When Eira saw how badly he was scalded she cried out. Bryn's face looked like raw meat on a butchers slab. At night they took turns keeping a bedside vigil in case he woke. Eira was sat reading on the fourth night when she heard a moan. Bryn had thrown back the bedclothes and his bandaged hands were in the air. He was trying to touch his face.

'Nye, come quickly, he's awake! Shhhh your mother's here,' she whispered and gently lowered Bryn's arms as she soothed him.

A week later, they took Bryn back to Vaynor. His convalescence was slow and painful but as the weeks passed the swelling on his face and hands went down, leaving strawberry scars he would wear for the rest of his life. But the steam had burnt deeper into his skull than any of them realised. It had affected his mind and disfigured it, like an acid, leaving him sullen and morose, afraid and guilty for surviving when his friends had died. Nye tried to talk to his son, to tell him to act like a man but Bryn wasn't listening. He didn't want to hear about others who were worse off or how lucky he was. His depression affected his mother most of all. When he ignored her, she got angry and upset with herself. No one knew what to do except wait and hope.

The Christmas of 1806 was subdued at Vaynor. Because of Bryn's depression no one felt like celebrating. Eira's cheerful attempts to lift family spirits had little effect while Nye retreated to the foundry to escape the gloom that had engulfed the house. The New Year passed unnoticed but in early January visitors arrived, bringing fresh hope and laughter.

It was early in the morning. There had been a heavy frost during the night and the ground was white when a carriage pulled up at the front of Vaynor Hall and two naval officers emerged. Eira watched them walk across the gravel. One was tall and walked with an air of authority whilst the second was shorter but looked equally confident. She heard the bell ring and listened as the footman went to enquire who the visitors were. There was muffled talking and footsteps. The door opened and the footman announced two gentlemen to see Mrs Vaughn. The taller officer stepped into the room and removed his hat. It was Rhys, home after four years at sea. Four years in which he had grown from a youth to a man. Eira hadn't recognised him until he took off his hat.

'Why didn't you tell us you were coming?' she said as she hugged him.

'We only have a few days. I wanted to come as quickly as possible,' replied Rhys. Cerys, who had heard the carriage, rushed into the room.

'Rhys,' she cried and ran over to him, 'you're home. I'm so glad to see you.' Rhys remembered his companion who was standing awkwardly in the doorway.

'This is my friend Captain Howard,' said Rhys.

'I'm pleased to meet you Mrs. Vaughn, Miss Vaughn.' said Captain Howard.

'Why is your uniform red?' asked Cerys.

'Because I'm a captain of marines,' answered the captain. The other striking feature of Captain Howard's appearance was his face. There was a large scar from his temple to the side of his jaw and he only had one eye.

'What happened to your face?' asked Cerys.

'Cerys, don't be impertinent. It's rude to ask questions like that,' scolded Eira.

'Don't worry Mrs Vaughn. The scar is a souvenir from Trafalgar. I got it when we boarded a French ship. I'm proud of it and I still have one good eye,' said Captain Howard and grinned.

'Where's father and Bryn? asked Rhys.

'Bryn's in his room and father is at the foundry. I'll send a messenger to fetch him,' said Eira.

'I read your letter telling of Bryn's accident. How is he?'

'He's very low in spirit. He seldom speaks and rarely comes out of his room,' answered Eira.

'Come, Howard. You must meet my brother,' said Rhys and led his friend upstairs.

They knocked on the door and entered Bryn's bedroom, without waiting for an answer. Bryn was in a chair by the window. He looked up.

'How are you Bryn? Are you pleased to see your older brother, home from the sea? cried Rhys. The brothers embraced. Then, Bryn saw Captain Howard and drew back in horror.

'I'm John Howard, a friend of your brother's. Don't mind my face. It doesn't bother me,' said the captain and offered his hand.

'Was it an accident?' asked Bryn starring at the scar.

'No. A French sailor slashed me with a cutlass. I'm lucky. A bit closer and he would have cut my head in two,' said Howard, 'How did yours happen?'

'A steam boiler burst, scalding me. Three other men died,' answered Bryn.

'Then we're both lucky. Look at us, a man with a sliced melon for a head and another with a strawberry face. We must walk down the street together. No one will forget us,' said Howard and laughed.

'You're a madman,' said Bryn.

Howard stopped laughing, 'I'm not mad. I thank God I'm alive. How do you cope?' Bryn didn't answer.

That evening Bryn dressed for dinner, the first time for many months, and ate with the family. He had changed. For the first time since the accident he engaged in conversation, asking about Trafalgar and talking about his own future. Bryn had decided to go back to Boulton and Watts' to complete his apprenticeship. John Howard's disregard for his injuries and his positive outlook had shamed Bryn and made him realise how lucky he was.

During their short stay, Rhys and his friend were made welcome everywhere they went and there were tears when they departed. Cerys was in love with John Howard with the intensity of a fifteen year old adolescent. Undaunted by his disfigured face, she dreamed of marrying Howard and imagined life as the wife of a naval hero. In return John Howard thought her childish and awkward looking but, being a gentleman, kept his opinions to himself.

Isaac Thomas studied the plans for the new foundry carefully. The design was good and he was particularly pleased with the layout of the furnaces. Raw materials were plentiful and choosing the Sirhowy Valley as the site offered another advantage. It was close to the Monmouthshire Canal. Thomas had negotiated discounted transport rates for using the canal which gave him an economic route to Newport and the sea. Sirhowy would be free of Vaughn's extortionate canal charges. The partnership with Tredegar's owner, Sir Charles Morgan, had been surprisingly easy to arrange. Sir Charles was also growing tired of paying Vaughn's inflated charges for transporting coal on the canal and wanted to enter the iron industry. To him, leasing the Sirhowy Valley, to Isaac Thomas, while taking a share in the business was the logical thing to do.

Isaac had also agreed to build a foundry at Rhymney in partnership with the Marquess of Bute but knew Bute was greedy and could not be trusted. The arrangement with Sir Charles Morgan was a way of insuring against Bute's

252

avarice. Isaac Thomas was manipulating powerful allies and using their money to build a business where the risks were spread and he would be in control, a business so large and complex no one could dictate terms or threaten him. Combined with Thomas' existing works, the two new foundries would make him the biggest iron producer in South Wales, one capable of taking back what Nye Vaughn had stolen from him.

The February board meeting at Castle Iron Works was guaranteed to be lively. Nye Vaughn was angry. Things had been happening which threatened the foundry.

'Read the letter again,' said Nye. The lawyer read it aloud.

Sirs,

The Marquess of Bute has instructed me to inform you that his assets, namely the facilities in Cardiff Dockyard, are not returning a satisfactory profit. Consequently he has no option other than to adjust the tariffs for using the port. The charges levied on all iron goods passing through Cardiff will increase by 100% in 30 days from the above date in accordance with our terms and conditions of trade. If the directors of Castle Iron Works prefer to take their business elsewhere, his Grace requires a similar period of notice to be given.

Signed
Alan Owen
Secretary to his Lordship

'If we prefer to take our business elsewhere! We can't go anywhere else. The canal goes to Cardiff,' bellowed Nye.
'Can Bute double the prices like that?' asked Will Jones.

'I've looked at his terms of contract and he can, providing he gives 30 days notice,' said the lawyer.

'Who signed the contract?' demanded Nye.

'Benjamin Griffiths but it's not entirely his fault. The small print is very complex,' explained the lawyer.

'What else can he do? Can he cancel the contract?' asked Nye.

'I'm afraid he can. He owns the docks. If he wanted to, he could stop you using Cardiff all together,' replied the lawyer. The room was silent as they contemplated the consequences.

'Why has he done it? He must know we'll react somehow,' said Paxton.

'The man's a bully. He's up to something and we need to find out what. I'm going to go and see him,' said Nye.

'What about the increase? Do we pay it?' asked Will.

'If you don't he can close the docks to you without giving notice,' warned the lawyer.

'There's a small dock at Barry. How far is it from Cardiff?' asked Nye. Will produced a map and unfolded it.

'It's six miles from Cardiff. Why?'

'We could cut an extension to the canal and move all the trade that uses Cardiff to Barry, coal, iron, limestone; everything that he earns revenue from. That would teach his lordship an expensive lesson,' answered Nye.

'It'll take time,' said Will.

'What are the other problems you wanted to discuss?' asked Nye.

'We're short of work in the foundry for March and April. Do we cut wages or lay off men?' asked Will. Nye Vaughn looked at Paxton and smiled.

'When we met a while ago, you told me I was acting like Isaac Thomas because I wanted to sack some troublemakers. Thomas sends men home without pay when there's no work but I'm not like him. Keep all the men

254

working on full wages and stockpile until things pick up,' ordered Nye. 'What's the other issue?'

'It's canal business really. Sir Charles Morgan has given notice that he intends to stop using the canal. I understand he's building a tramway to deliver coal from his mines to the Monmouthshire Canal instead,' replied Will, 'If he goes, others will follow.'

'Perhaps it's time we looked at how much we're charging and lower the prices,' suggested Paxton.

'I agree. Find out the Monmouth Canal tariffs and we'll undercut them,' said Nye.

Nye Vaughn made some enquiries before he visited Cardiff Castle. The Marquess of Bute seemed affable enough but Nye knew it was going to be a difficult meeting. Building a canal extension to Barry would be impossible because Bute owned land between the two ports. Somehow he had to negotiate new, more favourable, terms for using Cardiff Docks and avoid antagonising the marquess who, if he felt inclined, could strangle Castle Iron Works.

'I've come to discuss the tariff increase you are proposing for my company,' said Nye.

'I'm not proposing a tariff increase, Mr. Vaughn, I'm raising them in two weeks time,' replied Bute.

'Such an increase will cause Castle Iron considerable hardship. Our order book is diminished and we are already considering laying off men. Doubled charges will be difficult to pay,' said Nye.

'Your labour relations are no concern of mine,' said Bute.

'I have another problem. We have been notified that several of our canal users are switching to the Monmouthshire canal and will be shipping through Newport,' said Nye. The marquess was suddenly more interested in what Nye had to say.

'Which users?'

'You haven't heard? Sir Charles Morgan for one and Isaac Thomas. He's building a new foundry at Sirhowy and will be using Newport. It seems our loss will also be yours,' said Nye and waited for a reaction. Bute seemed surprised by the news of Thomas' Sirhowy foundry.

'How are you going to deal with your loss of trade, Mr. Vaughn?'

'We no longer have a monopoly and will be forced to reduce our tariffs in order to remain competitive. Of course, if we fail, you will have the same problem since my canal feeds your docks. Might I ask how you would deal with your loss of trade?' asked Nye.

The news that Isaac Thomas had deceived the marquess and goaded him into challenging Nye Vaughn, one of the biggest users of the docks, infuriated Bute but he would deal with Thomas later.

'It seems we need each other,' said Bute.

'If I can increase the volume of coal passing through Cardiff, will you help me in return?' asked Nye.

'I'll withdraw your price increase. I know coal exports will grow in the future and I want to control the trade,' said Bute.

'I'm relieved we are agreed and can tell you that my engineers have already made plans to extend the canal to serve other coal mines,' said Nye, 'but we need a new contract between us. One that ensures our relationship is permanent and neither of us does anything disagreeable. Shall I ask my lawyers to draft it?' The Marquess of Bute nodded.

Chapter 41

In July 1807 the Russian Tsar signed a peace treaty with Bonaparte when the two emperors met on a specially constructed raft in the middle of Neman River. The Prussians followed suit and made peace with France. The 'Treaties of Tilsit' as they were known gave Bonaparte control of most of Europe and much of Russia. Only Britain and Sweden stood against him. Portugal had ignored the continental blockade, ordered by Bonaparte and, on the 19th November 1807, a French army invaded. The Portuguese were not prepared for war. The country was quickly occupied and the Portuguese Royal Family fled to Brazil. Britain's treaty obligations required her to defend Portugal. By attacking Portugal, Bonaparte had dragged Great Britain into the European land war. Henry Shrapnel's dinner conversation when he predicted the only way to stop the French Dictator was for the British to defeat him in a land battle was going to be tested.

Nye Vaughn read the newspaper report and reached for an atlas. According to the paper, on the 29th July 1808, Sir Arthur Wellesley had landed in Mondengo Bay, Portugal with 9,000 men. There was no trace of Mondengo Bay on the map. Nye returned to the paper which said that Portuguese citizens, who had been crippled by French taxes, were revolting and the country was in turmoil. Bonaparte, it added, was rushing reinforcements in from France.

'So it's happened at last. We've landed an army in Portugal,' he said and handed the newspaper to Bryn.

'It seems a rather small army. Can 9,000 men defeat Bonaparte?' asked Bryn.

'No, but it's a start. More will follow,' replied his father.

'There's an obituary here for John Wilkinson. Says he died on the 14th July. I met him when I was working at Boulton and Watt. We used his boring machines for making steam engine cylinders,' said Bryn.

'There are two of Wilkinson's machines in the foundry. We use them for boring cannons,' said Nye.

'Listen to this Father. The corpse of Mr. Wilkinson whose sobriquet was 'Iron Mad Wilkinson' has been buried in a cast iron coffin in the grounds of his Castlehead home. His family have placed a 40ft tall iron obelisk weighing more than twenty tons there as his monument.'

'Future owners might not appreciate such an ornament. What are you doing today?' asked Nye.

'I'm in the forging shop today. The steam hammer isn't working properly and I think I know why,' replied Bryn.

'You should be learning the commercial side of the business. We employ mechanics to run the machines. I need you with me to manage the business,' said Nye.

'I will. I promise,' replied Bryn.

Nye's strategy for dealing with the Marquess of Bute was a success. Bute signed a new contract and, as promised, withdrew the price increase. Reducing the canal tariffs persuaded the mine owners to continue using the waterway and ship coal through Cardiff. Connecting the canal to more mines further boosted the volume of coal. Cardiff was becoming the centre of the international coal trade. The Marquess of Bute's ambitions were being fulfilled. He didn't forget Isaac Thomas' treachery and publicly accused him of being a liar and a scoundrel, a charge which Thomas denied. Hearing the accusations, Sir Charles Morgan, who was paying for the new foundry at Sirhowy Valley, instructed his accountants to inspect Thomas' records to make sure there were no improprieties. Construction was well under way and he had already parted with a considerable sum of money.

Cerys Vaughn's infatuation with the marine, John Howard, hadn't diminished even after a year apart. She wrote to him regularly and he was replying although the unreliable post resulted in long gaps between the letters. At first, the letters were awkward but as she became more confident, the communication between them grew into something more than just a young girl's idea of love. The letters going both ways were expressions of fondness between two people. The letters from John Howard were more frequent than Rhys' and contained news of their daily existence which Rhys thought of no interest and not worth reporting. Cerys hid the early letters from her family but before long she was sharing them with Eira who could see how important they were to her daughter. They learned of John Howard's background as a minister's son from Yorkshire and that his father had died while John was a boy. Much of the time, the Conqueror patrolled the coasts of Portugal and Spain looking for French ships to attack. They also searched for Barbary Pirates. The pirates had signed a peace treaty but were still harassing ships and taking unfortunate crewmen to be sold into slavery. From his letters, they learned Conqueror had escorted a fleet, carrying the Portuguese Royal Family and the country's treasures, to Rio de Janeiro. John Howard's last letter, dated 4th November 1808 said the Conqueror was coming home and Captain Pellew had promised his officers they would be granted shore leave. John Howard and Rhys expected to be in Merthyr for Christmas. The letter which was delivered to Vaynor Hall on the 14th December caused great excitement in the Vaughn household.

Eira was already organising for Christmas, when the news of Rhys' imminent arrival was delivered. The whole family would be together for Christmas for the first time in seven years and Eira was determined to make the holiday special. The Hall was decorated with holly, ivy and a large fir tree illuminated with tapers in the new German style introduced by Queen Charlotte. Invitations were sent to family and friends to attend a ball at the house. There were musicians to book, menus to prepare and servants to instruct. Guest rooms were opened and fires lit to air them. Her enthusiasm was infectious and soon almost everyone was helping. Cerys took charge of the decorations, Bryn organised a shoot while Nye retreated to the foundry.

Rhys and his John Howard arrived at Vaynor on the 21st. That evening there was a family dinner. Nye's brother and sister, Richard and Anwen had travelled from Llangadog, leaving a neighbour to tend the farm animals. They dined in candlelight and the flames reflected from the mirrors and the silverware. Rhys and John Howard competed to entertain the party, describing their adventures, exaggerating as young men sometimes do. The talk and laughter continued late into the night. The next day John Howard and Cerys went for a walk and other guests started to arrive. William and Anne Paxton and their ten children were first. The smaller children filled the house with noise. Captain Williams and Mrs Williams arrived soon after, followed by Will Jones, his wife and other important guests. Nye and Eira were surrounded by the people they loved and cared for.

The houseguests spent the afternoon playing games and, after supper, the gentlemen retired to the billiard room leaving the ladies to entertain themselves.

'Did you have a pleasant walk with Captain Howard? Where did you go?' asked Eira and winked at Anne Paxton.

'Yes, thank you. I showed Mr. Howard the gardens. He was particularly taken by the hot houses and said the pineapples are as fine as ones he once saw growing in Brazil,' replied Cerys.

'What else did he say?' asked Eira.

'Nothing much really. We talked about the weather,' said Cerys awkwardly. She was beginning to feel uncomfortable.

'Pineapples and weather! Is that all? He wasn't tongue tied last night at dinner. I think you have an admirer in Captain Howard,' said Eira.

'He follows you round like a puppy. Has he declared his affection?' asked Anne Paxton. Cerys blushed.

'He told me he cares for me and I replied with the same sentiment. Then he said, it's best that we just remain friends,' said Cerys.

'What a strange fellow. Why did he say that?' asked Anne Paxton.

'He says he would find life at sea intolerable knowing I was waiting for him,' replied Cerys emotionally and dabbed the corner of her eye with a handkerchief.

'He makes a valid observation. Think of this. Rhys has only been home twice in seven years. To be separated from a husband for such long periods would be extremely painful,' said Anne Paxton.

'I don't care. I don't want to be an old maid.'

'Cerys. You're sixteen. You have years to find a suitable husband,' said Eira.

'I was fifteen when I married and far too young. I was still a child,' said Mrs. Jones who, until then, had been sitting quietly.

'I'm seventeen in three days,' snapped Cerys.

'Yes, you'll be seventeen and still be young and in love. Now there are four of us, let's have a game of cards,' said Eira.

The men were up early the following morning to go shooting. They rode along the Taff Fechan Valley to the woods above Pontsticill where beaters were waiting to drive the birds towards the guns. After a good mornings sport during which Captain Howard demonstrated he was an excellent shot, the ladies joined them for lunch at the Red Cow Tavern. The afternoon was spent rough shooting on farmland, further up the valley. The shooting party returned to the Vaynor Hall tired but in good spirits, to bathe and dress ready for the evening's grand ball.

Carriages began to arrive at seven o'clock and the visitors were shown to the ballroom. It promised to be a glittering social occasion. The first dance was a minuet followed by 'Miss Smith's Hornpipe'. Next, the orchestra played a lively cotillion and, although it was frowned on in London society, onlookers clapped to encourage the dancers while the older women sat fanning themselves and muttering disapprovingly. Not all the dancers knew the intricate steps needed to change partners at the right moment but it all added to the merriment. Cerys had several young admirers and her dancing card soon filled up, a fact she made clear when Captain Howard asked her to dance. Rhys, who had two left feet, found himself dancing with Julie, the Paxton's eldest daughter, an attractive girl with a wicked sense of humour. She teased him when they danced the 'Caledonia Reel' so exuberantly that he nearly fell over but he didn't mind and they remained dancing partners for most of the evening. Nye Vaughn, who hated dancing, accompanied Eira onto the dance floor for 'The Campbells are Coming' and then, having done what he thought was expected, he excused himself, preferring to talk with the men. The last dance of the evening was 'Upon a Summers Day'. Almost everyone was on the dance floor including Nye who had been dragged away from the punch by Eira.

On Christmas Eve a choir from the foundry visited Vaynor Hall and Eira rewarded the choristers for their performance with mulled wine and modest gifts. The concert was followed by dinner and then the house party wrapped up in warm clothes, for it was a clear frosty night, and walked down the hill to Vaynor Church to celebrate midnight mass. Near the end of the service, when the minister opened the poor box, he was pleased to find it full and astonished to discover that someone had given twenty pounds. He searched the faces of the congregation but there was no indication of who the generous benefactor was.

Nye and his guests joined the Dolygaer Hunt at the Penyrheol Inn on Christmas morning, arriving just as the innkeeper emerged with hot toddies to warm the riders. The chase was good and they took three foxes, the last, a large dog fox, going to ground under a wooden bridge at the bottom of a gorge. They watched as the terrier men dug it out. Suddenly, the fox broke free and escaped along the riverbank. The dogs gave chase followed by the riders. The fleeing fox was strong and ran for six miles before it was cornered and despatched. In the evening, they celebrated Cerys' seventeenth birthday and, when they were alone, Captain Howard gave her a small box.

'What is it?' she asked.

'Open it and find out,' replied the captain. She opened the box and her eyes shone. Inside was a gold ring mounted with tiny intertwined hearts. Cerys slid it on her finger.

'Do you see the hearts? It's a fide ring. I give it to you as a token of our fidelity. Fide is Latin for faith. Will you wear it for me? asked the captain.

'Are you proposing marriage?' asked Cerys. Captain Howard lowered his eyes.

'Cerys, if you asked me to leave the sea I would, but you must understand, I have no other profession and would not be able to support you. I want us to marry but we must wait until I can find a way,' replied the captain. Cerys held her hand up and Howard kissed her finger.

'I believe you have just offered an engagement. I will wear your ring for as long as you ask, until you are ready to place a wedding ring on my finger,' said Cerys. Captain Howard hesitated before he spoke, 'If you wish, I'll speak to your father about our future but you must realise it may be a long engagement.'

On Boxing Day, Nye took his guests to view the foundry. They watched a steam hammer in the forging shop, rhythmically rising and falling while men positioned the red hot metal between strikes. The ground shook each time it dropped.

'The hammer weighs six tons,' shouted Nye, 'What do you think?'

'It looks dangerous work,' replied Captain Howard. Nye nodded.

'This is where we make the cannons,' said Bryn in the casting shed.

'That's a strange looking gun,' said the captain pointing to a cannon that appeared to be in pieces.

'It's my partner's project, said Nye as they approached the cannon.

'This is something I've have been trying to perfect for a while, a breech loading cannon,' said Will Jones.

'Does it work?' asked Captain Howard.

'Unfortunately not. We can't find a way to seal the breech. It won't contain the explosive charge,' replied Will.

'I saw a Ferguson Rifle at Chatham Arsenal. That was loaded through the breech. Only a hundred were ever made. Apparently the army used them during the American Revolutionary War but they were too expensive to manufacture so they were replaced with Brown Bess muskets. Muskets are cheaper and, in my opinion, more reliable,' said Captain Howard.

That evening, back at Vaynor Hall, Captain Howard asked to speak to Nye privately and Nye showed him to the study. Nye offered the captain a chair and poured two whiskies. He handed one to Captain Howard. The captain, who had shown no fear as he leapt aboard a French warship in the midst of battle, was feeling rather nervous and took a large mouthful. He shuddered as the malt liquor hit his stomach.

'What do you want to talk about?' asked Nye.

'Mr. Vaughn, I believe you know how fond I am of Cerys. I want to ask your permission for us to get engaged,' said Captain Howard. Nye had already guessed the reason for the private talk and had prepared his response. Earlier he had discussed the possibility with Eira who had told him not to embarrass the young suitor. He didn't intend to cause embarrassment but there were important questions to ask.

'How old are you Captain Howard?' asked Nye.

'I'm 24, Sir.'

'Do you have any money?'

'My father left me £300 when he passed away, I have £161 prize money from Trafalgar and I have my captain's pay.'

'And what are your prospects? Can you support Cerys?'

'If I stay in the marines I might rise to the rank of colonel. Yes I can support her, maybe not immediately to your standard but that's not what I'm asking.' replied Captain Howard.

'You said, you wanted to marry my daughter,' said Nye.

'I do, but that wasn't my question,' said Howard, 'I asked for your permission to get engaged. Cerys and I have discussed our future and agreed that we'll delay the wedding until we can be together and I can provide for her properly.'

'Are you thinking of leaving the navy?' asked Nye.

'I'm not sure, Sir. It would be a big step.'

'So is getting married. Forgive me for saying this but your plan seems rather vague. You say, you're going to wait but for how long? How long a delay are you talking about and more to the point, when you do marry, how will you provide for her? That's the question I must have an answer to,' said Nye. Captain Howard made no reply.

'I thought so, you have no ideas and no plan for the future,' said Nye, 'That's a serious problem and there is another we must consider. Cerys is only seventeen and, in my view, still a child.'

'That's the other reason I wanted to delay,' said the captain. Nye held a finger up to his lips and contemplated the situation.

'Here is what I suggest. I will agree to your engagement to Cerys but there are three conditions. The first is, the wedding cannot take place before a year has passed and she has reached her eighteenth birthday; the second is, if she changes her mind you will release her from the contract without penalty or disgrace,' said Nye.

'What's the third condition?'

'Before you marry my daughter you must obtain a position for yourself where there is potential for advancement and profit,' said Nye.

'That would mean resigning my commission,' Captain Howard paused, 'I'm willing to give up the sea for Cerys but where will I find such a position?'

'There's an opportunity at Castle Iron Works. It would involve learning the business but I believe in time you would make an excellent commercial manager, possibly, with enough experience, even a director,' said Nye.

'Your offer is unexpected. I'll need to think about it,' said Captain Howard.

'If you need time to think, I question your proposal. Which of the two is causing you concern? Your love for my daughter, or the sincerity of my proposition?' asked Nye.

'You're a hard man to refuse Mr. Vaughn but I'll not give you an answer immediately. I accept your first two conditions but the third is problematic. For one thing, your offer of a position would leave me in your debt and, for another, I'm proud of my life and what I've achieved. What's more, I believe Cerys would be happy as a sailor's wife,' said

266

Captain Howard. Nye was pleased with Howard's answer. It showed integrity and strength of character.

'So you accept the first two conditions.'

'I believe I've already said so.'

'Then I withdraw the third condition and give my consent to your engagement to my daughter. If you are interested in joining the business, later on, we will discuss it. Now, your fiancé and her mother will be getting anxious so I suggest we go and break the good news,' said Nye and shook Howard's hand.

Chapter 42

Isaac Thomas was on his way to inspect the construction site at Sirhowy when a rider approached and stopped his carriage. The building work at the foundry was nearly complete and Isaac expected to start producing iron within weeks. Isaac recognised the horseman; he was the master stonemason finishing the new furnaces. The stonemason's face was cut and bruised. He told Isaac a gang of ruffians had attacked the workmen, beaten them with clubs and driven them from the site. Questioning the stonemason further, he learned the gang had told the fleeing men that Sirhowy Foundry was being seized on the orders of Sir Charles Morgan. Isaac continued to Sirhowy and finding the foundry guarded by armed men, he rode to Tredegar House to obtain an explanation and an apology from Sir Charles.

Arriving at Tredegar, Isaac demanded to see Sir Charles but was directed, instead, to the estate manager's office, in an annex at the rear of the mansion. The estate manager, whose predecessor Evan Jenkins had mysteriously drowned in the canal some years earlier, kept Isaac waiting for half an hour. When, eventually, Isaac was admitted to the office he was in a foul mood.

'Why are there armed men at Sirhowy Foundry and why have my workmen been beaten?' shouted Isaac. The estate manger looked up from his desk.

'You're shouting, Mr. Thomas. There is no need. I have perfectly good hearing,' said the estate manager.

'I'll do more than shout if I don't get some satisfactory answers,' bellowed Isaac. The estate manager opened a drawer and produced a pistol which he placed on the desk.

'Really, and what more will you do?' said the manager calmly. Isaac looked at the gun.

'I want to know what's going on,' said Isaac. His voice was more controlled now.

'It's very simple. You've been caught swindling Sir Charles Morgan. His accountants have found large fraudulent entries in your ledgers for materials and labour that have been used elsewhere,' said the estate manager.

'That's a damn lie,' said Isaac.

'Think very carefully before you call me a liar,' said the estate manager patting the pistol, 'We have proof of your deceit. My men have followed deliveries, paid for by Sir Charles, to a foundry at Rhymney. You've been building another works with Sir Charles' money.'

'Rhymney is nothing to do with Sir Charles. I have a legal contract with Sir Charles to build Sirhowy. We're partners.'

'Not any more. Sir Charles has cancelled the lease and instructed me to take possession of the iron works. We don't need you to operate the foundry and if you, or any of your men, show your faces there you'll be shot as trespassers,' said the estate manager.

'You waited until it was nearly finished. This is robbery, I'll sue,' said Isaac.

'If you wish to waste money debating your dishonesty in the courts that's your prerogative. I believe our business is concluded. There's the door, Mr. Thomas. Good day.'

The Marquess of Bute, who was equally upset by Thomas' behaviour, reacted differently. Bute had invested some money in return for ownership of one third of Rhymney Foundry but he had also loaned money to the business, as an interest bearing loan, with no voting rights. Thomas believed Bute had parted with his money unaware that he would have no control over the business. In Thomas' view he could do as he pleased. It was a foolish mistake. Bute's lawyer had been fastidious and the contract had been carefully written to protect his client.

The first indication of trouble was a solicitor's letter which arrived at Thomas' office. The letter advised Thomas that the terms of the loan Bute had made to Rhymney Foundry had been breached and demanded repayment in full with interest within seven days. The letter continued, saying if the loan was not repaid in the aforesaid time, the Marquess of Bute would exercise his right, as laid out in the loan agreement, to convert the loan into voting shares. Isaac Thomas was in no position to give back the money; he'd spent it. Seven days later the loan was converted to voting shares and Isaac Thomas lost control of Rhymney Foundry.

Greed and dishonesty had cost Isaac two foundries. His plan to dominate the iron industry of South Wales was in tatters. Isaac still held shares in the foundry at Rhymney and Thomas Iron Works was still his but Bute wasn't finished. The next attack was designed to destroy Thomas Iron Works. It was notification that, in one month, Cardiff Docks would no longer accept shipments from Thomas' foundry.

Isaac wrote to Bute asking for a meeting and was relieved to receive a reply inviting him to Cardiff Castle. When Isaac arrived at Cardiff he was escorted to the marquess' state dining room and told to wait. A short while later the marquess entered with two other men.

'Good afternoon, Mr. Thomas. Sit down,' said Bute and pointed to a chair.

'Good afternoon, My Lord. Thank you for agreeing to see me,' said Isaac.

'This is my legal representative Mr. Ashton and the second gentleman, who will make a record of our conversation, is my secretary Mr. Owen,' said Bute, 'Now, we'll forego the pleasantries and get to business. Mr. Ashton will explain.'

'The marquess intends to buy a controlling share in Thomas Iron Works,' said the lawyer.

'How dare you. My father started Thomas Iron Works forty years ago. It's not for sale,' snapped Isaac.

'Mr. Thomas, without access to Cardiff Harbour your foundry is worthless. Come now, the marquess is not an unreasonable man. He will pay a fair price and you will still own part of the enterprise. The alternative is your foundry will close and you'll get nothing,' explained the lawyer.

'Why is the marquess being so generous?' asked Isaac.

'Because you're going to work for me, managing my iron works at Rhymney and Merthyr. You'll keep a share, as an incentive and to guarantee your future loyalty to me,' said Bute, 'Do you remember what I said? It's better to be part of something big.' Isaac wanted to shout at the three men, to leap up and tell them what he thought of them, to laugh in their faces but he didn't; he just sat there, a beaten man.

'I have already prepared the share transfer papers. All they need, to complete them, is the amount and your signature,' said the lawyer and placed a document on the table.

Rhys and John Howard returned to their duties at the end of January, Rhys back to the Conqueror while Captain Howard was summoned to the marine headquarters at Chatham Dockyard. The Royal Marines had a new task for John Howard, as an officer in the recently created Royal Marine Artillery. The navy was converting HMS Heron, a 16 gun sloop, into a bomb ship, designed for bombarding enemy shore installations. The existing ordnance was being replaced with 2 thirteen inch mortars, firing exploding shells. Captain Howard was ordered to join as the ship's artillery officer, in command of the marines manning the mortars. After the refit, the warship would be named HMS Volcano.

The Vaughns were eating dinner when the butler announced a visitor had arrived who wished to see Nye.

'Mr. Isaac Thomas, Sir. He says he needs to see you on a matter of great importance,' said the butler. Eira hadn't spoken to her brother for several years and his unexpected presence at Vaynor Hall stirred unpleasant memories. Nye put down his knife and fork and looked at his wife. He could see she was distraught.

'Do you want to see him?' asked Nye. She nodded.

'Show Mr. Thomas into the drawing room and tell him we'll join him in a few minutes,' said Nye.

'Shall I come with you?' asked Bryn.

'No. Your father and I will see what he wants,' replied Eira.

Isaac looked older than Eira remembered. He'd lost weight. His face was haggard and pale. His eyes were wide and staring.

'What do you want?' asked Nye abruptly.

'I've come to ask for your help,' replied Isaac.

'You come here expecting help from us, after what you did to Eira?' snapped Nye.

'I'm sorry for what has come between us, for what Delyth made me do. She's mad and clever with it. Because of her,

271

I've lost everything dear to me. I'm being punished and I have no one else to turn to. Eira, I'm so very sorry,' said Isaac.

'A pretty speech but your words are shallow. You're the creator of your own misfortune and you'll get no help from us,' said Nye.

'Nye, he's my brother. Can't you see he's in trouble,' said Eira.

'So what! He nearly destroyed you,' shouted Nye.

'I know, but it was a long time ago and he's still my brother. We must help him,' replied Eira. Nye struggled to control his temper. He was about to tell Isaac to leave when Eira looked at him imploringly and he knew he was beaten.

Isaac told them about the foundry he was building at Rhymney in partnership with the Marquess of Bute and how Bute had closed Cardiff Docks to blackmail him into giving up control of the foundry his father had built.

'Did you sign the shares over to Bute?' asked Nye.

'No. I told him I needed to think. He's given me seven days to agree or he says he'll ruin me,' replied Isaac.

'Tell me something and I want an honest answer. Did you alter your father's will?' asked Nye.

'No, it was Delyth. I didn't know anything until later, when father's lawyer began to blackmail her. By then it was too late to do anything about it. I'm sorry Eira. I was a fool,' said Isaac.

'Where's Delyth now?' asked Eira.

'She's living in an insane asylum.'

'Nye, we can't let the Marquess of Bute take over my father's foundry. He'd turn in his grave,' said Eira.

'If you want my help, you're going to return what was stolen from Eira. You'll sign a third of Thomas and Sons' over to me, as Eira's trustee. When you have done that, I'll sort this mess out,' said Nye.

'I don't want a third of the foundry. Isaac can keep it all,' said Eira emotionally. Nye put his hands on Eira's shoulders, looked into her eyes and said, 'Listen to me. Your brother and his wife swindled you out of your inheritance. He deserves to rot. If you don't agree, I won't help him.' Eira looked at her brother and nodded.

Nye and Isaac visited Cardiff the next day. The marquess was surprised to see them together. He'd always understood they were bitter enemies and wondered why Nye was there. Learning that Nye held a third share in Thomas' foundry and was Isaac's brother in law came as a shock and complicated his plans. Bute didn't feel strong enough to take on Nye Vaughn. He'd done that once before and knew he still needed Nye. Nye's solution gave Thomas and Sons continued use of the docks on the same terms as Castle Iron Works. In exchange, the Marquess of Bute acquired, for a fair price, Isaac's shares in Rhymney Foundry giving him outright ownership. To sweeten the deal, Nye offered to provide expertise to help Bute establish the new works.

Chapter 43

By August 1809, Arthur Wellesley's Peninsular Campaign was on the offensive. French troops were driven out of Portugal and Wellesley advanced across Spain until he was confronted by a reinforced French army of 30,000 men. Wellesley retreated to Portugal, leaving 1,500 wounded to the mercy of the French. As the year ended, the British commander was considering abandoning Portugal. Bonaparte's Grand Army seemed invincible. The following spring, the French advanced again, determined to finish the British. General Wellesley had moved his men onto the Lisbon Peninsular and constructed massive earthworks to slow the enemy. As the French attacked, the Royal Navy bombarded them from the sea. It was Captain Howard's first engagement using HMS Volcano's mortars. He watched as the shells flew in a high arc and exploded, tearing gaping holes in the French ranks. The French attack failed and their army withdrew in confusion. The British counter attacked and seized the initiative, driving the Grand Army back towards France.

As HMS Volcano returned to Britain, John Howard reflected on his life. His appointment as ordnance officer aboard HMS Volcano was interesting but the Volcano was a small ship and he missed the responsibility of commanding 100 marines on a first rate man of war. The prospect of spending more time on an uncomfortable bomb ship appalled him and, if he was truthful with himself, he had grown tired of fighting. More than a year had passed since the engagement and, judging by her letters, Cerys was still in love with him so there was no impediment to their marriage. As soon as the Volcano reached Chatham, John Howard resigned his commission. The resignation was refused and he was reminded there was a war which still had to be fought. He was, however, granted two weeks leave, enough time to return to Merthyr and get married.

1809 had been a busy year for Rhys. In July, HMS Conqueror sailed in a fleet transporting 40,000 troops to the Netherlands as part of a plan to open a second front against the French. The expedition was a disaster. The humid, warm weather encouraged mosquitoes to breed in huge numbers and the army was struck down with malaria. More than 8,000 men were infected. By December the British had had enough and withdrew leaving over 4,000 dead from the disease. The survivors were shipped to Lisbon to reinforce General Wellesley's army, bringing the disease to Portugal with them.

The marriage of Cerys and John Howard took place in Vaynor Church on the 12th June 1810 three days after Bonaparte annexed the Kingdom of Holland. There wasn't time for the reading of the marriage banns so Nye bought a special licence for the wedding. The bride wore a fine muslin dress, embroidered with primroses and a silk shawl, the groom his blue marine artillery uniform. It was a simple ceremony. Villagers watched as they emerged from the church. Isaac Thomas, having been forgiven his sins by Eira, if not by Nye, congratulated the happy couple. Then the family returned to Vaynor House for the wedding breakfast. The newlyweds had three nights as man and wife before John Howard kissed his bride goodbye and left for Chatham.

Shortly after the wedding, two Americans visited Castle Iron Works to negotiate the purchase of artillery. Mr. Franklin and his assistant represented the American Government. The American Congress was determined to protect its merchant vessels from foreign attack and had voted to build a fleet of warships to supplement their existing six frigates. The American merchant fleet had doubled in size in the last decade and was now the largest neutral fleet in the world. The order placed by the Americans was a large one and they readily agreed to Nye's request for payment in gold. In return, Franklin asked for an assurance from Nye that the business deal between them would remain confidential. No one, including the British Government, must learn of their arrangement. Nye Vaughn agreed and invited the Americans to stay at Vaynor Hall. He was interested to hear their opinion of the war with France.

'Your war in Europe has caused some problems for us. Your navy interferes with our ships and there's talk of war in Canada where the French are agitating,' said Franklin.

'You do realise we're fighting a madman who wants to conquer the world,' said Nye.

'For a madman, he's doing a pretty good job. His relatives sit on nearly every throne in Europe,' replied Franklin.

'It almost sounds like you admire him,' said Nye.

'Don't get me wrong. He sent an army to New Orleans and we weren't ready to fight. We bought him off but next time anyone messes with us they'll get a shock. The United States of America is growing up and will look after itself,' said Franklin.

'You said anyone. Does that include us?'

'We've given the British a bloody nose before. It could happen again,' replied Franklin.

Lord Mulgrave was a professional soldier who had seen action in the American War of Independence and against the French at Toulon. He watched as Bonaparte smashed the British defences to pieces with cannon fire. In 1810, the Prime Minister appointed Mulgrave Master General of Ordnance and asked him to examine reported shortcomings in the British army's artillery. His aides met on the 20th September to discuss the problem.

'General Wellesley says the 20 pounders require too many horses and are too heavy to move in difficult terrain. The guns can't keep up with the cavalry,' said Mulgrave's second in command.

'My understanding is the 3 and 6 pounders have neither the range or the punch of the French artillery,' added an aide, 'the French gunners can blast away with impunity, knowing they are out of range of our guns.'

'So, what's the solution?' asked Lord Mulgrave.

'There is only one possible answer. If we are going to defeat the French, we must re-equip the entire army with 9 pound field guns and do it quickly,' said the aide.

'Such a proposal would cost a fortune. We're facing an enemy with over 2 ½ million men under arms,' said Mulgrave.

'That is so, my Lord, but the 9 pounders are preferred by the horse artillery. The guns are easier to bring into action and the ammunition is half the weight of the bigger cannons. This is proving to be a war of mobility. We must have the 9 pounders. We can retain the bigger guns for static defensive positions,' explained the aide. Lord Mulgrave didn't need convincing. He'd witnessed the effectiveness of French artillery for himself, at Toulon.

'Start placing the purchase orders. I'll speak to the Prime Minister myself,' said Lord Mulgrave and closed the meeting.

Cannon production reached a new peak in 1811. Castle Iron Works was casting 9 pound field artillery pieces as quickly as possible. Bryn modified the cannon boring machines to speed up production and new furnaces were constructed to smelt the extra iron required.

On the 1th February 1811 Cerys Howard gave birth to a baby girl, she named Angharad. Days later, news reached Merthyr that King George III had gone mad and Parliament had appointed his son as Prince Regent with full royal powers. The creation of the Regency had little effect on the lives of the people of Merthyr. They had more immediate concerns.

A ringing bell signalled the end of the shift at Thomas and Sons. Patrick Murphy took off his leather apron and walked from the forging shop to the pay office to collect his wages. He waited in line to make his mark and receive sixteen coins. Each coin was embossed with the company name and a value, one shilling. Having received his pay, Murphy returned four shillings to the wages clerk to repay the credit he'd had the previous week in the company shop. He walked slowly home to his wife and children. Murphy's home was a single room five feet by seven feet which he rented from the company for five shillings a week. Living with two adults and four children in such a small space was difficult. There was no toilet, the gutter served that purpose and the only water they had came from a tap at the end of the street. The coal fire his wife cooked on, filled the room with smoke and covered everything with smut. Patrick Murphy had left Ireland because there was no work, the potato crop had failed and people were starving. Merthyr, he'd been told, was a place where a man could support his family and hold his head high.

Murphy greeted his wife, handed her the coins and sat on a box by the fire to eat his supper. A young child was huddled under a mound of rags in the corner, shivering and coughing.

'How's she been today?' asked Murphy as he wiped his plate clean with a chunk of bread.

'The cough's getting worse. Patrick, you must get a doctor,' said his wife.

'I told you, it's just a cold. She doesn't need a doctor,' snapped Murphy. They both knew the reason he couldn't fetch a doctor; doctors didn't want company tokens and they had no real money to pay a doctor's fee. That night the child's coughing stopped. It was still dark when the knocker-up hammered on the door. Murphy lit a taper, pulled a coat over his clothes and put on his clogs. Then, he wrapped the tiny corpse in hessian sacking and carried it outside without saying a word. He buried the child beside a stone wall, mumbled a prayer over the shallow grave and went to work.

It was early in the morning. Dark clouds filled the sky and there was a heavy Atlantic swell. HMS Conqueror was rolling as she sailed slowly east. The ship was returning from Jamaica. Eight bells had been rung and the middle watch had gone below when a lookout reported a sail on the horizon. Rhys was officer of the deck. He picked up a telescope and studied the ship in the distance. She was flying an American flag. Captain Fellows came on deck.

'What is she, Mr. Vaughn?' asked the captain.

'An American merchant ship. She looks like a brig,' answered Rhys. The captain looked through his telescope.

'She's sailing into the wind. Do you think we can catch her?'

'I do, Sir, unless she turns and runs before the wind,' replied Rhys. Captain Fellows lowered his telescope and smiled.

'Mr Vaughn, bring the men to quarters but keep the gun ports closed. We don't want to alarm our American friends. When she's in range fire a warning shot across her bow and order her to heave to,' ordered the captain.

It took half an hour for the ship to come within range. Conqueror fired the warning shot and signalled the American vessel to lower its sails. Rhys watched as the American brig turned. She was attempting to get away. Conqueror fired two more shots and opened her gun ports. The merchantman lowered her sails. Conqueror lowered her boats and Rhys led a boarding party across to the captured vessel. He climbed aboard and offered his compliments to the ship's captain.

'We are not at war. Lieutenant, by what right do you detain my ship?' demanded the captain.

'By the authority of his Britannic Majesty King George. I'm commanded to search your ship for any cargo that would help the French war effort and to impress able bodied men into the service of the king. Where are you bound?' replied Rhys.

'We sail to Charleston with a cargo of coal and my crew are all Americans with no desire to serve an English king,' answered the captain.

'We have many nationalities serving aboard our ship, captain. We'll leave your officers and enough crew to man

279

your ship,' replied Rhys and called a lieutenant of marines to join him.

'You are to select ten members of the crew to take aboard the Conqueror. If any resist, shoot them,' ordered Rhys. The lieutenant of marines nodded and called his men to assist in the task.

'I protest. You can't take my men,' shouted the captain.

'Your protest is noted Sir. Now, if you will allow, we shall let you get underway,' said Rhys and ordered his men to return to the boats with the pressed men.

Aboard the Conqueror, Captain Fellows addressed the American sailors.

'You men have been impressed and are now in the service of his Majesty King George. You are subject to navy regulations and, if there are any among you thinking of causing trouble or trying to escape, be warned, I'm not a tolerant man. Take them below.'

'They look able enough. Well done, Mr. Vaughn,' said Captain Fellows.

'It's a dirty business, Sir. Those men were going home to their families after two years away,' said Rhys.

'I agree but we are at war and war is a dirty business,' replied Captain Fellows.

Chapter 44

Two men stood on the old stone bridge. Below them was the road from Swansea to Merthyr. The men had been there for an hour and it would soon be dark. They watched as a carriage slowly climbed the hill towards them. When it got closer, they ducked behind the parapet, listening to the horse's hooves and the clatter of the metal clad wheels. The road levelled out and the carriage driver flicked his whip, urging the horses to a trot. As the carriage reached the bridge, the men pushed a large rock off the parapet. The rock smashed through the leather roof and punched a hole in the floor of the carriage, missing the passenger's feet by a few inches. Hearing a bang but not realising what had happened, the driver stopped. A second rock hit the road and shattered.

'Ride on. Ride on, before we're killed,' shouted Isaac Thomas from inside the carriage.

A search was made of the area but there was no sign of the stone throwing attackers. Realising he was in danger but with no idea who was responsible, Isaac Thomas began to take precautions. When he travelled by carriage, a guard armed with a blunderbuss sat next to the driver and a second with a brace of pistols accompanied him everywhere. Isaac had never trusted his workmen and after the attack he was suspicious of everyone. His paranoia resulted in spiteful behaviour. Men were sacked and evicted from their homes on the slightest pretext and sometimes for no reason at all. No one, except the attackers, knew the reason for the assault at the bridge but there were plenty who approved of it and sneered at Isaac Thomas behind his back.

It was June 1812 and Nye Vaughn was in London on business when news that the United States of America was at war with Great Britain arrived. Continual searching of American ships and the impressing of American seamen by the Royal Navy had caused resentment in America and triggered a declaration of war. Nye hurried back to Merthyr to make sure the last shipment, to Norfolk Virginia, had left Wales. To be caught supplying an enemy state with cannons would be treason and he was relieved to learn the cargo had left Cardiff a week earlier.

John Howard was aboard the Volcano, anchored off Lisbon, when a supply boat arrived with orders for the ship to return to England. General Wellesley's army was making good progress, clearing the French out of Spain and the admiralty was withdrawing ships to prepare for a new expedition against the Americans. HMS Constitution received similar orders at Gibraltar and put to sea.

At first, no one thought much about the new building at Thomas' foundry but as the stonework grew higher the foundry men wondered what it was. Some said the building was a furnace, others that it was the wrong shape. The building was circular and measured a hundred and twenty feet around the base. The walls were ten feet thick and two storeys tall. Cast iron frames encased windows a few inches wide. A thick metal door reinforced with iron bars was the only way in. There were slots with flaps in the door that could be locked shut from the inside. When open, a musket barrel fitted neatly through them. The roof was a cast iron dome covered in limestone. Nothing that could burn was included in the structure. When it was finished the building was filled with provisions, barrels of fresh water, muskets and powder. Isaac Thomas had built a citadel where he could take refuge, in case of attack.

On the 24th June 1812 Bonaparte responded to continuing trade between Russian and Britain by leading an army of half a million men across the Neman River into Russia. The Russians retreated, burning villages and crops as they went. Nothing was left that the French might eat or put to use. After three months and several bloody battles, the French had advanced more than six hundred miles to Moscow only to find the city had been evacuated and was in flames. By now the troops were starving and the Russian winter was approaching. Horses pulling the gun carriages were dropping dead. The men's boots had fallen to pieces and they had no winter clothing. Bonaparte ordered a retreat and hastily returned to Paris. The withdrawing army was harassed continuously by the Russians, discipline collapsed and the army became a rabble. Temperatures reached 30 degrees below zero. Men froze to death as they slept. Others were killed by peasants or died of hunger. The roads were covered with the corpses of men who dropped down and refused to walk any further. Of the 500,000 troops who invaded, 380,000 died and another 100,000 were captured by the Russians. Napoleon Bonaparte's reputation as invincible was shattered.

John Howard arrived unexpectedly in Merthyr on the 4th September and went straight to Vaynor Hall. He'd been away for over two years. Cerys was in the nursery when he bounded up the stairs, two at a time, to see his daughter. When he came out with Angharad in his arms, he was weeping.

'She's as beautiful as her mother,' he whispered and grinned like a fool. The family was complete when Rhys, who had been promoted and was now a naval commander, came home a week later.

'How long will you stay?' asked Eira as she hugged her son.

'I have three months. The fleet won't sail for America until after the winter storms,' replied Rhys.

'Then the Conqueror's in the same fleet as John,' said Nye.

'No. I have a new ship, my own command, a sloop, HMS Erebus,' said Rhys.

'How many guns?' asked Nye.

'24 carronades but they aren't her main armament. She has a battery in the hull that fires Congreve rockets,' said Rhys.

'Congreve rockets, I've never heard of them,' said Nye.

The winter of 1812 was a happy time at Vaynor Hall. Despite being apart for two years, John and Cerys were still in love. Bryn was taking more responsibility at the foundry and Nye had found a contentment he had never known before. Surrounded by her family, Eira was in her element enjoying every day of their precious time together. Their last morning was an emotional one.

'How long will you be away?' asked Eira.

'A year, perhaps two,' replied Rhys.

'Promise me you'll write more often.'

'I will mother,' said Rhys. Eira turned away to hide her tears. Cerys and John had said their goodbyes earlier and embraced in silence, neither wanting to let go.

'If you're going to get the stage, we have to go,' said Nye and opened the carriage door. The three men didn't speak until they were out of sight of the house.

'As soon as the war's over, I'm resigning my commission. Does your offer still stand?' asked John.

'For a position at the foundry? We'll talk about it on your return,' said Nye. The carriage travelled down the hill and past Castle Iron Works. A new shift was arriving for work and the street was crowded. Foundry men stepped aside and removed their caps as the master's carriage clattered past. The mail coach was waiting outside the Castle Hotel when they arrived. Rhys supervised the luggage being strapped down.

'You're both very dear to me. Stay alive, and come home safely,' said Nye and hugged them.

Chapter 45

The tap room of the Key Tavern was crowded with men, the air, thick with smoke and angry voices. Patrick Murphy listened to the brave talk. Men demanding something must be done, to unite and confront the masters, to take control and teach the masters a lesson. They talked of mutiny, rebellion and war. The iron masters were, they said, leeches drinking the blood of the working men and the worst master of them all was Isaac Thomas. His men hated him for his callous greed, the contempt he showed them and the way he stole from them.

'I can't afford to buy my children shoes,' shouted a man.

'He gets rich while my children starve,' yelled a voice.

'We live like dogs, on scraps from another man's table,' cried another.

'Why don't we hang him?' asked a voice. There was a roar of agreement. Murphy stood up.

'And which brave soul will put the noose around his neck?' he shouted and pointed to a man, 'Will it be you?' The man didn't reply, 'or you,' he said pointing to another. Again no answer came.

'I'll do it gladly,' said a voice.

'Aye, if you do, remember to bring two ropes because you'll be dangling alongside him soon enough,' said Murphy. 'Have you seen a man kicking as the life is choked from his body? I have.' The room was quiet.

'You see, we're all talk and nothing more. We deserve to live like dogs,' he sneered and stormed out.

The destruction of Bonaparte's army in Russia encouraged Prussia, Spain, Austria, and Sweden to join Great Britain and rise up against their French occupiers but they needed time to prepare. Castle Iron Works was swamped with orders to supply ordnance to Britain's new allies. Bonaparte had been beaten but not defeated. Bonaparte spent the next year raising a new conscript army and in August 1813 he attacked Dresden. It was a reckless gamble which cost the lives of

90,000 men. It was the bloodiest battle of the war and France was running out of young men to send to their deaths.

Bryn Vaughn was drinking with a friend, at the Castle Hotel, when he heard the hunting horn.

'It's the London mail coach. It'll be here in a minute,' said the friend. As he spoke a gun went off and the two men went outside to see what was happening. The coach rumbled into the yard. The driver and guard were shouting and a crowd, attracted by firing of the guard's blunderbuss, was gathering.

'It's over. We've taken Bonaparte prisoner. The war's over,' yelled the driver. The crowd cheered. A fuller account of Bonaparte's capture arrived days later. It said, 'The French were exhausted and sick of war. On the 2nd April 1814 they had deposed Napoleon Bonaparte when he ordered the army to march on Paris.'

'What will they do with him?' asked Eira. Bryn continued reading.

'It says Bonaparte is being exiled to an island called Elba and will in future be addressed as Emperor of Elba,' said Bryn.

'The Emperor of Elba. The man's a murderer. He should be put against a wall and shot,' said Nye. Cerys entered the room with Angharad. The little girl ran across to her grandfather and held up her arms. He picked up Angharad and sat her on his knee.

'All we need now is to make peace with America so Rhys and John can come home,' said Nye and bounced her up and down.

News from America arrived when a letter from Rhys was landed in Plymouth in October. It reached Vaynor Hall a few days later.

Dear Mother and Father

Please forgive my tardy behaviour and lack of regular correspondence but things have been very busy here. Admiral Cochrane ordered an attack to capture American ships sheltering in Baltimore Harbour. To approach, the fleet needed to pass Fort Mc Henry, a stout bastion manned by brave men. The fleet anchored a mile from the fort and began a bombardment on the 12th September using cannon fire, rockets and mortars. The Volcano was close at hand, during the attack and I saw John Howard directing the mortar fire. Tell Cerys he is well and in good heart.

Congreve Rockets fly through the air with a fearsome whoosh and there were so many that the sky turned black with smoke and flying projectiles. The attack continued for three days and nights. On the third day of the bombardment we expected the American's to surrender but they didn't. When the sun came up a huge American flag could be seen fluttering defiantly above the ramparts. Then we discovered they had blocked the harbour mouth with sunken ships. There was no way past the fort and we were ordered to withdraw. We didn't win but it was a glorious battle and I am proud to have been a part of it.

The great news of Bonaparte's abdication reached us last month. I wish I had been with you to celebrate. Now the war in Europe is over, we will be reinforced and can finish the war with America. I send my love to Cerys, Bryn and to you both. Give Angharad a hug from her uncle.

Your obedient son
Rhys.

Eira folded the letter and put in the box where she kept all of Rhys' letters.

'It seems like we have been at war for ever. When will it end, Nye?' she asked. He had no answer to her question.

On the 24th December 1814, negotiators from Britain and America met in Ghent, Belgium and signed a treaty ending the war between the two countries. There had been heavy losses on both sides and everyone was weary of the fighting. The treaty arrived in Washington the following February and was quickly ratified, ending the hostilities. News of the outbreak of peace didn't reach Merthyr until April.

Lieutenant General Sir Thomas Picton arrived in Merthyr in March 1815 and was welcomed as a hero. The general, who had fought his way from Lisbon to Paris and been instrumental in negotiating Bonaparte's exile, was returning to his Carmarthenshire home after an absence of six years and was invited to stay at Vaynor Hall. Across Europe men, of all nationalities, who had been killing each other for a decade, were going home to their loved ones. Although he was 56, the general was an active man with an enthusiasm for his profession.

'At the battle of Vitoria we were pounded by fifty French cannon. I lost 1,800 men that day,' said Picton.

'It sounds dreadful,' said Eira.

'I've witnessed the efficacy of cannon, loaded with a charge of ball behind double grape shot, on an advancing French infantry. The grape shot carried away the first four ranks and the ball sliced its way through twenty five men. Cut them to pieces,' said Picton. Cerys got up, excused herself and left the room.

'General Picton, we are at dinner,' said Eira.

'I apologise Mrs. Vaughn. It was thoughtless of me. I'm afraid war makes one blasé about such things,' replied Picton.

'Please excuse my daughter. Her husband and our son are fighting in America,' said Nye.

'What's Bonaparte like?' asked Bryn.

'He's of average height with delicate, almost feminine features and his hair's plastered to his temples. When I first met him I thought he was a servant but when he looks straight at you his appearance changes, he grows taller and commands attention. That's why men worship him and are willing to die for him,' said Picton.

'He sounds like a horrible monster,' said Eira.

'Quite the opposite, Mrs Vaughn. He's a charming man who can be witty and has a sharp mind,' replied Picton.

'You describe a dangerous man,' said Nye.

'Indeed I do. He's the most ruthless man I've ever met. Believe me, we are well rid of him,' said Paxton. The conversation hesitated.

'Now the war against France is over, are you retiring from the army, General Picton?' asked Bryn.

'I'm afraid the army's retiring me. It's time for me to hang up my general's baton,' said Picton.

'Would you be interested in a tour of the foundry tomorrow?' asked Nye.

'Indeed I would, Mr. Vaughn,' replied the general and drank some wine. The butler entered the dining room followed by a lieutenant of dragoons. His spurs clattered on the bare floorboards. He was caked with mud and sweating.

'What is it?' asked Nye.

'This gentleman insists on seeing General Picton immediately,' replied the butler.

'I have a message of the utmost urgency from His Grace the Duke of Wellington,' said the lieutenant and handed a letter to General Picton. The general broke open the seal, read the message and looked at his host.

'I'm afraid the tour of your works will have to wait until another day. I must return to France immediately. Bonaparte has escaped from Elba and the French army has rallied to him.'

The morning of Sunday the 18th June 1815 was wet and misty. The fields heavy with mud. Field Marshall Arthur Wellesley, 1st Duke of Wellington surveyed the landscape and gave his orders. They would stand and fight. An army of 67,000 men had been hurriedly assembled to engage the advancing French. Wellington's force had been retreating protected by a rearguard which included a battery of horse artillery commanded by Captain Cavalie Mercer. Captain Mercer was sitting under a tree smoking a cigar. His troop of 190 officers and men had recently been equipped with new 9 pound guns. Mercer was proud of his troop. His men were well trained and their horses were some of the finest in the army. Mercer's troop had been in action for the last twenty four hours, firing at the advancing French then hitching up the cannons, withdrawing at a gallop, and firing again to protect the retreating army. It was hot, exhausting work but 70,000 battle hardened Frenchmen, who had sworn an oath to die for their emperor, were approaching. An old man ambled up and asked Mercer how the day was going. The old man was wearing a shabby coat and a top hat. Mercer assumed he was a civilian spectator, wandering around the battlefield and curtly told him to go away. He was unaware the gentleman was Lieutenant General Picton who had just arrived from Britain, having lost his baggage and his uniform. Picton was looking for his regiment and wandered off to find his men.

The battle lasted the entire day. During it, Captain Mercer's troop fired their guns more than 3,000 times, were fired upon by their own side and overrun by French cavalry. General Picton found his regiment and led a charge that turned the tide of battle against the French. He was leading his men, still wearing his top hat, when a musket bullet struck his temple and killed him. During much of the fighting, Napoleon Bonaparte had sat in an armchair outside a tavern, a mile from the battlefield. His mood was dark. His generals were nervous of approaching their emperor. Bonaparte wasn't well. Ruptured piles and seventeen years of warfare had made him lethargic and short tempered. By the end of the day, when the French ranks broke and ran, the fields were littered with 75,000 dead and wounded men. Bonaparte had also gone, escaping in his coach. That night, small groups of survivors huddled together in the darkness listening to the wounded shouting for water and the screams as they were robbed and murdered by looters. The next morning, the remnants of Captain Mercer's troop retired from the field leaving behind dead gunners, horses and the guns they couldn't drag away.

'What is this place called,' asked The Duke of Wellington.

'Waterloo, Your Grace,' replied his aide.

The Duke rode across the field of battle littered with corpses and commented on the battle, 'It was a damned nice thing, the nearest run thing you ever saw in your life.'

Orders were issued to take Bonaparte dead or alive and a manhunt began to catch the emperor who was now declared an outlaw by his own people. He tried to escape to America but found British warships waiting at every French port. Bonaparte surrendered to the captain of HMS Bellephron, at Rochefort, on 15th July, asking for the protection of the British.

When Nye Vaughn arrived at Vaynor Hall, with a special edition of the London Gazette, Eira was subdued. She listened quietly while he related how Emperor Bonaparte was being sent to St. Helena, a remote island in the Atlantic Ocean, where escape was impossible. Eira said nothing when he read the reports of the battle. The news of General Picton's death caused no reaction. She just stared at the fireplace as if in a world of her own.

'We've won. Aren't you pleased?' asked Nye putting the newspaper on the table.

'Who won? Not the thousands of men who've died or their mothers or wives and the children. Did they win? Should they be pleased as well?' shouted Eira, 'And Rhys and John, will we be winners when they're killed?' Eira put her head in her hands and started to sob. Nye went to Eira and comforted her.

'Nye, I just want them home safely,' whispered Eira.

'The war with America's ended. We're at peace,' said Nye.

'So, where are they? Why isn't my son here?' cried Eira. Nye felt awkward. He tried to console Eira, to calm her anxiety but he failed. Nothing he said or did soothed her anguish.

HMS Volcano dropped anchor in Plymouth Sound on the 23rd September and John Howard arrived at Vaynor Hall two weeks later. His resignation from the navy had been accepted. He was a free man, ready to begin a new life with the family that had waited so patiently for his return. Cerys and four year old Angharad, were overjoyed by his return. The family celebrated John's homecoming but Rhys' absence hung, like a spectre, over them all.

292

Part 5 1816 - 1833

Chapter 46

The celebrations welcoming 1816 heralded a new age. Britain had been at war with France for twenty three years but Bonaparte was defeated and the war was over. Britain was at peace. No one realised the new dangers and the consequences that peace would bring to Merthyr. The end of the war brought a new challenge for Rhys who was given command of HMS Creole, a 36 gun sloop. The Creole was to join the West Africa Squadron with orders to capture slave ships and bring to an end the transportation of Africans across the Atlantic. John Howard quickly adapted to life in Merthyr and Nye was confident that his son in law would soon have a responsible role in the business. Cerys and John moved to a modest but comfortable house on the Swansea Road with a garden which contained a large oak tree. John hung a swing from the tree for Angharad to play on. It was her favourite place.

One morning, Angharad was sitting on the swing when she saw a man running along the road. She saw him again the following day and again the day after that. Angharad asked her mother who the man was and why he ran along the road. Cerys told her he was Thomas Llewelyn a foundry worker from Penderyn and he was practicing for the great race. It was said that Thomas Llewelyn was the fastest runner in the world and when his mother put the kettle on the fire, he could run from Penderyn to Merthyr to fetch a jug of milk and be home before the kettle boiled. Howell Richards, one of Nye's workmen, had challenged Llewelyn to a race along the Vale of Taff. The race, it was agreed, would take place on Trinity Monday, the day of the Waun Fair, when servants were hired for the coming year and the whole town would line the route and thousands of people would watch and cheer on the runners.

It was bright and sunny on the morning of the race. A noisy crowd had gathered by the river to see the red haired giant, Shoni Sgubor, defend his title of Boxing Champion of Wales. His opponent, a miner from, Pen-y-darren, fought bravely but was no match for Shoni who knocked him to the ground with a ferocious uppercut to the jaw that ended the match. With the fight over, the crowd made its way towards the canal towpath to watch the end of the race. The race had begun ten miles away in Abercynon, and the runners were neck and neck as they sprinted through Quaker's Yard.

'Who's going to win?' asked Eira, excitedly.

'It has to be Richards. The honour of Castle Iron is at stake. I've promised him two guineas if he beats Llywelyn,' replied Nye.

'We've been watching Llywelyn training. He's very fast. He's never been beaten. They say he's so quick he can blow out a candle and jump into bed before the light fades,' said John Howard.

'That's nonsense. Howell Richards will win, I tell you,' said Nye.

'Ten shillings says he won't,' said John. The two men shook hands.

'That's very disloyal of you John, betting against our man,' said Cerys.

'It's a friendly wager. There's no harm in it,' said Nye.

There was a roar of encouragement from the crowd. The runners had been spotted in the distance. They were a mile from the finish line and going at a furious pace. Suddenly Llywelyn stumbled and fell. The crowd groaned. Howell Richards streaked ahead.

'Would you like to pay me now or later?' asked Nye.

'It's not over yet,' replied John and yelled for Llywelyn to get up. Others were yelling and Thomas Llywelyn, the fastest man in the world, got to his feet and set off in pursuit of Richards who was now more than a hundred yards ahead. Richards heard the cheering and glanced back to see Llywelyn running with a look of grim determination. Richards increased his speed. His lungs were about to burst. He could see the finish line and the blur of yelling faces as he passed them. His shoes felt like they were filled with lead. Only a few more steps and the race was his. The crowd was screaming and Richards sensed his opponent was getting closer. Then they were running side by side. Howell Richards threw himself forward to cross the line but he was too slow. Thomas Llywelyn got there first. Nye took a ten shilling note from his pocket and gave it to John Howard.

'Look on the bright side. You've saved yourself two guineas,' said John and laughed.

Isaac Thomas didn't see the running race. He spent the day at his works with his ledger clerk. There was a problem and they had to find a solution. Isaac finished checking the ledger and put his pen down. He'd added up the figures several times and each time the answer was the same; the foundry was losing money. Without a war to fight there was no need for more cannons and the regular orders from the Board of Ordnance had stopped coming. Not only that but orders already placed had been cancelled. Unless he did something to stop the business haemorrhaging cash, Thomas' foundry would soon be bankrupt. He summoned his manager and told him what to do. Two furnaces were to be shut down and sixty men sacked. In addition, the remaining puddler's wages were to be cut from twenty five shillings a week to fifteen and the labourer's wages from sixteen shillings to twelve.

'The men will take it badly. You can't feed a family on twelve shillings a week,' said the manager.

'Feeding their families is not my responsibility. If they are hungry let the parish feed them. That's what we have poor laws for,' snapped Isaac. The manager said nothing.

'There's something else. I'm cutting your wages as well,' added Isaac. The manager stiffened and turned red. He was about to protest but, realising it would be futile and might even cost him his job, changed his mind.

'Have you heard? Thomas' foundry has closed down. He's cut the men's wages by half and the puddlers walked out. They're on strike,' said John Howard.

'What's our situation?' asked William Paxton.

'Not good. We have some orders but not enough to keep thirty furnaces working. Including the quarries and mines, our wage bill is £300,000 a year and we have 5,000 men on the payroll,' answered John.

'A strike might be a good idea. There would be no wages to pay,' said Paxton.

'We can't encourage the men to strike. Their families would starve and they are loyal men who have served us well for years,' said Will Jones.

'I agree with you, Will. Pushing the men into striking by cutting their wages isn't the answer. We must keep the foundry working,' said Nye.

'How can we do that with no orders to fulfil?' asked John.

'We will produce iron and stockpile it until things improve. Tell the men there will be no wage cuts at Castle Iron Works,' said Nye.

Patrick Murphy refused to join the strike. He had recently been promoted and was enjoying the higher wages of a puddler. The pay cut would be difficult to manage but at least it was something. On strike there would be nothing to give his wife. His eldest son had started work while his wife Colleen and daughters sold vegetables in the market. The women only earned a few pennies but between them they would manage somehow. They were eating supper when the door burst open and masked men dragged him from the room. The men blindfolded Murphy and frog marched him to the Patriot Inn where they hoisted him onto a seat. The men removed the mask and Murphy discovered he was sitting on a wooden horse surrounded by men wearing animal head masks.

'Who are you? What do you want?' cried Murphy.

'We are Scotch Cattle summoned here to punish you,' growled a man wearing a cow head mask.

'Punish me for what? I've done nothing wrong,' replied Murphy.

'You're a strike breaker and your women are penny capitalists making money while the rest of us go hungry,' yelled the man. There were shouts of agreement and someone said, 'Give him a good hiding.'

A man stepped forward and struck him with a leather strap. Another followed suit and more joined in. Murphy fell to the floor and they kicked him. It was a savage beating. When it ended Murphy was shoved into the street and left. He got up and staggered home to find his family cowering in the corner of the room. The door had been smashed from its hinges and the few pieces of furniture they possessed were smashed. Murphy didn't return to work. He didn't want another beating.

The strike was three weeks old when Nye Vaughn and Isaac Thomas were asked to a meeting of the parish council.

'Gentlemen, the parish is in a difficult position. We are obliged to pay poor relief to the men's families but have run out of money,' said the chairman.

'Then you must increase the poor rate to raise money,' said Isaac.

'We have considered doing so and levying a rate of 8 shillings on all cottages worth £6 but that would hit the workers who have no money. Instead we intend to increase the rate on your foundries to cover the expense,' said the chairman.

'That's an outrageous proposal. I shall not pay it,' said Isaac and stood up.

'Sit down Mr. Thomas,' said the chairman. 'You are the man who is responsible for this unpleasant mess and you should be willing to help these unfortunate people.'

'Help them? Why should I help them? They are out to ruin me,' hissed Isaac.

'Castle Iron will support the families living in the parish who are destitute. My wife is already giving food for distribution by the Methodist Church and the chapels near our works,' said Nye.

'You're a fool. The strike will go on forever if you feed them,' said Isaac.

'There has been some trouble. Strikers in animal masks have been intimidating men who want to work,' said the chairman.

'Send word to the Marquess of Bute requesting the Glamorganshire Yeomanry to be ready for action,' suggested Isaac.

'Soldiers in Merthyr? Do you think that's necessary?' asked the chairman, 'We could raise a militia of our own.'

'And fill its ranks with foundry men who can't be trusted. I don't think so,' said Isaac.

'We are getting ahead of ourselves. The best course of action is to calm things down. Thomas, you need to make a gesture of some kind. Talk to the men. Reduce the amount of the pay cut and get them back to work,' suggested Nye.

'I've heard enough. There will be no gestures on my part,' announced Isaac and stormed out.

Isaac Thomas retreated to his fortified tower with a loaded musket by every window. When the men realised he was intransigent and would never back down, their resolve wavered and the strike collapsed. The men returned to work, sullen, humiliated and broken. Isaac Thomas had won and his victory brought more grief to the men who worked for him in the form of revenge. Suspected ringleaders were sacked and their families evicted from their homes. Minor indiscretions were dealt with in the same ruthless way. A wayward look or a comment was all that was needed. Bailiffs carried one old lady into the street on her sickbed and tipped her into the gutter. She died of pneumonia where she lay. Isaac Thomas inflicted hardship and suffering on anyone who crossed him and his workmen hated him for it.

Chapter 47

The news that income tax was being abolished now that the war was over was announced on the 16th September, the same day as a letter arrived from Rhys.

Dearest Mother and Father

I write this letter while sitting at a small card table on the quarterdeck of HMS Creole. She is a lovely ship that handles well and my crew, who are all volunteers, are in good spirit. Having no pressed men aboard my ship is a relief. There is nothing as sour as a man taken by force from his loved ones.

On the 27th August last, a combined force of Dutch and British ships bombarded Algiers to force the Dey of Algiers to release slaves he had taken. Seeing the mortars in action reminded me of John during the attack on Baltimore. We freed more than 3,000 Christian men and women from the Dey's clutches and got a solemn promise from him to cease the barbaric trade. The man is a heathen and untrustworthy. I doubt if he will honour his pledge and believe we will have to return to deal with him return again in the future.

Your letters telling of the trouble in Merthyr did not surprise me. I have heard of similar troubles in other places where soldiers and sailors returned home to find there was no work for them. That is why so many want to stay at sea, where they are fed and have purpose. Tell Angharad I have a beautiful pair of embroidered slippers for her, with turned up toes, which I will bring when I return home.

We sail south for the winter to patrol for slavers in the Atlantic. Some of them carry more than 600 slaves crammed in the holds like salted herrings in a barrel. The stench of a slaver can be smelt from miles away. Many of the slaves die and are thrown overboard during the voyage. It is a dreadful, inhumane business and we will be well rid of the trade.

I hope to return to Wales next year. It will have been five years at sea without seeing you all, a long time, but the last Christmas we spent together is as fresh in my mind as yesterday. The ball you threw was a wonderful evening even if father's dancing made us all laugh.

My first lieutenant has just told me that the supply boat is about to sail for England with the mail so I must finish.

I send to you my love and affection.

Your obedient son Rhys.

Rhys' return home was still a year away but Eira was already making plans for his visit. The foundrymen of Merthyr had other things to think about. They had seen how ruthless the ironmasters could be and were aware that there was not enough work for the foundries to continue as they were. Somehow the men had to organise themselves and find a way to survive. Following the strike, Isaac Thomas had raised the prices in the truck shop, forcing starving families to look elsewhere for the essentials they needed. Unscrupulous traders offered credit to the unwary and, when they couldn't pay, the bailiffs stripped them of everything. Thieving became commonplace and the streets of Merthyr grew increasingly dangerous. No one walked alone. Starving men stole and those who still had jobs lived in fear that they too would soon be in the gutter. It was time for the workers of Merthyr to stand together.

The puddlers were the first to organise a friendly society. They held a secret meeting at the Patriot Inn. Patrick Murphy, recovered from his beating, called for direct action. He had witnessed Isaac Thomas' vindictiveness.

'My family is expected to live on twelve shillings a week,' he cried.

'I heard the masters pay themselves a thousand pounds a week,' yelled another.

'We're being robbed at the truck shop. They're stealing the bread from our mouths,' said another.

'Not all the masters are bad. Vaughn hasn't cut our wages and his wife has been feeding the poor,' said a man from Castle Iron.

'Vaughn is a master and they are all the same. He'll squeeze you dry to save his own skin when the time comes,' said Murphy. There were shouts of agreement.

'Brothers, we must keep calm and stay together. Arguing amongst ourselves will get us nowhere. I propose we swear an oath of loyalty to protect each other and elect a committee to find a way to take what is rightfully ours,' said William Teague. It was the first time the firebrand had spoken at the meeting and his words were welcomed. The oath they swore that night was full of glorious promises and threats of wrath to any dissenters. Later, the oath would be written in blood.

At first, Nye was unconcerned when he learned the puddlers had formed a secret friendly society. His men were still at work and there was no obvious unrest at Castle Iron. In his opinion, a friendly society which looked after its member's interest and supported the families was harmless and could be ignored. Eira had a different view. She wanted to encourage the friendly society and suggested the members be offered the use of the meeting rooms at the works. Nye offered the rooms but they were immediately rejected by the men and, for the first time, Nye felt hostility from his own men.

The Howards were on their way to Vaynor Hall when their carriage came to an obstruction. The coachman pulled up the horses and surveyed the scene. A chest of drawers lay on its back in the road. Clothes were scattered in the mud. A prostrate woman was sobbing beside the chest. Four men emerged from a house carrying a table and chairs. The woman stood up and tried to push them back into the house. One of the men hit her with a stick and knocked her to the ground. Cerys made Angharad look away. John Howard jumped down from the carriage and advanced towards the men.

'What is going on here?' he demanded.

'Mind your own business,' answered the man with the stick. John snatched the stick from the man and raised it above his head.

'I'm making it my business. I'll ask you again. What is going on here?' The man grinned at his colleagues, reached into his pocket and produced a piece of paper.

'Here,' he said and thrust the paper at John. It was a warrant from the Court of Requests to seize goods to the value of five shillings from Mrs Price. The man took back the paper.

'It's all perfectly legal,' said the man.

'I only borrowed a shilling. They're stealing everything I own,' sobbed the woman.

'What's your name?' asked John Howard.

'Charles Walsh. I'm the Court Bailiff,' replied the man.

'Is it true, the woman only borrowed a shilling?'

'How should I know? I'm just doing my job,' replied the bailiff.

'And, I suspect, making a tidy profit,' said John Howard. Carys had stepped down from the carriage and helped the woman up.

'John, give the man five shillings,' she said. John Howard took two half crowns from his pocket and offered them to the bailiff.

'Take it and leave this poor woman in peace,' he said. The bailiff looked at the coins for a moment and at John. He considered throwing the two coins in the gutter but decided against it. He nodded to his men to leave.

'Just a minute. You will put Mrs Price's belongings back where you found them and give her a receipt for the five shillings,' ordered John. Charles Walsh shrugged and told his men to take the woman's furniture back into the house. He was angry. The table and chairs were well made and he'd planned to keep them for himself. The bailiff took a stub of pencil, scribbled 'paid' on the warrant and tossed it on the ground. After the bailiffs had gone, John pressed a shilling into the woman's hand and helped her indoors.

When they reached Vaynor Hall, Cerys told her mother about the incident.

'It was horrible. The bailiff was beating her with a stick,' she said.

'You know who Charles Walsh is, don't you?' said Eira.

'No, I've never seen him before in my life,' replied Cerys.

'He's related to your Uncle Isaac. Isaac's wife Delyth, the one who was in the asylum, is his cousin,' said Eira.

'I didn't know Delyth was in an asylum,' said Cerys.

'She must be dead by now,' said Eira.

'Whoever he is, he's a nasty brute. He was robbing the poor woman,' said John as Nye arrived home.

'Who's robbing a poor woman?' asked Nye. The story was repeated for his benefit.

'The Court of Request is being used to steal from those who have nothing to start with. It's a disgraceful state of affairs,' said John.

'The problem is the truck shops. People are borrowing money to buy food elsewhere and the shopkeepers are using the court to recover what they are owed,' said Nye.

'Do you have a truck shop at the works?' asked Eira.

'You know I don't. I have always paid our men coins of the realm. They can shop where they please,' replied Nye indignantly. Eira was surprised by the sharpness of Nye's reply.

That evening, as they were retiring, she asked him what was wrong.

'When I was in Merthyr this morning a woman screamed, 'There goes the Devil' and pointed at me. I don't even know who she was,' said Nye.

'She's probably touched in the head. Don't let a mindless comment upset you,' said Eira.

'It isn't just what she said. There's an air of hatred brewing, I can feel it. It's like a damp fog sticking to everything, unpleasant and dangerous. Worst of all, I can't see my way through it,' said Nye.

304

'What do you mean you can't see your way through it?'

'These are difficult times and I don't see how they will end. I'm trying to protect the men but without a new market for iron we will be lost. We can't keep producing without customers. We already have 10,000 tons in stock,' said Nye.

'Then you must find new customers and while you are doing that we must do everything we can to keep the works operating.' They lay in silence for a while.

'Why don't you close the truck shops,' said Eira suddenly.

'They aren't mine to close.'

'Get the law changed and make them illegal.'

'That would need an act of parliament,' said Nye.

'Nye, why are you so negative? It's not like you. If it needs an act of Parliament, get one.'

'I'm not a politician. Merthyr doesn't even have a Member of Parliament,' replied Nye.

'Then it's about time it did. Another thing, it's about time you joined the Parish Council and sorted out the poor law payments. Talking about positive things we can do, I have decided to open a lace factory to employ pauper girls. Merthyr is full of young women with no means of support except to sell their bodies,' said Eira. Nye sat up. He was surprised by his wife's passion and felt ashamed. She was right. There were positive things they could do.

Chapter 48

Nye Vaughn quickly learned that he had little chance of obtaining a seat in Parliament. The constituency of Glamorganshire was controlled by the Marquess of Bute. He used his power as a landlord with the gift of leases and threats of rent increases to ensure his preferred man would remain the sitting Member of Parliament. Merthyr had grown from a population of 4,000 to 27,000 people. By any reasonable measure, the town deserved its own representation but Bute was determined to resist. Other influences were also in play. The Marquess of Bute supported The Duke of Wellington who was opposed to any reform of the poor laws. Facing such powerful opponents, Nye abandoned any ideas he had of entering Parliament. If he wanted to change the law, it would have to be done through others. Nye began to canvas for political support for the abolition of the truck shops.

Eira leased a building next to the workhouse and her lace factory opened in the spring of 1817. Initially, it engaged seven girls. Many were supporting families where they were the only breadwinners. While Nye financed the factory, Eira took a close interest in its management and would spend time encouraging the girls to improve themselves. One in particular showed promise. Mary Murphy, daughter of Patrick and Colleen Murphy, was an enthusiastic, intelligent girl with dark hair and a radiant smile. She could be flippant without being impudent. Mary stayed after her work was done to attend a class teaching the girls to read and write. She was a quick learner and Eira made her a leading hand, responsible for organising the others. Word spread and before long girls were queuing outside the gates asking to be taken on. Eira found it difficult to turn them away. By the end of the year, the factory was employing sixty five women and losing money.

Rhys Vaughn arrived back in Merthyr in February 1818. He was no longer in uniform having been placed on the reserve list of captains, available to be recalled to active service and maintained by the Admiralty on half pay. Unless there was another war, Rhys would be unlikely to get another ship to command. His income was sufficient to allow him to retire but Rhys found life ashore increasingly boring. Nye tried to interest him in the business but Rhys would not be drawn. When Bryn invited him to see how the foundry had grown, Rhys agreed to come but didn't turn up. No longer in command of a ship and with little prospect of a return to active service, Rhys was lost. After sixteen years at sea he knew no other life and had no other ambitions. The unemployed sea captain drank and played cards at the Castle Inn while he waited, in vain, for a summons from the Admiralty.

It was late November and cold. The trees had lost their leaves and the first heavy frosts of winter turned the ground white. It was eight o'clock in the evening. Rhys Vaughn had been in the Castle Inn since lunchtime and was on his second bottle of wine. The game of vingt-et-un was beginning to irritate him. He had been winning all afternoon and was ready to return home when a man he didn't know asked to join the game. A chair was produced. The stranger sat down and placed a neat pile of silver coins on the table. The next hand was dealt.

'What's your name?' asked Rhys.

'Charles Walsh,' replied the stranger and asked the dealer for a card. The name meant nothing to Rhys. He looked at his card. It was a five. He tossed a shilling into the pot and the dealer handed him another card; a four.

'I'll buy another,' said Rhys and put another shilling in the pot. The card was a jack. Rhys put the cards face down on the card table.

'I'll stick with these,' he said. The dealer finished the round and turned his card over. It was a seven. He drew a second card, a six of spades and a third, a king. The dealer shrugged. His hand was bust.

'The bank pays,' said the dealer. Charles Walsh won the bank during the next hand and continued to win. At first his luck seemed unusual, then extraordinary and then unlikely.

When Rhys' five card trick was beaten by twenty one for a second time he lost control. Two bottles of wine had dulled his reason. He knew Walsh was cheating and thought he had seen the man drop a card on the floor. Charles Walsh grinned as he leaned forward with his arms outstretched to gather up his winnings.

'You're a cheat. I saw you drop a card on the floor,' said Rhys and stood up. Charles Walsh stood up and the two men glared at each other across the table.

'Does anyone else say I'm a cheat?' snapped Walsh. The other players remained silent.

'You're drunk. If there are any cards on the floor, you probably dropped them yourself. Thank you for an entertaining game Gentlemen,' said Walsh and started to pick up the money. Rhys grabbed his arm but Walsh pushed him away. The men began to scuffle. When they were parted the gamblers looked under the table and found four cards on the floor.

'They aren't mine,' said Walsh. Rhys lunged at him again. By now the landlord had entered the room.

'That's enough. If you want to fight like animals, do it outside,' he yelled.

'You're a drunkard. Go home and sleep it off,' sneered Walsh. Rhys went for him again but was held back by the others.

'Let's settle this outside like men or are you a coward as well as a cheat?' snarled Rhys. Charles Walsh was angry but he was a careful man. It would be simple enough, he reasoned, to kill this drunken fool and there would be enough witnesses to prove he was acting in self defence.

'Alright, I'll fight you,' said Walsh.

'You can't fight him. He can hardly stand,' said a man. The protagonists were followed into the street and a group gathered around them. Someone handed Rhys a sword and the onlookers fell back to form an arena illuminated by
308

burning torches. Rhys focussed on Walsh. He was about to attack. Rhys spread his feet apart and steadied himself. He wasn't thinking anymore. Instinct and experience had taken over. Walsh slashed the air with his sword and jumped forward. Rhys parried, stepped aside and drove his sword hard into his enemy's body. He heard a scream, felt a searing pain in his side and then nothing.

When Rhys woke he was in bed at Vaynor Hall. Eira and Nye were sitting in the room. Rhys tried to move but there was a burning sensation in his chest. It was tightly bandaged and he couldn't breathe properly.

'What happened?' asked Rhys groggily.

'You had a sword fight with the court bailiff, Charles Walsh,' replied Nye. Rhys tried to move again. Eira handed him a glass of water.

'How badly am I hurt?'

'Your left arm is cut above the elbow and you have two fractured ribs. The doctor says you'll live,' said Eira.

'What happened to Walsh?'

'You stabbed him in the abdomen. He died this morning,' replied Nye. Rhys tried to collect his thoughts but his mind was numb.

'There's something else you should know. The magistrate says he is going to charge you with the murder of Charles Walsh,' said Nye.

That afternoon constables came to Vaynor Hall to arrest Rhys but were refused entry by Nye and John Howard saying Rhys was too sick to move. Faced with a powerful ironmaster and his son-in-law, brandishing pistols, the constables withdrew. They returned with the magistrate. Nye invited the magistrate inside to discuss the situation while John Howard remained on guard by the door to ensure the constables didn't push their way in. After Nye gave an undertaking to guarantee Rhys would not abscond and offered a substantial bond, the magistrate agreed terms for bail. Rhys would remain free until the trial. Before the trial, there would be an inquest to determine the cause of death. Nye sent for his solicitor and set him to work preparing Rhys' defence.

The solicitor interviewed the witnesses and collected statements. Then he made enquiries into Charles Walsh's background and character. He wanted information to discredit the bailiff. The impending trial of Rhys Vaughn for murder was front page news in the Cambrian News and a salacious report of the death of Charles Walsh was printed in the Times Newspaper in London. In it the men had agreed to fight to the death and fought a savage duel where no quarter was given. It described Rhys as a Hero of Trafalgar and Charles Walsh as an upstanding officer of the Court of Requests responsible for protecting the financial security of the traders of Merthyr. Reading the Times article gave the solicitor an idea and he searched his law books to find a precedent. He found the case law he wanted in the papers for 'Ashford v Thornton', a trial for murder that had taken place earlier in 1818. If all else failed it would have to do and might, as a last resort, save Rhys from the gallows.

The Vaughns listened to the solicitor as he explained how the defence would proceed.

'Our first opportunity to stop the trial is before it starts. If the coroner's jury decides death was caused by something other than Rhys sword thrust, there would be no case to answer. The trail would be abandoned,' said the lawyer.

'How might they be persuaded?' asked Nye.

'It shouldn't be difficult. Walsh was very unpopular. He was extorting money from the unlicensed beer shops and everyone knew he was stealing from the victims of the loan

310

sharks. The man was a bully and a cheat,' replied the solicitor.

'The fact he was a bully or a cheat is irrelevant. I ran him through,' said Rhys.

'Not according to the witness statements I have collected. They say you were drunk, staggered and fell against him. Any cut was accidental and not a mortal blow,' said the solicitor.

'So what did he die of?' asked Rhys.

'That is a matter for the jury to decide with a little help from us,' explained the solicitor.

'You're suggesting we place men sympathetic to Rhys in the jury,' said John Howard.

'That would be illegal and I didn't propose it,' said the lawyer adding, 'but there are plenty in Merthyr who are loyal to Castle Iron.' The lawyer shrugged and continued explaining his plans for the defence if the case came to court. While he suggested using Abraham Thornton's defence to escape the noose there was silence.

'It was quite simple really. Thornton had raped and killed a girl named Mary Ashford and stood accused of the murder by her brother, William Ashford. The Court of the King's Bench upheld the right claimed by the defendant to 'trial by battle' but there was a problem. William Ashford was a puny fellow and Thornton a brute. Sensibly, Ashford refused to fight. With no challenger to contest his guilt, Thornton was declared innocent and released. Walsh had no friends. I doubt if anyone would want to defend his honour.'

'Trial by battle; it sounds medieval!' said Rhys.

'It is medieval justice but the case law was established this year so there would be no argument,' said the solicitor.

'Let's hope it doesn't come to anything as drastic as mortal combat,' said Nye.

Chapter 49

The coroner's inquest was convened in February 1819. The court was crowded with spectators and the room was noisy. The coroner had to call for silence several times and there were frequent interruptions. The magistrate was getting increasingly frustrated and threatened to clear the court to restore order. His shouts for quiet made no difference and, with only two constables in attendance, he was forced to continue, despite the noise. After hearing evidence from the witnesses and legal arguments, the jury was instructed to retire and consider its verdict. They returned to the court after just a few moments.

'Have you reached a verdict as to the cause of the death of Charles Walsh?' asked the clerk of the court.

'We have. We find the deceased died from the effusion of blood into the abdomen, but the cause of the injury is unknown,' replied the foreman of the jury. There were cheers from the spectators. Rhys' solicitor winked at his client. The coroner leaned over and whispered to the clerk.

'This is a strange verdict. I am unable to rule on it. There is a partisan influence against the deceased in this town. There would be no prospect of a fair trial if it was held here. I direct that the trial of Rhys Vaughn for the murder of Charles Walsh be transferred to Cardiff Quarter Sessions. The High Sheriff in Cardiff will select his own jury,' ordered the coroner. 'Now that the defendant is well, I revoke his bail conditions and order him to be taken into custody.'

'Damnation. He didn't need to do that,' said Rhys lawyer.

Rhys was taken straight from the court to Cardiff and the gaol beneath the court house on the High Street. Nye and the solicitor visited Rhys the following day. They walked along St Mary's Street, past the gallows and knocked on the heavy doors of the prison. The jailer led them along a passage and down a steep flight of stone steps to a small iron door. The turnkey unlocked the door and opened it. Nye had to duck under the lintel to enter Rhys' cell. The cell contained a rope sprung bed, a straw mattress, a chair and a bucket. A small grating in the ceiling provided the only light. Nye sat next to Rhys on the bed and the solicitor took the chair.

'How are you?' asked Nye.

'I'm hungry,' replied Rhys. Nye opened a basket and produced a pie.

'You're mother sent some food and some clean clothes,' he said and handed the pie to Rhys.

'Do you know when the trial is?' asked Rhys between mouthfuls.

'It will be at the end of March when the quarter sessions are held,' replied the solicitor.

'So I'll be in this stinking cell for six weeks and then freedom or the rope. They were hanging a man yesterday when I arrived. Did you see the gallows on the way in?' Nye nodded.

'You must be strong. You will survive this ordeal,' said the solicitor. Rhys snorted.

'I'll give the jailer some money to get you some bedding and make sure you eat properly,' said Nye. They talked about little things for a while and then it was time to leave.

'I'm sorry, father. I've been a fool,' said Rhys and they hugged.

'I'll get you out of this, I promise,' said Nye and released his grip on his son.

'You always were the impetuous one,' he added and hurried from the prison cell.

Isaac Thomas' reaction to the coming trial was surprising. He visited Eira at Vaynor Hall and promised to do everything in his power to help secure Rhys' acquittal. Eira thanked him for his support and listened politely to his suggestion. She was unaware that, years before, Isaac had been robbed by Walsh and in turn had beaten Walsh senseless to steal Delyth's inheritance from her Aunt Lily. His motives for offering to help Rhys were unclear to her and it was only when he said he knew the presiding judge that she began to pay proper attention.

'Judge Travers will hear the trial and he can be persuaded to look favourably on the case,' said Isaac.

'Why would he do that?' asked Eira.

'He owes me money. I hold a promissory note of his for £500,' said Isaac. Eira looked at her brother and wondered if he was telling the truth.

'Are you suggesting that we bribe him?'

'Certainly not but if I tore it up as a sign of goodwill he would be very grateful,' said Isaac.

'But you would be out of pocket by £500.'

'Surely your son's life is worth £500,' said Isaac. Eira was beginning to understand.

'How much do you want Isaac?' She asked.

'£1000 including the £500 to cover the promissory note,' he replied.

'You bargain to make money in return the life of my son? I could go straight to the judge and pay him the £500.'

'I wouldn't advise it. He doesn't know you and wouldn't trust you. If he did, your hands would be dirty. I have a reputation for, shall we say, sharp practice, he'll deal with me,' said Isaac. It was a loathsome offer but Rhys' life hung in the balance.

'I'll have to discuss it with Nye,' said Eira.

'Is that wise? He hates me and doesn't trust me.'

'I have to. I don't have £1000,' replied Eira.

Nye refused to contemplate Isaac's plan when Eira explained it to him. The idea of bribing the judge appalled him and the thought that the crime was to be committed with Isaac as an

314

accomplice made him angry. He reminded Eira of her brother's character and said it was improbable that the judge would be indebted to Isaac. The whole thing was more likely a deceit, thought up by Isaac to make money. Eira didn't care. She had made up her mind. Her son's life was worth the risk. Eira enlisted Cerys' help to wear down Nye's resistance to the plan and eventually he reluctantly agreed. Nye withdrew a thousand pounds from the bank and gave it to Eira.

'Tell Isaac, if he cheats us and Rhys hangs, I will make him pay,' said Nye. Eira said nothing. She had already considered the possibility and decided what she would do if her brother double crossed her.

Rhys Vaughn's trial began on Tuesday 5th April 1819. Judge Horace Travers was presiding.

'What person brings this prosecution?' asked the Judge.

'I do, my Lord. The deceased, Charles Walsh, was an officer of mine in the Court of Requests,' replied the magistrate from Merthyr. Rhys pleaded not guilty to the crime and the magistrate began describing the evening when Charles Walsh was accused of cheating. He told how the defendant was determined to pick a quarrel and accused Walsh unfairly of cheating at cards. Then he produced two witnesses who swore under oath that Rhys had been the aggressor and had struck the fatal blow. The magistrate went on to talk of Rhys' naval career as if he were a blood thirsty pirate and concluded by demanding the death sentence. It was a convincing performance.

Rhys' defence lawyer offered another version of events. The picture he painted showed Walsh was by nature a bully and a cheat. Character witnesses were called to prove the man was a thief who had used his position as an officer of the court to seize people's property and keep it for himself. The lawyer went through the events that took place that evening and produced witnesses who gave a different version of events; saying that Walsh was the attacker and Rhys had acted in self defence. The next witness to take the stand was Admiral Thomas Foley of Abermarlais.

'How long have you known Captain Vaughn?' asked the lawyer.

'I have known Rhys Vaughn for seventeen years, since he joined the Navy in 1802,' replied the admiral.

'Tell us your opinion of his character.'

'He is a man of outstanding honour, a brave man who has risked his life for his king and country many times. At Trafalgar he was one of the first to board a French ship to seize the vessel and capture Admiral Villeneuve. I vouch for his integrity as an officer and gentlemen,' said Admiral Foley.

'That's a glowing tribute admiral. As a naval officer would he be trained in the use of weapons?' asked the magistrate.

'Of course, officers in the Royal Navy are fighting men,' replied Foley.

'Fighting men! So you describe Captain Vaughn as a fighting man. Thank you Admiral,' said the magistrate. Nye noticed the judge make a note of the answer.

The final person to take the stand was Rhys. He was dressed in his captain's uniform and looked confidently around the court as he swore to tell the truth. Rhys described what happened that night and the confusion as he was pushed into the street. He admitted he didn't remember who gave him the sword or the details of the fight when the magistrate questioned him.

'Did you strike Charles Welsh with your weapon?' demanded the magistrate.

'I believe I must have done so,' replied Rhys.

'We must be perfectly clear Captain Vaughn. Do you admit striking the deceased?' asked Judge Travers.

'Yes my Lord, I do, but it was an act of self defence,' answered Rhys without losing his composure.

'Do you have any more questions?' asked the judge.

'No my Lord, Captain Vaughn's confession is sufficient proof,' replied the magistrate.

'Quite so. We will adjourn for one hour. Take the prisoner back to his cell,' said the judge and dismissed the court.

The family waited in the street outside the courthouse. Eira was distressed, convinced that Rhys would be found guilty. Nye was unsure what was happening and angry. Isaac had said he would be at the trial but he was nowhere to be seen.

'Why has the judge adjourned the trial?' asked Bryn.

'I don't know. It's very odd. I don't understand,' replied the lawyer. Eira began to weep.

'We must all stay calm and pray for the best,' said Nye.

'So it might be 'trial by battle' after all,' said John Howard.

'I hope not. It was a fanciful idea in the first place,' said the lawyer.

'Not so fanciful. I fancy Rhys would have no trouble beating the magistrate,' said John. As he spoke a carriage pulled up, the judge got out and hurried up the steps into the courthouse and the carriage drove away.

'I wonder where he's been?' said Nye.

'Did you see who else was in the carriage? I think it was Isaac Thomas,' said Bryn as they returned to the courtroom.

The clerk of the court told everyone to stand while Judge Travers took his seat.

'Gentlemen of the jury, this is a case where clear evidence requires me to direct you to give a specific verdict. You have heard confusing versions of what happened. You have also heard that Captain Vaughn is an honourable man and a fighting man all of which add to the evidence but none of which are proof of guilt of innocence. There is however one piece of evidence that is conclusive and that is Captain Vaughn's admission that he stabbed the deceased with a sword. It may not have been premeditated, indeed the fact that he did not go armed with a sword, suggests it wasn't but the fact remains; he struck the lethal blow. I direct the jury to find Captain Vaughn guilty of the crime of murder,' said Judge Travers. Eira clutched Nye's hand.

'How say you?' asked the judge. The foreman of the jury looked at his peers and shrugged.

'Guilty,' replied the foreman.

'Before I pass sentence does Captain Vaughn want to say anything?' asked the judge.

'My Lord, this is most irregular,' shouted Rhys' lawyer.

'Be quiet. I wasn't asking you,' snapped the judge.

'My Lord, if it be God's wish that I hang for this crime I will go to the gallows knowing I am innocent. Beyond that, I am in your hands,' said Rhys and smiled at his mother. The clerk stepped forward and offered the black cap to the judge. He looked at it for a moment and waved it away.

'I have carefully weighed the evidence before me. Charles Walsh was an unsavoury character and was almost certainly cheating at cards on the night of his death. The verdict of the coroner's jury proved how despised he was. I am satisfied with Admiral Foley's opinion of Captain Vaughn as a courageous and honourable man. To be proficient in the use of weapons is no crime, indeed, without such brave men we would all be learning to speak French. The accused will stand,' said Judge Travers. Rhys got up and stood to attention.

'Captain Vaughn, the court sentences you to a fine of one shilling for the murder of Charles Walsh. When the fine is paid you will be released from custody. I also judge that the prosecuting magistrate has no claim against the defendant for damages and will pay his own costs,' said the judge.

Chapter 50

Rhys returned to Merthyr a free man. The ordeal of the trial was over. Eira visited Isaac to thank him and ask what had happened. He told her the judge had at first refused and had only agreed to help after Isaac offered him more money. Rhys' admission that he had struck the lethal blow left the judge with no choice except to find him guilty. He had adjourned the trial to think, to find a way out of the dilemma and it was Isaac who had suggested a small fine.

'Why weren't you in the courtroom?' asked Eira.

'I was listening from the judge's chambers. He left the door open,' said Isaac.

'But Bryn saw you in the carriage with the judge.'

'When he adjourned we went for a short ride. It was the only place we could talk without being overheard,' replied Isaac.

'How much money did you give the judge?' asked Eira.

'That's a matter between him and me but I'll tell you this, it was more than you gave me,' said Isaac. Eira looked at her brother, wondered if he was telling the truth and realised it didn't matter.

'Thank you for saving my son,' she said. Isaac nodded and smiled. It was the first time she had seen him smile in many years.

Rhys was relieved to be free but he was a convicted murderer and it annoyed him. Nye decided Rhys needed something to occupy himself and asked him to manage a campaign to change the law and make it illegal for factory owners to use truck shops. Rhys accepted the challenge and began to plan. His first move was to arrange a public meeting to gather public support. To publicise it he had posters printed and pasted up around the town.

Word spread quickly and men from all the foundries went to the meeting. The hall was packed and latecomers, who could not get in, stood in the street. There were three speakers. The first was the radical owner of the Swan Inn, William Teaque. His oratory worked the men into a frenzy. Rhys realised the meeting was being hijacked and he was losing control. He hadn't expected Teaque's extreme views and calls for revolution. The second speaker was Morgan Williams a chartist leader who wanted truck shops abolished and working men to be given the vote.

'They build chapels by their works, to ease their consciences while they deny us the freedom to buy food and other essentials at a fair price. I say enough of this slavery,' he cried. There were shouts of agreement and loud applause. Rhys Vaughn was the last to address the audience.

'I speak as the son of a master who has never paid his men with truck shop tokens and vows he never will. In England people call them Tommy Shops that sell Tommy Rot. Whatever the name, they are an evil that must be done away with so honest men can be paid the king's money and spend it where they please,' said Rhys.

'Your father has got plenty of money to spend where he pleases,' called a voice. Rhys ignored the interruption and carried on.

'We can get rid of the truck shops if we work together and avoid violence.'

'When did you ever work in a foundry?' shouted a man from the back of the hall.

'Listen to me. If we all sign a petition to Parliament, asking it to outlaw truck shops they will have to listen,' said Rhys. The men were getting agitated. Rhys was no longer being heard. Morgan Williams stood and raised his hands. The hall went quiet.

'Brothers, Captain Vaughn is a decent man. Remember, it was Vaughn who confronted the robber Charles Walsh and removed him from our midst. What he says is true. He doesn't deserve your abuse. We should hear him out. If he can help us get rid of the truck shops it will be a good thing. If he can't, what have we lost?' said Williams. The question hung in the air until a voice replied, 'Nothing,' and there were shouts of agreement. The meeting ended with the men agreeing to present a petition to Parliament. Rhys thanked Morgan Williams for his intervention and support.

'I believe you mean well, Captain Vaughn but you have made a pact with the men and they are a force you cannot control. I warn you, they will turn on you and your kind when the time comes,' said Morgan Williams as they parted.

While Rhys continued with the truck shop campaign Nye and Bryn were looking for new markets for Castle Iron. When Bryn read about the new road linking London to Holyhead being built by Thomas Telford he saw an opportunity. The only way across the Menai Straits was by boat and Telford planned to build a bridge suspended on cast iron chains high above the channel. It would be the first bridge of its type in the world. Nye approached Telford and asked for a chance to quote for the work. When the tender documents arrived he was surprised at the scale of the project. The bridge required sixteen huge chains. Each chain included 935 cast iron links and weighed 121 tons. It was the type of casting Castle Iron Works was built to do. John Howard's costing was checked and rechecked. There was no margin for error. Castle Iron's offer would be to produce the chains and sell them at cost. Profit, Nye decided, would be sacrificed to keep the foundry working.

Nye and Bryn travelled to Llangollen to see Telford, discuss the construction of the bridge, present the quotation and persuade the engineer to give them an order. They arrived a day early for their appointment and took rooms at the Wynnstay Arms. With an afternoon free, they decided to visit Pontycysyllte Aqueduct which had been built by Telford in 1805. Nye started along the footpath that crossed the aqueduct but had to turn back. The height of the narrow path made him feel sick. Nye watched from the safety of solid ground as Bryn strolled to the far end of the aqueduct and back. They marvelled at the height of the arches and tried to guess which foundry cast the iron channel that carried the canal through the air so high across the valley. Returning to the hotel they discussed how to approach the next day's meeting and agreed that Nye would do most of the talking. They knew Telford was a genial Scot in his sixties with a sense of humour and, despite his age, inclined to be impulsive. The next morning they walked across the River Dee to the Bridge End Hotel where Telford had established a temporary site office. Telford was studying a map and discussing with his assistant which route the new road would take over Horseshoe Pass. He appeared distracted and in no mood to discuss the Menai Bridge. It was going to be a difficult meeting. Telford thanked Nye for taking the trouble to come so far and apologised saying he had earlier arranged for the casting of the chains to be done in a Birmingham foundry. Nye tried to explain why Castle Iron should make the chains but Telford was glancing at the map and not paying attention. Nye looked at Bryn and raised his eyebrows.

'We went to see Pontcysyllte Aqueduct yesterday. It's a beautiful piece of engineering Mr. Telford but there's one thing I don't understand. How did you seal the cast iron plates that carry the canal across the valley?' asked Bryn. Telford stopped looking at the map.

'It's an interesting question. What made you ask it?' said Telford.

322

'When I was in the boiler shop at Boulton and Watt, getting a reliable seal was always a problem. We spent a lot of time trying different materials as a sealant,' said Bryn.

'So you're an engineer Mr. Vaughn. We had the same problem. The aqueduct had to be completely watertight. Believe it or not the sealant is Welsh flannel impregnated with white lead and iron filings,' said Telford and grinned, mischievously.

'Judging by the width of your smile I believe you are teasing us Mr. Telford,' said Bryn. Thomas Telford roared with laughter.

'I promise you on my dear wife's life, it is true. What's more, after we bolted the sections together, we filled the aqueduct with water and left it for six months to prove it was watertight,' said Telford.

'If I say I believe you, will you believe me when I promise you that Castle Iron should cast the chains for the Menai Bridge?' asked Bryn. Telford grinned again and asked to see the quotation. He read it and instructed his assistant to make out a purchase order to Castle Iron Works for 2,000 tons of cast iron chain to be delivered to the Menai Bridge. After saying goodbye, Telford returned to his map and the assistant showed them out.

'You should know Mr. Telford is married to his work. He doesn't have a wife,' whispered the assistant.

'So he was teasing us about the sealant,' said Bryn. The assistant grinned and returned to his master. He saw no reason to reveal that Thomas Telford had told the truth about the aqueduct.

The order for bridge chains was useful but it would only keep the foundry working for a few weeks. More orders had to be found to slow the rapidly growing pile of stock iron accumulating at the works. Nye and Bryn talked at they rode south and Bryn raised an idea he wanted to discuss with his father.

'Do you remember the steam engine Trevithick built for Isaac Thomas?' he asked.

'Yes I do, why?' replied Nye.

'Why didn't it work?' asked Bryn.

'The cast iron rails couldn't take the weight of the locomotive and snapped under the load. I must admit, it was a good idea though,' answered Nye.

'If it was a good idea, did you try and make the rails stronger?' asked Bryn.

'That's a silly question. We saw the potential. Will Jones spent months trying but the metal was too brittle,' said Nye, wondering where the conversation was leading.

'The reason I ask is that an engineer in Northumberland named John Birkinshaw, has applied for a patent to roll wrought iron rails. According to the patent his rails are tougher than cast iron, strong enough to support a moving steam engine and they don't shatter when shock loaded,' said Bryn.

'That's interesting. How can we make money out of his invention?' asked Nye.

'There are already plans for railways using locomotives. It's the future of transportation. The market for rails will be huge. We need to get a licence from Birkinshaw to make them,' explained Bryn.

'I like the idea Bryn but we must be careful. Let's keep this to ourselves for the moment. If word got out someone else might get to Birkinshaw before us,' said Nye.

Rhys' campaign was gathering momentum. The foundry men collected 7,000 signatures. Nearly half of them were from Castle Iron Works where the men were encouraged to sign when they collected their pay. In January 1820 a delegation led by Morgan Williams travelled to London and delivered the petition to the Houses of Parliament. It received a cool reception in the Prime Minister's office where regular reports were arriving describing workers organisations which were causing trouble. At Peterloo, cavalry had charged a crowd of workers, demanding the right to vote, killing fifteen and injuring hundreds. Luddites were smashing textile looms in Lancashire. The Prime Minister, Lord Liverpool, had no time for workers grievances or secret societies and regarded the petition with distain. The Marquess of Bute had spies in Merthyr and was sending monthly reports to London on the state of the town. Liverpool's attitude hardened further when a second petition arrived from Merthyr, supporting the use of truck shops. Isaac Thomas and the other ironmaster in the town had ordered their workers to sign the petition or risk losing their jobs.

The delegation returned to Merthyr with sad news. King George III who had reigned for over fifty nine years had died at Windsor. Merthyr was garlanded in black and the town mourned the loss of a monarch who, although mad, was a popular king. Morgan Williams told Rhys that the delegation had been promised the petition would receive fair consideration and they should wait for a response. Rhys, however, was moving forward and widening his campaign, searching for a politician who would fight the cause in the House of Commons. He travelled to Malvern and met William Huskisson, a Member of Parliament who supported the removal of corn import tariffs to lower the cost of bread. Huskisson opposed the Corn Laws introduced after the war to protect British farmers saying workers' families were starving as a result of the tax. The MP was supportive but unwilling to lead the fight for the abolition of truck shops. The two men agreed to keep in contact. The fact that there was a world glut of cheap corn which was unavailable because of an import tax, introduced by rich landowners, was a revelation to Rhys and he began to feel a political motivation of his own.

Nye Vaughn visited John Birkinshaw in Northumberland and negotiated the rights to manufacture wrought iron rails using Birkinshaw's patented method. Although they were from opposite ends of Britain, Vaughn and Birkinshaw had similar backgrounds. They were both iron men and got on well. Birkinshaw told Nye about a locomotive engineer named George Stephenson who was about to built a railway to transport coal from collieries at Shildon to Stockton on Tees. Nye made a detour and called on Stephenson on his way home.

George Stephenson was a self taught engineer who had improved Trevithick's ideas to manufacture locomotives. He owned a foundry producing cast iron rails but suffered the same problem as Trevithick had done at Merthyr eighteen years earlier; the rails cracked under the weight of the engines. Nye wasn't surprised when Stephenson told him he intended to use Birkinshaw's more expensive wrought iron rails for the new railway. Stephenson's ambitions impressed Nye and his plans to build a railway system joining major cities were exciting. Bryn had been right when he said railways would provide the new market that Castle Iron needed.

Chapter 51

Mary Murphy was walking home from the lace factory when she began to feel uncomfortable. She felt hot and her head ached. As Mary removed her coat her nose started to bleed. She pinched it to stem the flow and hurried on. Then she began to cough. Mary's mother held a flat iron against the back of her neck to cool the blood and put her to bed. Mary's condition worsened. By the end of a week she was hallucinating and picking at imaginary spots on the blankets. Her anguished shouts kept the family awake at night and the tiny room they all shared smelt stale, as if a fish was rotting in the rafters. Mrs Murphy fed her daughter a potion of ground marchalan mixed with honey to ease the pains in her abdomen but the sickness got worse and, fearing Mary would die, her mother sent for the doctor.

When he arrived Mary was tossing and turning on her mother's bed. The doctor didn't enter the house. Instead, he stood in the doorway asking questions and telling Mary's mother what to do.

'Do you have a shilling for my services?' asked the doctor. Mrs. Murphy handed the doctor a silver coin.

'How long had she been ill?'

'It came on as she was walking home last week,' replied Mrs Murphy.

'Put the back of your hand against her forehead and tell me what it feels like,' said the doctor. Mary's mother did as she was instructed.

'It feels hot and damp.'

'Lift the bedclothes and look at her belly. Are there any blotches?' asked the doctor. Mrs. Murphy looked at her daughter's stomach. It was distended and covered with large red spots. As she replaced the covers there was a loud gurgling noise from Mary's gut.

'Are there spots?'

'Yes, they look like rose petals,' said Mrs Murphy.

'Tell me how regular her bowel movements are.'

'She goes five or six times a day.'

'Are the motions watery and green?' Mary's mother nodded.

'Your daughter has typhoid fever. I'll give you a tincture of mercury to purge the poison from her body and a willow

327

bark powder to thin her blood and reduce the fever. You must scrub the room clean with lime and wash the bedclothes every third day,' said the doctor.

'But we have no other bedding,' said Mrs Murphy. The doctor looked around the room and pretended not to hear.

Ten days after the doctor's visit, Mary Murphy's intestines began to haemorrhage. That night, while her family tried to sleep around her, she let out a long plaintiff moan and expired. The next day, her mother's nose began to bleed.

The typhoid epidemic took hold quickly, spreading through the slums of Merthyr like wildfire. Frightened families fled to the countryside unaware they were carrying the sickness with them. No one knew the cause of the disease that was killing so many.
Isaac Thomas took advantage of the epidemic, sacking men who didn't show up for work. Any that arrived looking unwell were sent away and told never to return. It suited him to reduce the workforce and he showed no compassion for the men or their sick families.

Eira took Cerys and Angharad to stay on the family farm at Llangadog away from risk of infection. It was a wise decision. The fever showed no respect for social divisions. When, eventually, the epidemic ended, prayers were said in the churches and chapels of Merthyr and the priests and minister alike thanked God for intervening, unaware it was the cold winter weather that had saved them. Patrick Murphy didn't offer a prayer to God. He saw no reason to give thanks. The fever had taken his entire family from him, leaving him a bitter man.

Merthyr Tydfil began 1821 in a state of shock. The typhoid epidemic was over but it would take years for the town to recover. Nye Vaughn was also in mourning. The fever had taken his oldest friend, Will Jones. He called a board meeting to discuss the situation with his directors.

'How many men did we lose?' asked Nye.

'Sixteen from the casting sheds, twenty one furnace men and I'm told the mines and quarries have lost about thirty men between them,' replied John Howard.

'Bryn, can you take over Will's work?' asked Nye. Bryn nodded.

'The men's families, we should do something for them,' said William Paxton.

'I agree. John, pay them four weeks wages and tell them they can stay in their homes rent free until they can find somewhere else to live,' said Nye.

'We need to talk about our finished stock. We have over 18,000 tons of unsold iron and the inventory is growing every week,' said Bryn.

'When are the orders for rail tracks going to begin making a serious difference?' asked Paxton.

'Not as quickly as I would like. The Stockton to Darlington Railway is the first but others are coming. How soon they will make a difference to us, who knows,' said Nye.

'Do we shut down some furnaces? It would avoid tying up more money in stock,' said Bryn. Outside a steam whistle sounded the end of the working day. Nye stood up and went to the window. It was raining and men were hurrying across the yard.

'No. Keep them working. Has there been any more talk of unions?' said Nye.

'I've heard nothing since the petition went to London. The men have had more immediate things to worry about,' said Rhys.

'What happened to the petition?' asked Bryn.

'The government has ignored it, as I thought they would, but I'm seeing John Moggridge next week. He's a mine owner from Blackwood campaigning for the abolition of truck shops,' said Rhys.

'You should talk to Jeremy Bentham. He's a radical committed to social reform. If anyone can change public attitudes it's him,' said Paxton.

Eira returned from Llangadog in March with the news that Nye's brother, Richard, was engaged to be married to Irwen Jones, a widow from Carmarthen. It was a small wedding attended by family and close friends. Nye and Eira gave them a Queen's Ware pattern Wedgwood dining set, destined to be proudly displayed on the kitchen dresser but too precious for eating from. Irwen had two sons from her previous marriage and Richard extended the farmhouse to accommodate them.

On the 17th June 1821 Nye celebrated his 60th birthday. Eira arranged a gathering at Vaynor Hall and the guests were toasting his good health when a rider arrived from London with dramatic news. Napoleon Bonaparte had died in exile on St. Helena.

'I raise my glass to the demise of the Corsican Corporal. May he rot in hell where he belongs,' shouted John Howard. There was a cheer. Nye held up his hands and the room went quite.

'Corsican he certainly was but a corporal, never! Napoleon Bonaparte was the Emperor of most of Europe and, strange as it seems, although we feared him, he did us a great service. If Bonaparte hadn't fought a twenty year war with Britain, Castle Iron Works would have been nothing more than a cooking pot factory so I offer you another toast. To Napoleon Bonaparte, Emperor of France, the man who made Castle Iron the biggest foundry in the world,' said Nye and drained his glass.

Trading conditions in the iron industry continued to decline. Iron masters fought for business, reducing their prices while the men suffered. Nye Vaughn's policy of manufacturing for stock kept Castle Iron working while his financial contributions to the parish poor laws helped keep the unemployed alive. The first rail of the Stockton to Darlington railway was laid on the 22nd May 1822. During the ceremony George Stephenson announced he was opening a new locomotive factory and would shortly begin construction of a railway linking Liverpool and Manchester.

In September 1823 the radical thinker Jeremy Bentham published the first edition of the Westminster Review, a quarterly magazine with left wing views. In it, he included an article written by Rhys Vaughn. It was a vitriolic attack on the political system and the governing classes. Rhys discussed the arguments for widening the right to vote. He asserted the politicians were protecting their own interests and betraying the people. 'How could it be fair?' he asked, 'that a few rich landowners controlled the kingdom's laws, because of an accident of birth?' The article, which was carried on the front page, included six demands;

1. That every man over the age of twenty-one, who is of sound mind and not a convicted criminal, be given the vote.
2. That the ballot be secret, to protect the voters from intimidation.
3. Property qualification to enter parliament be removed to allow rich and poor candidates an equal opportunity to represent the people.
4. Members of Parliament to be paid a salary to enable honest tradesmen to serve the interest of their country.

5. The constituencies to be made of equal size giving Merthyr as an example where there was no representation because the one seat for the country was controlled by the Marquess of Bute.
6. That there should be parliamentary election every year instead of every seven years to remove members who didn't represent their constituents.

The article in the Westminster Review was an opening shot in a political campaign against powerful vested interests. Rhys had laid down a marker and declared himself a supporter of the rights of ordinary men in front of a national audience. The prime minister, Lord Liverpool, invited Rhys to Downing Street.

'I read your article with interest. You make some interesting observations but I don't think you grasp the difficulties this country faces,' said Lord Liverpool.

'Which particular difficulties are you referring to, Prime Minister?' asked Rhys. Lord Liverpool went over to the fireplace and pulled a bell cord. The prime minister's secretary came into the room.

'Fetch me this morning's reports,' ordered the prime minister. The secretary went out and returned with a folder which he placed on the prime minister's desk. Lord Liverpool opened it and thumbed through the papers. He selected one and passed it to Rhys. It was a letter from the High Sherriff of Derbyshire naming troublemakers planning to destroy weaving machines at Cromford Mill. Liverpool handed another document to Rhys; a report from the Marquess of Bute concerning industrial unrest in Thomas and Sons Foundry in Merthyr.

'You seem to have spies everywhere,' said Rhys and returned the papers.

'We are in a state of anarchy. If the government doesn't contain the situation there will be revolution. Radicals have already tried to assassinate government ministers and there are constant attacks on property,' said Liverpool.

'And your cavalry cut down unarmed workers at Peterloo,' said Rhys.

'It was a seditious meeting. The riot act was read, warning the people to disperse,' said Liverpool.

'60,000 men, women and children being starved by your tax on corn, asking for help and you call it sedition,' said Rhys angrily.

'You're a traitor to your class. Your father must be ashamed of you,' snapped Liverpool.

'My father started with nothing. He wasn't born with a silver spoon in his mouth,' retorted Rhys. The two men glared at each other.

'Why did you ask me to come here?' asked Rhys.

'To ask you to restrain your opinions. None of us want civil war and your article is inciting revolt,' said Liverpool.

'What if I don't?'

'Continue and you may find yourself facing a charge of treason. On the other hand, a more moderate approach would be welcomed in the house and I have a seat available. Are you interested in advancing your position?' said Lord Liverpool.

'I would like a seat in parliament but not through your patronage. I want to represent Merthyr but the town, with 27,000, people doesn't have a seat. How can that be fair when a constituency like Gatton in Surrey has a seat with only 23 houses and 7 voters?' The Prime Minister didn't answer.

'Prime Minister, you opposed the abolition of slavery and lost the fight. Now you oppress free men and you will lose unless you change your policies. I'm no traitor. I oppose violence against the state and I promise you I will promote the rule of law but the laws must be made fit for the 19th Century,' said Rhys.

'I was warned you are a man who harbours strong opinions, Captain Vaughn. It has been a useful exchange of views,' said the Prime Minister and concluded the meeting.

The prime minister's private secretary showed Rhys out and returned to the prime minister's office.

'He's a man with principles who thinks he knows the answers, that makes him dangerous. We'll have to watch Captain Vaughn carefully,' said Lord Liverpool.

Chapter 52

The spring 1824 edition of Westminster Review carried an article by Rhys Vaughn, describing the appalling conditions factory workers faced and calling the truck shops, employed by factory owners to boost their profit, legal robbery. He followed a call to outlaw the truck shops with the case for abolishing the Corn Laws, to lower the price of bread. Agitation from Rhys and other activists was shifting public opinion which was beginning to press for a change in government policy. Lord Liverpool astutely responded by repealing the 'Combination Acts,' passed earlier to prohibit trade unions. The political climate was beginning to change.

Eira and Nye travelled to London in June. Nye had been invited to a dinner at the Board of Ordnance to celebrate the anniversary of the Battle of Trafalgar and they planned to stay with William and Anne Paxton at their London home in Russell Square. Nye grew bored with the endless after dinner speeches. When the Lords of the Admiralty began to toast each ship, he slipped away and called for his carriage. Returning along the London streets, Nye enjoyed the gas lighting and remembered his first visit to the capital with its black, torch lit, streets where thieves and prostitutes lurked. Was he really the same brash young man who was prepared to take on the world? It seemed like another life. He thought of the night he had dinner with Paxton's partner, Charles Cockerell and wondered if he was still alive. Nye smiled as he remembered the book of wagers at Brook's Club. Did Lord Derby ever have his way with a woman in a balloon and win his 500 guinea bet? The carriage stopped. Nye had arrived at Russell Square.

Eira met him in the hallway as the butler was taking his cloak. She looked concerned.

'What is it?' asked Nye.

'It's William. He's been taken ill. Anne has sent for a doctor. He's in the drawing room,' said Eira and shook her head. Nye understood. William Paxton was laid half upright on a settee. His face was drawn and he was in pain. Anne was kneeling beside him.

'How are you old friend?' asked Nye and knelt beside Anne.

'I have a stomach pain. It was probably the fish,' whispered Paxton between shallow breaths. Nye took hold of his friends hand and was surprised at the strength of his friends grip. Anne Paxton buried her head in her husband's lap.

'Don't eat the fish, Nye,' said William Paxton. He closed his eyes; his grip of Nye's hand weakened and with a gentle sigh he passed away. Anne bent down, kissed his brow and turned away with tears streaming down her face.

William Paxton was buried in the catacombs beneath St. Martin's-in-the-Fields. The funeral was a large affair, reflecting Paxton's prominence in the business world. Although his new money made acceptance by high society impossible, he had, during his eighty years, made many friends who came to pay their last respects. After the funeral, Nye and Eira returned to Merthyr.

'What will Anne do?' asked Nye as the carriage travelled west.

'She told me she's going to live in Tenby. William's last will and testament requires Middleton Hall to be sold immediately and his estate divided equally between the children. He's already provided for Anne and made a number of charitable donations,' said Eira. Nye looked out of the window and contemplated his friend's death. Too many of his friends seemed to be dying.

'She said something else. Apparently, William often remarked on your first meeting in the hotel in Llandeilo and how you stood your ground when he demanded our room. He admired you greatly for that and was proud to have your friendship,' said Eira. Nye sniffed and concentrated on the view. He didn't want Eira to see the tear in his eye.

In August, the directors of Castle Iron received an invitation to ride on the inaugural passenger service of the Stockton to Darlington Railway. They travelled north to County Durham and took rooms at the Eden Arms Hotel. The hotel was crowded with visitors. A few had tickets for the railway but most had arrived hoping to see a train for the first time. The following morning, the 27th September, the carriage drove them the five miles to Shildon Lane End where Stephenson's locomotive No.1 and 21 coal wagons, fitted with seats were waiting. They watched as 12 more wagons, loaded with coal were lowered down Brusselton Incline by a stationery steam engine and attached to the rear of the train. Nye, Rhys, Bryn and John Howard presented their invitations and boarded the carriage behind the engine, reserved for dignitaries. They watched as the rest of the train filled with passengers. George Stephenson had allowed seating for 300 but the crowd got out of control. Nearly 600 people squeezed aboard and refused to get off, many of them squatted on the coal. Men whose job it was to operate the brakes climbed onto the couplings between each wagon. The driver eased open the steam valve and the train started to move. In front of it rode a horseman carrying a red flag. Other riders accompanied the train until it gathered speed and left the horsemen behind. The passengers gripped their hats and thousands of bystanders cheered as the train crossed Skerne Bridge.

'How quickly are we going?' called Nye.

'I've no idea but if a horse can't keep up, it's fast,' said Bryn with a grin and stood up to watch the driver. Suddenly there was a jolt and the train slowed. The last carriage had lost a wheel. It was uncoupled and left behind. The train stopped briefly for a repair to the engine before finishing the journey to Darlington. As they arrived, Rhys did some hurried calculations.

'I don't know the top speed but we averaged 8 miles an hour,' he announced.

The dignitaries went for refreshments while the coal wagons were unloaded and the passengers disembarked. George Stephenson told his men to give the coal away to the poor and fill the train with new passengers for the return journey. The train was greeted in Stockton by over 10,000 spectators. That evening there was a dinner for invited guests at the town hall. Nye asked Stephenson how fast the train went and was astonished when he heard they reached a top speed of 15 miles an hour as the train crossed the turnpike approaching Stockton. When they were alone, Rhys related how, during the journey a man, clinging to the side of a wagon, had fallen under the train and lost his foot. Despite the accident, the railway was considered a success and Nye returned home satisfied that railways were the future for Castle Iron.

It was late afternoon on Friday 4th February 1825. The queue of men in Thomas and Sons yard was growing longer. Some had been waiting for an hour and it had begun to snow, turning the men into frosted white statues. They stamped their feet to keep warm and complained to each other. At the front of the queue, men banged on the tarnished shutters and shouted for them to open. The clerk hidden behind the shutters was also waiting and growing increasingly nervous with each passing minute. He glanced at the clock on the wall. The candle on his desk flickered. A fist hammered the shutter and an angry voice threatened to beat him to a pulp. Isaac Thomas had left before it got dark saying he would return with the men's pay but he hadn't returned and the clerk's safe was empty. The clock struck six and the banging on the shutter got angrier. The clerk pulled on his coat, wound a scarf around his neck and slipped quietly out of the back door of the office. On his way home he threw the safe keys into the river. Tomorrow, he decided, he would walk home to Swansea and find a new employer.

Not long after the pay clerk abandoned his desk, the men broke into the office. Finding the office deserted, they dragged the safe into the foundry and placed it under a steam hammer. It took four blows before the door sprung open revealing the truth; there was no money nor even tokens for the truck shop. Men grabbed makeshift weapons and ran across the yard to Isaac's fortress tower. A labourer struck the iron door with a metal bar and there were shouts,

'We know you're in there.'

'We want our money.'

'Come out you coward and face us,' they yelled. A small flap in the door slid open. The end of a musket barrel appeared. There was a flash of powder as the gun discharged. A foundry man fell to the ground. The others fell back, leaving their comrade writhing on the floor. The flap snapped shut. Two men crept forward, dragged the wounded man clear and held him until, minutes later, he died.

338

The foundry men set a guard outside Isaac's citadel, to stop him escaping and sent a message to the men of Castle Iron to join them, invoking the oaths of loyalty they had sworn together. Others began to loot the offices looking for anything of value. When they heard about the shooting, the men of Castle Iron were reluctant to get involved and sent a man to find out more. News of the death reached Vaynor Hall as the Vaughn's were having supper. Nye ordered a horse to be saddled and said he was going to see for himself. John Howard arrived as Rhys and Bryn were trying to dissuade their father from acting foolishly. Nye agreed to let them accompany him but got angry when John said they should arm themselves. The four men rode down the valley from Vaynor. They could see flames rising from the offices of Thomas' works and heard the men rampaging through the foundry.

Nye and his sons rode into the yard. Men were milling about. Sullenly, they backed away from the horsemen and glared at the riders. Nye looked at the dead man on the ground.

'What evil has happened here?' he shouted. Patrick Murphy stepped forward.

'We've not been paid and Thomas killed young Davis there,' said Murphy pointing to the body. 'Shot the boy down like a dog. He's skulking in his fort, too afraid to show himself, like the coward he is.' Nye surveyed the scene. The men were edging towards him.

'Nothing good can come of this. You all know me. I promise you that tomorrow you will be paid what you are owed. Return to your homes, I beg you, before there is more bloodshed,' shouted Nye. There were murmurs of approval.

'What about Thomas? He's a murderer,' demanded Murphy.

'Isaac Thomas has nowhere to run. He's going nowhere. Let him stew where he is until the magistrate can consider his crime. Better that than to storm his castle and pay for his capture in blood,' said Nye. Patrick Murphy turned to consult his comrades. After a whispered debate he spoke again.

'Mr. Vaughn, will you speak in our defence that it was Thomas who caused this trouble and killed Davis?' asked Murphy.

'I give you my solemn word that I will tell the truth in this matter. What's your name?' said Nye.

'Patrick Murphy.'

'Mr. Murphy, I will return at ten o'clock tomorrow morning with my cashier to pay every man's wages with coins of the realm. Is that satisfactory?' asked Nye. Murphy smiled and the men began to disperse.

Riding back to Vaynor Hall, Nye told his companions they had been lucky and might easily have been attacked by the mob.

'I don't think so,' said John Howard and opened his riding coat to reveal two saddle pistols.

'Always the marine, John,' laughed Rhys and produced a carbine.

'Are you really going to pay them?' asked John Howard.

'I gave my word. I'll get the money back from Isaac Thomas, somehow,' replied Nye.

The next morning Nye arrived at Thomas' foundry and found the Glamorgan Militia had arrived. A line of soldiers with fixed bayonets, at the ready, stood confronting the foundry men. Isaac Thomas had emerged from his citadel and was talking to the major in charge. Nye dismounted, approached the officer and introduced himself.

'What is your business here?' asked the major.

340

'I've returned to keep a promise I made to these men last night,' said Nye deliberately loudly so the men could hear.

'You were here last night? Point the ringleaders out to me,' ordered the major.

'He's one,' said Isaac pointing to Patrick Murphy.

'Sergeant, arrest that man,' ordered the major.

'Before you do anything rash major you should establish what happened,' said Nye.

'Mr. Thomas has already acquainted me with the facts. He was attacked by a mob and forced to defend himself,' replied the major.

'Did he tell you the cause of the dispute; that the men hadn't been paid?' asked Nye.

'He did not,' answered the major.

'Who sent for you?' asked Nye.

'Mr. Thomas' urgent request for help arrived in Brecon at 6 o'clock yesterday evening. I marched my men here through the night,' said the major.

'Then you should arrest Isaac Thomas for the premeditated murder of Mr. Davis,' said Nye.

'Who is Mr. Davis?' said the major, obviously confused.

'Mr. Davis is the unarmed man Thomas shot in cold blood,' said Nye. The major looked around the yard and wondered what he should do next.

'Might I have a private word?' asked Nye and took the Major to one side.

'There was nearly a riot here last night and it was caused by Thomas. These men have reasonable grievances and are not to blame. Your soldiers should put up their weapons or there might be more trouble,' whispered Nye

'My men's muskets aren't loaded. We didn't come to fight a war,' said the major.

'I'm pleased to hear it, major. I suggest you take Mr. Thomas with you, back to Brecon, for his own safety. I will pay the men and they will disperse. Let the magistrate deal with the consequences of last night,' said Nye.

'Very well!' said the major quietly, adding in a loud voice, 'No one will be arrested until the magistrate has had the opportunity to investigate what really happened.' Then he ordered his men to shoulder their arms. As they did so the foundry men relaxed and the confrontation was diffused. Nye told Isaac he was being removed for his safety, made him sign a loan note for the money that was about to be distributed and watched the soldiers march away with Isaac. When they had gone, he set his cashier to work. The men collected their pay and hurried away to buy food for their families.

'Why have you done this?' asked Patrick Murphy. Nye looked at the Irishman and wondered the same question.

'Did you know I worked here once?' replied Nye.

'You worked for Isaac Thomas. But you're a master,' said Murphy.

'I wasn't always,' replied Nye and mounted his horse.

The major released Isaac Thomas when they were out of sight of the foundry and Isaac hurried home, unaware that he had been seen and followed by two of the men. One was Davis' older brother and the other a friend. They knocked at the door. When the housemaid answered the two men seized her by the throat and demanded to know where Isaac Thomas was.

'Up there,' she hissed and pointed to the stairs. The men covered the stairs, noisily, two at a time. There was no thought of stealth. They found Isaac in the bedroom. A half filled carpet bag was on the bed. Davis' brother jumped across the bed. Isaac grabbed for a pocket pistol on the dresser. He was too slow. The first stab was in his side. Others followed to his chest and stomach. It was a frenzied attack by a man out of control, who wanted revenge, to kill the man who murdered his brother. When his friend pulled him away, Isaac Thomas was dead. Released from the killer's grip, the lifeless form slipped to the floor leaving a trail of blood down the wall. The killer and his accomplice fled.

The brutal murder of Isaac Thomas, described by the Cambrian Newspaper as a wealthy ironmaster and well respected gentleman, was national news but the search for his killers proved fruitless. They were never caught. Davis and his friend escaped to Swansea where they hurriedly signed up as crewmen aboard a collier, bound for Valparaiso. The captain, who was short of men, wasn't interested in their past. When the vessel reached South America, they jumped ship and vanished.

Chapter 53

Going through Isaac's affairs, it became clear that his foundry was on the point of collapse. Suppliers hadn't been paid for months and he had mortgaged everything to try and survive. With no money to pay the men's wages Isaac must have known that the business his father had proudly started was finished, ruined by a lack of orders and his own stupidity. The day after his funeral, the banks foreclosed, sacked the men and put the foundry up for auction. Cerys helped Eira go through Isaac's private papers and they made a surprising discovery. They found a bill for the nursing care and maintenance of Delyth Thomas. Isaac hadn't spoken about his estranged wife for years and Eira had almost forgotten her. The unpaid invoice for £9. 15s 0d. was for three months stay as a private patient at Sneinton Lunatic Asylum in Nottingham.

'What will happen to her if it isn't paid?' asked Cerys. Eira didn't know but suspected the worst; Delyth would be put on the street. It was Cerys who suggested they visit

Nottingham. She had never seen her aunt and was curious to find out what she was like.

'How old is Aunt Delyth?' asked Cerys.

'She's older than me. She must be about sixty five,' answered Eira.

Cerys left Angharad with her father and accompanied Eira to Nottingham. Sneinton Lunatic Asylum had been built by the parish to accommodate 80 lunatics. Some were paid for by the parish but fees for private patients, who were charged fifteen shillings a week, contributed to the upkeep of the asylum. Delyth had been the first private patient to be admitted when it was built in 1812. Before arriving at Sneinton, Isaac had kept his wife at Liverpool Asylum but moved her because the warden had declared her sane and wanted to set her free. Sneinton had admitted her without asking questions. In all, Delyth had been behind bars for 26 years.

Sneinton Asylum was a long three storey building, surrounded by high walls encircled by poplar trees to hide it from view. Eira shuddered as the high wooden gates slammed shut behind their carriage. A group of men were tending some vegetables near the wall. Others were playing quoits. She looked up at the building. It was bigger than she had imagined and cleaner. 'Sneinton Asylum could almost be a country house,' she thought, 'except for one thing; all the windows had bars.'

A man dressed in a frock coat emerged from the building and came towards them.

'I'm Doctor Storer, the hospital physician. Are you Mrs. Vaughn?' he asked.

'Yes I am and this is my daughter Mrs Howard,' replied Eira. Laughter drew her attention back to the men playing quoits.

'Who are those men?' she asked.

'They are some of our patients. We encourage them to spend time gardening and exercising,' explained the doctor, 'You look surprised. An asylum isn't all straightjackets and padded cells you know. Most of our patients appear quite normal. Follow me. Your sister in law is expecting you.' The doctor led them along a corridor to a small room furnished with several chairs.

'Please sit down. Before I bring Delyth to see you, I must ask you not to expect too much from her. She hasn't had a visitor for over twenty years and may get agitated when she sees you. There will be two nurses outside the door in case of trouble,' said the doctor and smiled.

'What sort of trouble?' asked Cerys. Doctor Storer appeared not to hear the question. He got up and briskly left the room, closing the door behind him. They could hear a woman shouting obscenities somewhere in the building. Cerys gestured to the wall and Eira noticed the iron rings anchored in the brickwork.

Eira stood up and peered through the bars. The window looked onto a small courtyard where women were sitting on chairs knitting. The sun was shining and the scene in the courtyard, like the rest of the building, struck her as unreal. Just then the door opened and Eira turned around. There was an old woman standing beside the doctor. Eira recognised Delyth immediately. Her black hair had turned white and she was smaller in stature than Eira remembered. Then Delyth spoke and there was no doubt, the voice was the same. Eira moved forward to hug Delyth.

'No touching, please,' ordered Doctor Storer and directed Delyth to a seat on the far side of the room.

'Why have you come?' asked Delyth. The directness of Delyth's question and her piercing eyes unsettled Eira.

'This is my daughter, Cerys,' said Eira.

'Why have you come?' repeated Delyth.

'We've bought you some sad news. Your husband Isaac is dead,' said Cerys.

'Isaac, dead. I didn't know,' said Delyth and shifted her stare to the empty wall.

'Do they treat you well here?' asked Eira.

'I'm not insane. I should be after so many years here but I'm not. I'm not mad, Doctor Storer, am I?' said Delyth.

'We shouldn't talk about such things Delyth or your sister will think you paranoid,' said the doctor.

'Eira's not my sister, she's my sister-in law, Doctor Storer and she knows I'm not paranoid, don't you Eira,' said Delyth sharply.

'I don't think you're paranoid Delyth,' replied Eira. Before Delyth could pursue the conversation further, Doctor Storer interrupted her, announced the meeting was over and escorted Delyth back to her room.

Cerys looked at her mother. Eira was angry.

'This is an evil place. We must get Delyth away from here,' whispered Eira.

'Did you see her eyes? She can see into your soul. She frightens me,' said Cerys. Doctor Storer returned to the room and sat down.

'What's the matter with my sister-in law?' asked Eira.

'It's a sad case. Mrs. Thomas has hereditary insanity, which brings on sudden mood swings. Sometimes, like today, she appears normal. On other occasions she can be very angry,' replied the doctor.

'Has she ever been violent?' The doctor shook his head.

'I believe you'd be angry after being locked in a lunatic asylum for 26 years, Doctor Storer. With Mr. Thomas dead,

346

there is no one to pay your account so what will become of her now?' asked Eira. The doctor hesitated and then explained that if there was no money to pay for her keep, she would be discharged.

'Pack her things. We're discharging her,' ordered Eira and stood up.

Nye was disturbed when Eira returned from Sneinton with Delyth. Her arrival brought back painful memories and he hadn't forgiven Delyth for her treatment of Eira or the theft of Eira's inheritance. Eira brushed his objections aside and insisted they find a small cottage for Delyth to live in. Cerys' opinion of Delyth remained the same and she was determined not to trust her aged aunt. Delyth's new home was on Market Street in Dowlais where she settled down to live a quiet life. At first her personality was cold and acerbic but, as she grew accustomed to life outside the asylum, her guard relaxed and she became more agreeable. Delyth's gimlet eyes could still intimidate the unwary but her stare was sometimes softened with a smile.

Nye and Bryn went to the auction at Thomas' foundry. There were few bidders and they acquired a steam hammer that was only four years old for its scrap value. Sacked men loitered outside the yard. Nye saw Patrick Murphy and went over to him.

'What's your trade?' asked Nye.

'I was a puddler once,' replied Murphy.

'Good. Do you want a job?' Murphy nodded.

'Go down to the foundry first thing in the morning and see the manager. I'll tell him you're starting tomorrow. 25shillings a week,' said Nye and left Murphy with his mouth open.

By the end of 1825, work was nearing completion on Telford's Menai Bridge. The twin towers supporting the centre section were finished and the suspension chains had been hoisted across the void. Moving each chain into position had needed 150 men and taken two years to complete. The roadway was hung from the chains in the autumn and the bridge opened on the 30th January 1826. Telford's reputation as the most talented bridge engineer in the world was assured and he wrote to Nye to thank him for the work Castle Iron had done;

My Dear Vaughn,

You will be pleased to learn that the bridge at Menai is finished and was opened to mail coaches last month. I confess the admiralty demand to hang the road a hundred feet above the sea to allow sailing ships to pass beneath was a daunting requirement. However the bridge is built and, I must say, I am proud of it. It seems I am to be known as the 'Colossus of Roads'. An odd name don't you think? Your iron chains were a devil to hang across the straits but they are firm and there is little movement when the coaches pass across, although some of the horses are unsettled by the drop. Thank your son for his suggestion to coat the chains in linseed oil to protect them from corrosion. His idea has proved better than the lead paint we planned to use. To be doubly sure we have done both. When he proposed linseed oil I believed he was repaying me for teasing you in the sealing of Pontcysyllte Aqueduct. I hope you forgive my jest. Please accept my compliments and thank your foundry men. Tell them we found no flaws in the links we tested. When I am next in need of heavy castings I will call on you.

My very best regards,

Telford.

Nye showed Telford's letter to Bryn and asked him to take it to the foundry for the men to see their work was appreciated. The friendly tone of Telford's letter lifted Nye's spirits in days filled with depressing news. The quantity of unsold iron stock was growing at an alarming rate. It had reached 40,000 tons and financing it was becoming a problem. The Marquess of Bute had learned of Nye's difficulty and offered to help. He saw a chance to benefit from the situation. Following his mother's death, the marquess' father had married Frances Coutt and the Coutt's family was looking for investment opportunities. John Howard travelled to London with the marquess and negotiated a £100,000 loan from Coutt's Bank but the interest rate was high and the loan repayable after one year. Nye's refusal to shrink Castle Iron and cut the men's wages was damaging the business. The high interest and harsh penalties for default, demanded by Coutt's Bank, made Nye realise that Castle Iron was in trouble but there was more bad news. An official enquiry into Isaac Thomas' death concluded the men responsible for his murder were members of a secret society, a union of workers. The report was seized upon by the Prime Minister. Lord Liverpool used it as an excuse to reintroduce punitive legislation, outlawing workers unions. The men at Castle Iron were preparing for the worst and waiting to see what Nye would do. Would he enforce the new law or ignore it? Nye decided to do nothing, for now.

Rhys Vaughn's political ambitions were still evident but there was a new interest in his life. Rhys was in love with Christine Paxton. They married at Vaynor Church on the 31st March 1827. It was a bright spring morning. Green shoots were appearing in the hedges and the banks that lined the small lane leading down to the church were carpeted with yellow daffodils. In the field above the lane, early spring lambs played together and explored their strange new world. Eira welcomed her new daughter-in law and the family celebrated. It was a chance to forget, for a moment, the growing problems at Castle Iron.

That night, as the Vaughn's enjoyed the wedding party, there was a large gathering at the Patriot Inn. Men had come to hear Lewis Lewis, from Penderyn, who some knew by his Welsh name Lewsyn yr Heliwr (Lewis the Huntsman). Lewis was popular and outspoken, a natural leader who shunned responsibility, preferring to agitate from within the ranks.

'We must confront the masters and make them concede to our demands,' shouted Lewis.

'They won't listen,' cried a voice.

'You are right. They don't listen. Do they listen when you say you can't afford to buy bread?'

'No,' said a man.

'Do they listen when your child of nine is crippled in the mine?'

'No,' came the reply, louder this time.

'Do they listen when you have no money to buy new tools?'

'No,' shouted the men. Lewis paused and then continued.

'They will if we speak as one. Together we have the power to force them to listen. The puddlers have joined together to protect themselves. The colliers of Penderyn have a union. We call it a friendly society. The forge men have a union and the labourers at Castle Iron have a sick club. What use are these congregations of men when they are illegal, when they dare not speak? I will tell you. They are gestures of resistance that can be swept aside or ignored.'

'What can we do?' asked a man.

'Act together. Form a National Association for the Protection of Labour and demand our rights. I tell you, there is a force which explains the truth of what I say. We are all social beings and must stand together. The force that gives us unimaginable power is socialism. Together we will march into Satan's furnace and emerge victorious,' cried Lewis. The room erupted with cheers.

Nye listened to Patrick Murphy's account of Lewis' speech and asked Murphy's opinion of the men's mood in the foundry. Murphy replied that the men were afraid and reluctant to join the revolt. Nye's support of Thomas' men, when their wages hadn't been paid and his continuing refusal to cut wages, would keep his workers loyal. If the men from Castle Iron, the town's biggest employer, didn't strike, the revolt was unlikely to happen. Nye thanked Murphy for the information and asked him to warn if there was going to be trouble.

Lewis Lewis continued to agitate but his calls for a National Association failed to gather momentum. None of the men had the ability to organise such a body. Despite this, attitudes had hardened. The relationship between the masters and the men was worse than ever before. Merthyr was a toxic mix of resentment and hatred, likely to explode at any moment.

In October the loan from Coutt's Banks was due for repayment. Nye was unable to settle the debt and travelled to London to ask for an extension. The stock of finished iron was still growing and had reached 50,000 tons. The directors of Coutt's appeared sympathetic as they listened to Nye's plans for the future and agreed to a new loan of £180,000 repayable after three years. The longer term would give Castle Iron time to sell the stock as rails. To protect their investment, Coutt's took a charge over the unsold stock and the fixed assets of the company. Nye returned to Merthyr knowing he was exposing the business to the risk of failure and he didn't like it. Everything depended on one thing, the coming of the railways. Castle Iron would have to struggle to survive until things picked up.

Chapter 54

Christine Vaughn gave birth to a boy in June 1828. They named the infant John and he was christened at Vaynor Church when he was a month old. The Vaughn women rarely travelled to Merthyr anymore, preferring to stay at home, away from unpleasant shouts and sneering glances. During the last year, Nye had become increasingly involved in parish affairs. He had taken over the management of the parish poor fund when the minister was exposed as an embezzler and vanished, taking the money with him. Business was improving at Castle Iron. Most of the rails for the Liverpool to Manchester railway had been delivered and the track was due for completion within a year. The mill owners of Manchester were pushing for it sooner. The 35 mile line would have two tracks which, together with sidings and marshalling yards, was a valuable order for the works. To reach the Manchester terminus the engineers designed an iron girder bridge and Nye identified a new product. In time, Castle Iron would produce large numbers of iron girders for railway bridges. Work on the Bolton and Leigh railway had started, other routes were being surveyed and there was talk of a national network. The increasing trade enabled Nye to start repaying Coutt's Bank. It seemed, Castle Iron would survive and was returning to better times.

Shortly after the christening, Rhys was visited by the M.P. for Monmouthshire, Sir Charles Morgan of Tredegar. Sir Charles had closed his iron foundry at Sirhowy and concentrated on his political career. He had been reading Rhys' articles in the Westminster Review and been impressed by them. Sir Charles needed a cause and the nationwide abolition of truck shops, promoted by Rhys, suited his purpose. Sir Charles planned to bring the argument before the House of Commons and fight for legislation to do away with their use. Rhys said he would help, supplying facts and developing the argument. In return, Sir Charles agreed to press for electoral reform to give Merthyr its own Member of Parliament. Rhys Vaughn had, at last, found an ally to champion his cause.

Eira looked at the royal crest on the envelope, replaced it on the tray and wondered why Nye had a letter from the palace. She wanted to open the letter but it wasn't addressed to her. Eira left the letter but her curiosity got the better of her and she returned, carefully opened the letter and read it. Nye had been summoned to Windsor Castle to be dubbed a Knight Batchelor by King George IV for his services to the admiralty. Excitedly, Eira resealed the letter and replaced it on the tray. She tried to appear disinterested when Nye came home. She watched as he opened the envelope and read the contents.

'Would Sir Nye care for a glass of wine?' she asked with a grin.

'You read my letter,' said Nye and hugged her.

'I shall need a new dress and you must have a new coat,' said Eira.

'A new dress, what for?'

'To wear at the investiture, what do you think?' asked Eira.

The ceremony took place on the 19th February 1829. The king arrived late and had been drinking. Afterwards, Sir Nye and Lady Vaughn went to Bognor Regis and stayed at the newly opened Norfolk Hotel. Their bedroom overlooked the

353

beach. From it they could see bathers entering the sea from bathing huts wheeled into the water. Nye laughed and said the water would be freezing when Eira suggested joining them. Later, they went to the bathhouse in Steyne Street and bathed in the heated seawater. On the way home they visited Portsmouth and stayed at the Sallyport Hotel. The channel fleet was anchored in the Solent and the streets were full of seamen. Their tour continued with a stop in Gloucester where they strolled through the cathedral, enjoying the brilliant sunshine illuminating the stained glass windows. When the Dean pointed to a window depicting a golfer, Nye asked what golf was and was surprised to learn it was a game. They arrived in Merthyr on the 12th March and the family greeted them like conquering heroes. Nye quickly grew tired of being called Sir Nye and bowed to. He knew his sons found the title amusing and were teasing him. Nye told them to stop but his irritation encouraged them even more and made matters worse. Eventually, he stopped complaining and ignored the mockery.

In September 1830 John Howard, Bryn and Rhys travelled to Liverpool for the opening of the railway and stayed with William Huskisson, the M.P. for Liverpool. During dinner Rhys enquired how Huskisson's campaign against the corn-laws was progressing.

'Not well. Now that the Duke of Wellington has become prime minister I see little chance of them being repealed. The duke has no interest in helping the working class and, since I spoke on the matter in the house, no time for me,' said Huskisson.

'I believe the duke will be there tomorrow,' said Bryn.

'He will and I'm riding in the same carriage,' replied Huskisson.

'Another chance to press your case,' said Rhys.

'I think not. Wellington would not be amused,' said Huskisson and the conversation moved on to the following day's events.

The next morning, the 15th September, the party rode to Edge Hill and boarded the special train which was to take them to Manchester. William Huskisson took his seat in the front carriage while the others climbed into the second carriage. The Duke of Wellington and his entourage arrived and joined Huskisson in his carriage while a crowd cheered. A band at the end of the platform played Rule Britannia.

'The engine is called the Northumbrian. She was built by Stephenson. Isn't she beautiful?' said Bryn.

'George Stephenson?' asked Rhys.

'No, his son Robert. They say he's a better engineer than his father,' said Bryn. The train pulled slowly away from the station and up through Broad Green towards Huyton. The train gathered speed along the Rainhill Flat and slowed to cross the viaduct at Newton le Willows. The turnpike below the viaduct was crowded with spectators. The driver closed the steam valves and brought the train to a stop at Parkside. Rhys looked around. They appeared to be in the middle of nowhere.

'Why have we stopped?' he asked.

'To take on more water,' replied Bryn and pointed to the tower beside the track. A door on the front carriage opened and William Huskisson climbed down, followed by a second passenger. They walked a short distance along the track and then returned to the train. The second man resumed his seat while Huskisson remained on the track looking up at the carriage. Rhys could hear him talking to the Duke of Wellington. A train was coming on the other track. John Howard shouted a warning and others yelled at Huskisson to get clear. He turned, saw the approaching train and tried to climb to safety. Huskisson slipped and would have fallen if he hadn't seized the door. It swung open, carrying the unfortunate Huskisson into thin air. His legs thrashed and there was a look of terror on his face. The oncoming engine struck him and dragged him under the train. He screamed as his legs were crushed. Rhys, Bryn and John Howard gently lifted their friend onto the Northumbrian's tender.

'I have met my death,' whispered Huskisson. They uncoupled the rest of the train.

'My father will take him to Eccles,' said Robert Stephenson and they watched as the locomotive steamed away with the injured man aboard.

George Stephenson drove William Huskisson to Eccles where he was carried to the vicarage. Huskisson was given a dose of laudanum to ease the pain, and told he was dying whereupon he dictated his will and died a few hours later.

A replacement engine arrived at Parkside and was hitched to the waiting train. The journey resumed but the euphoria of the day was gone, replaced by a melancholy gloom. As they drew closer to Manchester a brick hit the train, followed by another. Mill workers, angered by the Peterloo Massacre which the Duke of Wellington had said was unfortunate but necessary, had gathered to express their opinion of him. The attack intensified. Soon a hail of missiles was hitting the train. When it arrived at Liverpool Road Station in Manchester a hostile crowd had surrounded the welcoming committee on the platform. They waved banners and pelted the train with vegetables. The Duke of Wellington refused to leave the train and ordered it to return to Liverpool immediately. The civic reception planned in Manchester was abandoned. Obstructions placed on the track and more attacks slowed the return journey and the train arrived in Liverpool 6½ hours later than originally planned.

Bryn, Rhys and John returned to Merthyr, saddened by the death of a decent man. William Huskisson's obituary in the Cambrian Newspaper, reported he was struck by the Rocket, a locomotive built by Robert Stephenson and was the first man to be killed in a railway accident. His death, which was widely reported, generated considerable interest in the railway and within months, regular passenger trains were running between Liverpool and Manchester. It was the breakthrough Nye had been waiting for. Because of a tragic accident, the speed of railway construction was about to accelerate.

Andrew Dickie, a director of Coutt's bank, came to Merthyr in October to discuss the balance of Nye's loan. Dickie had started work in the bank as a humble clerk but his skill with numbers and an uncanny ability to see profitable opportunities earned him promotion. Harriot Coutt had seen his potential. When her husband died she relied on Dickie to keep her informed and when she married the Duke of St. Albans in 1827 she rewarded Dickie with a seat on the board. He was utterly loyal to her and ruthless. Dickie arrived with the Marquess of Bute which Nye thought strange. Why had the banker brought Bute with him? Nye had repaid some of the loan during the last three years but, including interest, there was still £148,000 outstanding and he didn't have the money. With the market for rail track improving Nye saw no problem. Bankers were reasonable men. Coutt's had renewed the loan before and would do so again. Another year was all he needed. Andrew Dickie and Bute were served coffee in the board room.

'As you are aware Sir Nye you are required to repay the outstanding amount before the end of the month. That is ten days from now. Here is a summary of the interest and capital sum I require,' said Dickie and handed Nye a sheet of paper. Nye looked through the figures. They appeared to be correct.

'I'm not in a position pay you at the moment. You must give me more time,' said Nye and placed the sheet of paper on the table.

'I'm afraid that isn't possible. My board instructs me to recover the debt. If you can't pay we will foreclose and take assets sufficient to recover our money,' said Dickie. The abruptness of the man unsettled Nye.

'I have a mountain of finished iron, over 50,000 tons in stock. You're welcome to it,' said Nye.

'The price of iron has collapsed. Your stock has no interest to us,' said Dickie.

'You're well informed. It's true the price of iron is down but it will go up again very soon,' said Nye. He was starting to feel uncomfortable.

'Sir Nye, what the price of iron does in the future is irrelevant to our discussion. We require payment of £148,000 by the 31st October. If you don't pay, Coutt's Bank will liquidate your business,' said Dickie.

'My business is worth nearly £2 million,' replied Nye angrily.

'That is a matter of opinion but I assure you that in a forced sale it is worth considerably less.'

'Perhaps I can help, Sir Nye. I might be willing to buy a stake in your business for say £148,000,' said Bute. Nye felt cornered. Bute had shown his hand. He wanted the foundry.

'How much of a stake, my Lord?' asked Nye.

'Fifty one percent,' replied Bute, without hesitating.

'That's ridiculous. I would lose control of my own company.'

'Better to lose control and keep trading than lose everything. Those are your options,' said Bute arrogantly.

'With fifty one percent, you could do as you please. You could sack me the following day,' said Nye. He wanted to punch Bute in the face.

'Why would I do that? I want you to run the foundry for me,' said Bute. Nye clenched his fists under the table and stared at the two men opposite him. He had been a fool to give Coutt's a charge over his assets and in ten days time they could do as they pleased. He would be powerless to stop them. Bute had introduced Coutt's and waited for Nye to get into difficulty. Perhaps they had planned it together.

'Sir Nye, I must ask what you intend to do?' asked Dickie. His question interrupted Nye's thoughts.

'Gentlemen, I still have ten days. I will give you my answer before the end of the month,' said Nye and asked his visitors to leave.

Somehow Nye had to find £148,000. He had already spoken to other banks and none of them were willing to lend the money. Nye spent the next three days going from bank to bank but it was hopeless. Nye went to Sir Charles Morgan and asked for help. Sir Charles politely declined. His own experience in the iron industry had cost him a lot of money. It was becoming clear to Nye that there was no confidence in the state of the iron industry. Everyone expected him to go bankrupt. With four days left, he called the family together to discuss the situation. They met in the drawing room at Vaynor Hall. After Nye explained the problem everyone agreed that the Marquess of Bute should be stopped from getting control of the foundry. Rhys and Christine offered her inheritance of £10,000.

'It's a pity your father isn't alive. He would have lent me the money,' said Nye.

'Why not ask my mother?' suggested Christine.

'Would she have that much money?' asked Nye.

'What about Paxton's business partner?' said John Howard.

'Charles Cockerell, he must be dead by now,' said Nye.

'He might be dead but I believe his merchant bank is still trading,' said John. It was a long shot and would mean getting to London and back but it was worth a try.

'Christine, would you and Rhys go to Tenby and ask your mother? While you are there, Bryn and I will go to London. We'll leave now and ride through the night. We must be back here before the 31st,' said Nye.

Anne Paxton listened to her daughter and offered £50,000. It was all the money her husband had left to her. She signed a cheque and wrote a covering letter to her bank instructing them to proceed with the transaction immediately. They hurried back to Merthyr with the money. Nye and Bryn rode hard through the night and reached Cheltenham the following morning. They had changed horses three times and were exhausted. The London mail coach was about to leave. They quickly bought two pies from a butchers shop and boarded the coach. Bryn woke his father as the coach arrived at Charing Cross. Nye took out his watch. It was 7 o'clock in the evening, too late to visit the bank.

Nye and Bryn were waiting at the offices of Paxton, Cockerell, Trail and Co when the ledger clerk arrived to unlock. He showed them to small office and said Mr. Trail was expected shortly.

'What's the date?' asked Nye.

'It's the 29th and that's the fourth time you have asked,' replied Bryn. Nye took out his watch and opened the cover. It was quarter past nine. At half past ten the clerk appeared and said he was sorry but Mr. Trail had not arrived which was unusual since he was a punctilious man. At noon, Nye was pacing up and down. The door opened and a small man with spectacles introduced himself as Mr. Trail. He was holding a bloody handkerchief to his face and apologised for keeping them waiting. During the night a toothache had started and he had been to a barber to have the broken tooth pulled out. Nye introduced himself and Mr. Trail said he knew of him. Nye began to explain the reason for their visit. When he mentioned Coutt's and Andrew Dickie, Mr. Trail became animated.

'The man is a rogue. He encouraged Davidson's Bank in Pall Mall to over extend itself and then took it over. It was a mean trick, unworthy of a gentleman,' said Trail.

'I fear he plans the same for us,' said Nye.

'How much do you need and what security are you offering?' asked Trail.

'We need £148,000 and I offer a personal guarantee the money will be repaid as soon as possible,' said Nye. Mr. Trail explained Nye's assurance was not enough. He would need a mortgage on the foundry. Nye agreed and they shook hands.

'We have to get back to Merthyr before the 31st or Coutt's will foreclose,' said Nye as Trail wrote a draft for the money.

'No need for that. I'll send a runner to Coutt's with the money. Their office is on the Strand, not far from here,' said Trail. His suggestion made sense and gave Nye an idea.

'I'd like to deliver it myself,' he said. Mr. Trail looked at his client for a moment then he stood up and handed Nye the banker's draft.

'I'll come with you and show you where Coutt's office is. It will be a pleasant surprise for Dickie,' said the banker. He grinned and covered his mouth with the handkerchief.

Andrew Dickie was surprised to hear that Nye Vaughn was in the banking hall with two other gentlemen. At first he considered having them brought to his office and then changed his mind. He would see them in the main hall. He didn't want Vaughn grovelling in his office. Seeing him in a public space would be easier.

'Sir Nye, it's a pleasure to see you again,' said Dickie and held out his hand. Nye ignored it. Dickie saw Mr. Trail standing a short distance away and wondered why he was covering his face with a cloth.

'Trail, what are you doing here?' asked Dickie.

'I'm here with my new client. He has something for you,' said Trail. Nye handed Dickie the bankers draft and said,

'I require a receipt and you can tell the Marquess of Bute, Castle Iron Works is not for sale,' whispered Nye. Dickie asked a bank teller to write a receipt, gave it to Nye and started to say something but Nye ignored him, turned on his heels and strode out of the building followed by Bryn and Mr. Trail.

Returning in the mail coach, Nye told his son they would repay the loan from Trail quickly and once it was paid he would never risk the foundry again. Nye Vaughn had nearly lost everything and it had made him realise that the benevolent way he had run the business had almost destroyed it. There would be no more charity. The business was going to make a profit every month whatever it took to achieve it.

Nye and Bryn didn't reach Merthyr until the 2nd November and their late arrival caused considerable panic followed by relief as Nye explained what had occurred in London. He sent Christine and Rhys back to Tenby with Anne Paxton's money and a letter of thanks. They took John with them to see his grandmother.

Nye ordered an inventory of the mines, quarries and the foundry to find a way of turning the business around. John Howard spent days writing plans and making suggestions to save money. During the next four months economies were made but a more radical solution was needed to meet Nye's demand to make the business pay its way. Nye summoned his works managers and told them he was going to reduce the overheads and make Castle Iron profitable. Hearing the news that there would be a 10% cut in wages made them angry. When he ordered three furnaces to be shut down and the stockpiled iron used instead, they objected.

'The furnace men and the puddlers won't like it,' said the furnace overseer. Nye looked at him for a moment.

'Who is the master here?' he asked. There was an edge of irritation in his voice.

'You are, Mr. Vaughn,' replied the overseer. Nye ignored the man's answer and produced a box of papers.

'These are pledges which I require every man who works for Castle Iron to sign confirming he is no longer a member of a union or secret society,' said Nye and handed copies to the manager. The room fell silent as they read the document.

'What if a man refuses to sign or put his mark?' asked a mine manager. Others repeated the question.

'He will be dismissed,' said Nye adding. 'I expect you to set a good example. There are pens and ink by the door. You gentlemen can sign the pledge as you leave.' Satisfied with his threat, Nye closed the meeting and refused to discuss anything further.

Chapter 55

Lewis Lewis waited for his week's wage. He owed money to a shopkeeper who was demanding payment. Men were coming away from the pay office grumbling about their pay packets. The 10% pay cut was hurting and there was angry talk. Lewis presented himself at the window and said his name. The pay clerk handed him a small envelope. Lewis ripped it open and counted the coins.

'It's short. There's only 21shillings here. I can't live on that,' said Lewis. Then he read the note, folded inside the pay packet. He'd been sacked for refusing to sign the pledge.

The arbitrary cut in pay and the sacking of 83 men stunned the workforce at Castle Iron. A meeting at the Patriot Inn that evening was loud and hostile but no one could decide what to do. The unthinkable had happened; Nye Vaughn had done the very thing he had promised never to do. He had followed the other iron master's example and cut the men's wages. The men's anger festered for five days until Wednesday 31st May when the bailiff from the Court of Requests visited Lewis' house to demand money or goods. Neighbours heard Lewis arguing with the bailiff and ran to help him defend his home. The situation became a standoff and Mr. Bruce the magistrate was sent for. Confronted by the magistrate Lewis agreed a compromise and let the bailiff take a trunk away.

Next morning Lewis, with his hunting horn around his neck, led an angry crowd to the shopkeeper's premises and recovered his trunk by force. From there the mob visited other shops, recovering goods seized by bailiffs. They visited the bailiff's house and ransacked it. Next they called on Thomas Lewis, a hated moneylender, and made him promise to write off debts. As the mob moved through the town more men from Castle Iron Works joined the demonstration. Realising the situation was out of control, the magistrate hurriedly enrolled 70 special constables but they were powerless to stop the damage. The mob went to the house of Mr. Coffin, the President of the Court of Requests, to demand his records. They arrived waving a white flag with 'reform' painted on it. Lewis climbed onto his trunk and gave a speech. The mob smashed Coffin's windows. Men armed with pickaxe handles carried Coffin's books and furniture into the street and set them alight. The rampaging continued throughout the night as the rabble drank and the town burned.

The following day Castle Iron Works was attacked and shots were fired from the mob. Nye Vaughn sent a message asking for military help and ordered the special constables to retreat to the Castle Hotel in the centre of Merthyr. The rest of the town was in the control of the rioters who had blocked the roads leading to the town. A rider was given a letter to take to London to ask for additional assistance.

Eighty men of the 93rd Argyll and Sutherland Highlanders were force marched to Merthyr. They arrived at 10 o'clock in the morning of the 2nd June. John Howard rode along the Brecon Road to meet them. The mob confronted the soldiers jeering, 'Go home and put your trousers on.' Led by Major Falls, accompanied by John, the soldiers held rank and pushed their way through the yelling crowd.

John Howard took the troops through side streets to the Castle Inn. The rioters, armed with clubs, iron bars and fence rails followed. Nye Vaughn was with the magistrate watching them approach from an upstairs window of the hotel. Shopkeepers, fearful for their lives had gathered downstairs. Some of the soldiers lined up outside the hotel facing the crowd. Other took up positions at different windows. A sea of angry faces glared at the hotel. The High Street was full of men and women who wanted revenge on the shopkeepers, the moneylenders and the ironmasters who had done them down.

'How many do you think?' asked Rhys.

'More than 10,000 I should say,' replied the magistrate. The mob began to chant,

'Give us bread.'

'I believe it is time to disperse them. We must read the riot act,' said the magistrate and slid open the sash window. A stone hit the wall nearby. The magistrate produced a paper from his coat and read the contents out loud,

'Our Sovereign Lord the King chargeth and commandeth all persons, being assembled, immediately to disperse themselves, and peaceably to depart to their habitations, or to their lawful business, upon the pains contained in the act made in the first year of King George, for preventing tumults and riotous assemblies. God Save the King!' There were jeers as he read it a second time, in Welsh. The magistrate closed the window. A missile hit the window and smashed it.

'What now?' asked Rhys.

'Now the riot act has been read. If rioters don't disperse the soldiers are authorized to open fire,' said the magistrate.

'You fool, 80 men aren't going to stop 10,000 rioters,' said Nye, 'These are my men. I'm going to speak to them.' He opened the broken window and put his head out. A defiant roar echoed across the street. A man waved a flag.

'Don't fear the soldiers. The game is ours,' yelled Lewis Lewis triumphantly. Nye tried to speak but was shouted down. He waited until eventually the noise died away.

'This will end badly for everyone unless we all calm ourselves,' yelled Nye.

'Bugger off,' cried a voice followed by laughter.

'You have grievances. I understand you are angry but if we are to settle our differences we must talk. Choose some men to represent you and let them come into the hotel to meet with us. I will listen and see what can be done to satisfy your cause,' said Nye and withdrew his head. He watched as a small group of men huddled around Lewis Lewis and then walked towards the hotel door where John Howard was standing with his pistols. He stepped aside and the delegation, led by Lewis went into the hotel.

Nye, Rhys and the magistrate went downstairs and met them in the tap room.

'We have four demands. If you agree to them and give your solemn word we will ask the people to go home,' said Lewis.

'What are your demands?' asked the magistrate.

'The Court of Requests is to be suppressed, the wage cut reversed and reform to reduce the price of bread,' said Lewis confidently.

'And the men sacked by Mr. Vaughn are to be reinstated,' added Patrick Murphy.

'Murphy, I didn't expect to see you here,' said Nye.

'Our cause is just. Those men were loyal. There was no need to deprive them of their livelihoods,' said Murphy. The magistrate glanced at Nye.

'I can do something about the excesses of the Court of Requests,' said the magistrate.

'What about the price of bread? People are starving. We need reform,' said Lewis.

'I don't control the price of bread but I will pass on your complaint to the government. The other matters are a question for Mr. Vaughn,' said Mr. Bruce, the magistrate.

'Go home and I will reinstate the men but, for now, the wage cut stands. When the price of iron goes up again we can look at increasing wages,' said Nye. The delegation argued but Nye would not change his position.

'This talking is a waste of energy,' said Lewis and stormed out.

Nye went upstairs and watched Lewis climb onto his chest. The crowd waited in silence.

'They refuse our demands. We must take what we want,' cried Lewis before seizing the flag and waving it above his head. The rioters surged towards the hotel overwhelming the soldiers outside and wrestling their muskets away from them.

John Howard fired both his weapons and ran into the hotel followed by rioters. Soldiers in the windows fired into the rioters. There were screams of pain. Some of the crowd fell back. Others came forward. The soldiers continued to shoot into the crowd. Men were fighting with pickaxe handles and bayonets in the lobby. A rioter tried to stab John Howard in the stomach with a knife. He parried and clubbed the man with his empty pistol. As the rioters reached the stairs a volley of musket fire, from the landing, stopped them. Nye saw a rioter run into the street with a soldier's musket. He pointed it at Nye and pulled the trigger. The musket misfired. A hail of stones hit the back of the hotel. The attackers were feet away. Musket fire drove them back. The fighting lasted a quarter of an hour before the rioters broke and ran, leaving the High Street littered with wounded and dead. A weeping woman cradled her dead son in her arms.

The defenders held a council of war and decided that the hotel would not withstand another attack. Shots were being fired at the hotel from a nearby cinder tip.

'Help is on the way. The Marquess of Bute is sending more troops,' said the magistrate.

'I suggest we withdraw to Penydarren House,' said Rhys, 'It will be easier to defend if they attack again.

'They have seized thirty muskets from my men. The muskets are the king's property. We are dealing with treason,' said Major Falls. Rhys volunteered to carry a report to Cardiff and ask for every military unit available to be sent to Merthyr. Major Falls ordered his men to advance on the cinder tip and recapture the stolen weapons. As they approached, the major was shot and wounded. The soldiers carried the major back to the hotel, firing as they withdrew, where he issued new orders. The men gathered together all the food they could find and quietly escorted Nye and his companions away from the Castle Hotel. As they left, they passed families searching among the bodies for relatives. The Cambrian newspaper reported 18 killed and seventy wounded but the real number was higher. Many were carried away and secretly buried by their relatives. One old woman was shot as she sat in her room, knitting. The bodies of wounded who had crawled away were being found for weeks after in ditches and under hedges.

The Glamorgan Militia arrived in Merthyr at 7 o'clock in the evening. The commanding officer, Lieutenant-Colonel Richard Morgan, found the town abandoned and quickly located Nye Vaughn and the remnants of the Argyll and Sutherland Highlanders at Penydarren. He sent the wounded soldiers away in coaches, escorted by cavalry to protect the convoy from marauding rioters. Having got the wounded away they prepared for a new attack.

Lewis Lewis and the other rioters had moved to high ground above the town and were drilling with the stolen weapons. Others roamed the countryside taking fowling pieces and rifles from farmhouses. Shops were looted for weapons, gunpowder and shot. Arms that had been secretly collected during the previous week were cleaned and loaded. The rioters slaughtered a calf and bathed their flag in it. Then they returned to the Castle Hotel to kill the occupants. At their head marched the flag bearer, his arms red with blood. When the armed men reached Merthyr, the hotel was deserted.

Nye looked across the valley to the rioter's fires burning on the mountain.

'What is your opinion of our situation, Colonel Morgan?' asked Nye.

'We are strong enough to hold this position but the enemy control the town and we don't know their intention,' replied Colonel Morgan. To hear his foundry men called enemies stunned Nye.

'I am sure reinforcements will arrive in the next couple of days but we have things that need doing. We need more provisions and we need intelligence,' said the colonel.

'We have a few trustworthy men who can walk freely through the town and spy for us,' said John Howard.

'That's a good idea, captain. Will you arrange them? You are a captain are you not?' asked Colonel Morgan.

'A retired captain of marines and my brother-in-law is a Royal Navy captain on half pay. We are at your service,' replied John Howard.

'Excellent. Captain Howard. Will you take command of the rear of the house. If they attack from there your duty is to keep the rioters out,' said the colonel. John Howard nodded.

'Captain Vaughn, you know the town. If I give you ten men, can you forage for supplies?' asked the colonel.

'It will be a pleasure, Sir,' said Rhys.

'Sir Nye, I must enquire after your family. Are they secure?' enquired Colonel Morgan.

'I have sent the women to our family farm at Llangadog. They will be safe there,' said Nye. The colonel appeared satisfied with his plans but Nye had another idea to propose.

'I believe we should take the initiative. There is a small press in our print shop we might use to publish a proclamation. Handbills, threatening reprisals, spread about the town will unsettle the rioters and may split the weaker ones away from the ringleaders,' suggested Nye.

'If you write the words, father, I'll go down to the works, set the type and print some copies,' said Bryn.

The next morning, forty soldiers of the East Glamorgan were escorting a wagon loaded with ammunition from Brecon to Penydarren. As they approached Dan-y-Craig boulders rolled down the mountain blocking the road and hundreds of armed men attacked. Outnumbered the soldiers retreated abandoning the much needed ammunition. Later a woman on horseback rode across the mountain to warn Lewis and his men that more soldiers had been seen approaching along the Swansea Road. The Swansea Yeomanry had been ordered to Merthyr. Lewis and his men hurried back across the mountain and concealed themselves beside the road. As the troops approached one man stood up and beckoned to the soldiers. The commander rode over to the man to see what he wanted and was surprised to find it was a trick. He ordered his men to surrender while the man covered him with a loaded pistol. The capture and disarming to the Yeomanry emboldened Lewis and he sent a message to the besieged men at Penydarren demanding talks.

Bryn returned the following morning with 500 copies of the proclamation which read;

WORKMEN OF MERTHYR TYDFIL
No one can lament more deeply than your masters do the occurrence of yesterday!

They are grieved beyond measure that the blood of their industrious men should be spilled by the rash attempts you made to disarm the soldiers brought here only to protect our property and persons, against your threatened violence.

That you should have been led on by the speech of one violent man to commit such daring attacks as you did, with no thought of the heartbreaking result which followed, and which we shall all of us, masters and men, regret to the end of our lives.

There are now ten times the number of soldiers, to protect us and our property, than were here yesterday and we implore you to consider the devastating effects of continuing your present unlawful proceedings.

For your own and your families' sakes at once come to Penyderren in a small number and meet us to assure us of your immediate reliance upon our justice and feelings.

Return to your work and put an end to this dreadful state of affairs which must end and will worsen with every hour it continues.

YOUR FRIEND AND MASTER NYE VAUGHN

Rhys' foragers left copies of the proclamation around Merthyr and returned to Penydarren with a wagon load of supplies. Riding back they had been shot at and one soldier wounded. Later, two foundry men approached Penydarren House waving a white flag. It was a deputation from Lewis asking for talks. One of the men was Patrick Murphy. Colonel Morgan received them in the hallway.

'Your position is hopeless. We have come to ask for your surrender,' said Murphy.

'Our position is far from hopeless. We are well provisioned and prepared. As we speak reinforcements are approaching from Swansea and Brecon. It is you who should be surrendering your weapons,' replied Colonel Morgan.

'Your reinforcements have been beaten back. We have their weapons. There are no reinforcements coming. Our terms are simple. We require a written guarantee that our wages will be increased and there will be no intimidation when we return to work,' said the second man. Colonel Morgan looked at his companions. If it were true about the weapons the situation was dire.

'A demand for a pay rise, that's rich!' said Nye. Suddenly, Murphy clutched his stomach, complained of a pain in his

372

bowel and asked to use a latrine. Rhys escorted him outside to the toilet and waited by the door.

'Tell Mr. Vaughn I'm sorry. This was never meant to happen. Tell him it's a trick. Lewis doesn't want an agreement. He's going to attack in the morning with all his men,' hissed Murphy through the door. Rhys took Murphy back to the meeting. Colonel Morgan was about to decline the terms and tell the men to leave. Rhys stopped him.

'Colonel Morgan. I believe we should give careful consideration to these men's terms. They have some merit. I suggest we ask them to return in an hour to hear our answer,' said Rhys. The colonel, who was a good judge of character, realised Rhys had a reason for making such a proposal and agreed.

Shortly after, Captain Howard's spies returned and confirmed the ammunition and advancing yeomanry had been taken. A second delegation appeared one hour after the first. This time there was no sign of Murphy and the two men looked less confident than their predecessors. The proclamation written by Nye was working and the rebels had started to argue. Some, like Lewis and the hotheads supporting him, wanted to storm Penydarren but other men were getting cold feet and waking up to the dangers they faced. Nye decided to speak to the deputation.

'I cannot give the men a pay rise or take back what has passed before. Tell the men, I have no malice for those who return to work and it is better to end this peacefully. There will be no retribution for them or their families. However, any who are foolish enough to follow Lewis Lewis further along the road of treason will suffer the full consequences of their actions and treason is a hanging offence,' said Nye. He saw the men stiffen at the word treason. The delegation left, disappointed by the response but saying they would relay

Nye's message. After they had gone, Colonel Morgan prepared his men for the following day's attack.

In the morning, a third delegation arrived at Penydarren and repeated the demand for an increase in wages. This time, instead of saying a pay increase was impossible, Nye Vaughn suggested it might be possible to reach an accommodation over money and asked the men to return and tell their friends he wanted to find a way out for everyone. As the men were leaving, a large crowd, led by Lewis Lewis, approached Penydarren, firing guns into the air and shouting. Colonel Morgan ordered his men to stand to and they formed up in three ranks facing the mob. The delegates met the rioters at the gates and announced that Nye would consider their demands. The mob hesitated. A few melted away. Lewis Lewis urged them on, calling the deserters cowards. The mob advanced through the gates towards the house. Colonel Morgan ordered his men to fix bayonets and the mob slowed. More slipped away. When the soldiers lowered their muskets and took aim Lewis Lewis seized the red flag and waved it to rally his comrades and encourage them on. He turned. Behind him, rioters were throwing down their weapons and running away. The sight of ranks of soldiers prepared to open fire had broken their resolve and panic had taken hold. Lewis Lewis dropped the flag and fled.

Chapter 56

In the afternoon, 300 dragoons arrived in Merthyr and cleared the last of the rebels from the streets. The following day more reinforcements reached the town increasing the number of soldiers to more than 800. That evening Nye prepared a list identifying 16 ringleaders and a manhunt to capture them began. Nye offered a £5 reward for information leading each man's arrest. Soldiers accompanied constables from house to house searching for the fugitives. Men suspected of being involved in the riots were shackled in irons, forged at Castle Iron for the slave trade. Lewis Lewis escaped from his home when the constables came for him but was captured in nearby woods after a violent struggle. His nephew Richard Lewis, known by his friends as Dic Penderryn, was also taken. Others, who had fled, were captured in Carmarthen and Swansea. By the 10th June more than 600 men had been interrogated and released while 26 of the most serious offenders were marched to Cardiff goal in chains.

The furnaces of Castle Iron were relit on the 11th June but the men who returned to work were sullen, intimidated by the patrolling troops. 150 Argyll and Sutherland Highlanders guarded the works against sabotage. Eira, Cerys and John came home from Llangadog the following week and the family reunited at Vaynor Hall.

'What is the state of the town? Is there much damage?' asked Eira.

'Most of the shops have been looted and a lot of buildings have been gutted by fire. It'll take time to rebuild Merthyr,' said John Howard.

'And the men, are their grievances settled?' asked Cerys.

'Far from it. Father has refused all their demands. I fear we face continuing trouble unless we make peace with the men,' said Rhys.

'I will not be bullied by a mob,' snapped Nye, angrily.

'The Swansea Militia is being stood down and the Glamorgan Yeomanry are returning to Brecon. How can we stay safe without the protection of troops with bayonets at the ready?' said Rhys.

'I have written to the Prime Minister offering to pay for new army barracks and asked for a permanent garrison in the town. He has replied accepting my offer,' said Nye.

'So we are to live our lives under siege. Father, it's a ridiculous idea. We must find a way to placate the men. Their complaints are not unreasonable,' argued Rhys.

'You forget. They wanted to kill us,' said Nye heatedly. 'If their complaints were reasonable, why are the ringleaders being tried for treason? If they were reasonable, why is Richard Lewis on trial for wounding a soldier?'

'I know Lewis. He's a gentle giant. I don't believe he would harm anyone,' said John Howard.

'What is he accused of?' asked Cerys.

'Stabbing a soldier in the leg with his own bayonet, outside the Castle Hotel,' said Rhys.

'I was outside the Castle Hotel when the soldier was stabbed. I didn't see Richard Lewis there,' said John Howard.

'There are witnesses who say different. I hope he hangs,' sneered Nye. Eira looked at her husband. He looked older than before and the compassion he had always shown had gone, replaced by hostility and sourness.

'Nye, the men need your leadership to recover from what has been a terrible time. You must talk to them if you want to rebuild a working relationship with some trust,' she said.

'A working relationship with some trust,' shouted Nye. 'I ran Castle Iron at a loss to help those men. I borrowed money and we almost lost everything to help those men. How did they repay me? They tried to kill me. No, Eira. I was a fool. They need to be shown who the master is and I'm going to do it.'

'What are you going to do?' asked Eira.

'When I wrote to the Prime Minister I told him I want the ringleaders to be hung,' said Nye.

'Nye, that's a terrible thing to do,' said Eira and stormed from the room.

'What did the Prime Minister reply?' asked Rhys quietly.

'He agrees. We will make an example of them to stop the unrest spreading to other parts of the kingdom,' said Nye.

The inquests into the deaths during the riots began on the 17th June when the coroner, who had travelled from Swansea, ordered the dead to be exhumed to confirm how they died. Many had been quickly buried by their families. His orders outraged the people of Merthyr who protested that the decomposed bodies would be a health risk and unlikely to reveal a cause of death. Facing more than 300 miners and workmen who had attended the inquest the coroner ordered one exhumation, of John Hughes who had been shot outside the Castle Hotel. The body was dug up and the rotting corpse was carried into the inquest. The jurors glanced at it for a moment and returned a verdict of 'Excusable Homicide.' Emboldened, the coroner instructed that a woman be exhumed next. Told that another man had just died of his wounds and facing a hostile court, the coroner changed his mind and sent for the fresh corpse. A second verdict of 'Excusable Homicide' was quickly given and the coroner announced that he was satisfied with the verdicts which would apply to all the remaining inquests. He left Merthyr hurriedly the same afternoon.

The trial of 28 rioters including 2 women began on the 13th July. The first three cases were stopped by the judge because of insufficient evidence. The next case was to try Lewis Lewis and Richard Lewis who were jointly charged with stabbing a soldier outside the Castle Hotel. Several witnesses identified Lewis Lewis as being several yards from the soldiers and unable to have committed the crime. Then a constable took the stand and swore to tell the truth.

'Tell us what you saw,' ordered the prosecution lawyer.

'I saw a man seize the soldier's musket and stab him in the leg with the bayonet,' said the constable.

'Can you identify the man who stabbed the soldier?' asked the lawyer.

'It was Dic Penderyn.'

'You're a liar,' yelled Richard Lewis.

'You mean Richard Lewis. Why did you call him Dic Penderyn?' asked the lawyer.

'Because he comes from Penderyn,' replied the constable. A ripple of laughter went around the court.

'Do you know Lewis?' asked the judge.

'I do your honour. He's a bad one. I've dealt with him before.'

'You're a liar and blackmailer. Tell them why I thrashed you,' cried Lewis.

'The prisoner will be quiet or he will be removed from the court,' said the judge. The soldier who had been stabbed was called but could add nothing new. He didn't see his attacker. The judge summed up, referring to the evidence of the constable as reliable and describing Richard Lewis' outbursts in court as proof of his temper. The jury deliberated for nearly an hour before declaring Richard Lewis guilty of the attack. The judge called for his black cap and told Richard Lewis to stand.

'Richard Lewis, you shall be taken hence to Cardiff Prison and from there to a place of lawful execution where you will be hanged by the neck until you are dead and thereafter your body will be buried within the precincts of the prison and may the Lord have mercy on your soul,' intoned the judge.

'I didn't do it,' shrieked Richard Lewis as he was led away. The judge had done his duty and made an example of Lewis but the work sickened him. He discharged the next ten defendants and gave the others appearing before him lenient sentences.

378

News of Richard Lewis' sentence reached Merthyr the next morning. Rhys went to his father and asked him to use his influence and intervene. Nye shrugged and refused to help. Rhys hurried to Cardiff to see the Marquess of Bute and plead for Lewis' life. Bute refused to see him. Rhys waited all day until a horse was led to the door and the marquess emerged from his house. Bute was mounting the horse when Rhys grabbed the bridle.

'You must stop the hanging. I'm sure Lewis didn't attack the soldier,' said Rhys.

'Let go or I'll strike you,' snarled Bute and raised his riding crop.

'Do you believe he did it?' asked Rhys.

'What I believe doesn't matter. We have to hang someone,' snapped Bute. Rhys released the bridle.

'So you agree with my father.'

'The prime minster sent me a copy of his letter. I agree with his sentiments. We must show who the master is,' said Bute then he turned his horse and trotted away.

'By hanging an innocent man?' yelled Rhys. Bute ignored him.

In Merthyr public opinion was behind Richard Lewis. A crowd broke down the door of the constable's house who had given evidence and dragged him from his chair. They knew he was a liar.

'Murderer! Hangman!' they shouted as they beat him. Fearing for his life, the constable signed a confession that he had perjured himself in revenge for a beating Richard Lewis had given him. A petition was started calling for clemency or a pardon. Eira pleaded with Nye to add his name to the 10,000 already there. He refused. On the 21st July, the judge responsible for passing the sentence of death received the constable's confession. He wrote to the prime minister and asked for the execution to be stopped. The judge no longer saw any purpose in killing Lewis. The prime minister, Lord Melbourne threw the letter away. The petition from Merthyr reached him on the 27th. He ignored it.

The date for Richard Lewis' death was set for 30th July. As the day approached he continued to claim he was innocent. Rhys and John Howard rode to London with a copy of the constable's confession. They arrived at Downing Street on the 28th and asked to see the prime minister. His secretary refused saying the prime minister was busy in Parliament. Rhys and John ran along Whitehall and into Westminster Hall. Lord Melbourne was talking to Members of Parliament.

'Prime Minister, we must speak to you. It is a matter of life and death,' said John Howard. The prime minister ignored him.

'Lord Melbourne, an innocent man will hang,' added Rhys.

'Who are you, sir?' demanded Melbourne.

'My name is Vaughn and you must see this,' said Rhys and thrust the constables confession into the prime minister's hand. Lord Melbourne read it.

'It's a judicial matter. There is nothing I can do,' said Melbourne and handed it back.

'You can save him, if you want. At least delay the execution so this can be investigated,' pleaded Rhys. Lord Melbourne shrugged, summoned a scribe and dictated a letter ordering a stay of execution until the 13th August. They had 48 hours to get back with the letter and save Richard Lewis' life. They arrived in Cardiff as Richard Lewis was climbing the gallows steps.

The Cambrian newspaper reported that Lewis Lewis had been taken to a prison hulk with other accused men and was waiting to be transported to New South Wales. In Cardiff,

Richard Lewis continued to deny he had stabbed the soldier. The jailers began to believe him.

'There is still time to save him, father,' said Rhys. 'You must write to Lord Melbourne. He'll listen to you.' Nye refused. Cerys added her weight to the argument but Nye was resolute and would not change his mind.

On the night before the execution, a crowd gathered outside Vaynor Hall shouting there was to be a hanging. Eira listened to the cries of 'Murderer' and covered her ears. Returning from town, Rhys was threatened. A stone was thrown at his horse as he rode past the crowd. The animal reared up and kicked a man. Rhys drew a pistol and the crowd backed away. No one slept at Vaynor Hall that night.

Early the following morning the jailer sent a message to the Marquess of Bute asking if he had heard from London. Bute replied he had not and to proceed with the execution. A new cast iron gallows had been erected on Mary Street. Richard Lewis stood on the trapdoor and looked around. A crowd had gathered to watch his end. Farmers had brought their families on carts. Children, on their way to school, stopped to see the spectacle. Shopkeepers had closed their shops and come to watch.

'Oh Lord, this is injustice,' cried Lewis as the trap door opened. His leg caught the side of the scaffold. The executioner jumped down, grabbed Lewis' legs and pulled downwards to hasten the death. Richard Lewis kicked and struggled for two minutes before he expired. As he died a thunderstorm broke and the crowd dispersed. His body was taken down at 9 o'clock that evening and buried in un-consecrated ground the following day.

Nye Vaughn finished reading the account of the hanging in the Cambrian. He folded the newspaper and got up from the table.

'They say a white dove landed on his coffin as he was being interred,' said Eira. Nye walked from the breakfast room without answering. At the works none of the men would speak to him. Nye gave some orders and left early. The following day he stayed in his bedroom with the door locked. The tray of food left on the landing went uneaten. He ignored Eira's calls to unlock the door. Nye emerged that evening while the family was eating supper. John Howard and Cerys were visiting Vaynor Hall.

'Are you coming to the works tomorrow? I have some new orders you should see,' said John.

'No,' said Nye.

'When are you coming?' asked John.

'Never, I'm finished with Castle Iron Works,' said Nye and pushed his plate away. 'I don't want to see the place ever again.'

'Father, you're being unreasonable. Come to the foundry tomorrow,' said Rhys.

'Rhys, because of my pig headedness an innocent man was hung. I don't care about the foundry any more, or the men working there. They know what happened. I could had stopped the hanging. How can I face them,' said Nye.

Nye's depression deepened during the coming weeks. Vaynor Hall became Nye's, a place where he did not feel the men's scorn. He would sit in his study doing nothing for hours and ignored all Eira's attempts to raise his spirits. She felt him growing away from her and the void between them was like a dagger in her heart. Despite the master's absence, Castle Iron moved on like an unstoppable monster with a will of its own.

382

Following the riots, the Electoral Reform Commission recommended that a new parliamentary constituency be created for Merthyr Tydfil and Rhys Vaughn put himself forward as a candidate for the general election to be held on the 8th December. He campaigned hard, promising to end truck shops and stop young children working in the mines.

On the 26th July 1832 the Mary Ann berthed in Swansea with two dead sailors on board. The men had passed away the previous morning. The ship's captain and mate had died during the voyage from Calcutta and been buried at sea. The crew, none of whom could read a chart, had managed somehow to sail home and enter port, unaware of the rules of the sea regarding quarantine. They didn't anchor offshore or fly a yellow flag to warn that sickness was aboard the ship. The dead men were removed and quickly buried. The vessel was fumigated with smoke and nearby houses scrubbed with lime but the precautions were of little use. A virulent disease, never before seen in Wales, had come ashore with the unwary crew; Asian Cholera and it was a deadly.

By August 16th the cholera had claimed the lives of 56 Swansea residents and the disease had spread to Carmarthen and Llanelli. It reached Merthyr in September. Hundreds of people were infected. John Howard chaired a local board of health and ordered all ministers of religion to attend to the dead and dying. A mass burial ground was opened at Pant. Laudanum, given to relieve the pain, sent some sufferers into a coma and a new fear gripped the town; of being buried alive. On the 3rd December a gardener at Vaynor Hall became ill. The next morning, his daughter, a scullery maid vomited a clear, fishy smelling, liquid and collapsed. By noon her skin had turned a clammy blue, she was incontinent, had convulsions and was gasping for breath. The doctor bled her and gave her opium but to no avail. She died later that afternoon. Nye Vaughn showed symptoms of the disease at 11 o'clock on the morning of the 7th December. He passed away in Eira's arms, three hours later.

For a wealthy man, Nye's funeral was a modest affair. People were afraid to leave home and struggling with their own family deaths. He was hurriedly buried in Vaynor churchyard the next day. Two days later the result of the general election was declared. The turnout had been low but the result was beyond doubt. Rhys Vaughn had been elected the first Member of Parliament for Merthyr Tydfil.

The Vaughns returned to Nye's grave the following spring to view his monument, an eight ton slab of pink granite surrounded by iron railings. Eira walked to the grave with her sons and read the epitaph containing her husband's last words.

Nye Vaughn – Ironmaster
Born 17th June 1762 - Died 7th December 1832
God Forgive Me